HOW TO USE SOCIAL WORK THEORY IN PRACTICE

An Essential Guide

Malcolm Payne

First published in Great Britain in 2020 by

Policy Press
University of Bristol
1-9 Old Park Hill
Bristol
BS2 8BB
UK
t: +44 (0)117 954 5940
pp-info@bristol.ac.uk
www.policypress.co.uk

North America office:
Policy Press
c/o The University of Chicago Press
1427 East 60th Street
Chicago, IL 60637, USA
t: +1 773 702 7700
f: +1 773-702-9756
sales@press.uchicago.edu
www.press.uchicago.edu

British Library Cataloguing in Publication Data
A catalogue record for this book is available from the British Library

Library of Congress Cataloging-in-Publication Data
A catalog record for this book has been requested

978-1-4473-4377-6 paperback
978-1-4473-4378-3 ePub
978-1-4473-4380-6 ePDF

Infographics by Carly Powell Design
Cover design by blu inc, Bristol
Front cover image: Stocksy.com

Printed and bound by CPI Group (UK) Ltd, Croydon, CR0 4YY

Contents

	List of infographics	viii
	Some of the terms that I use in this book	ix
	How to use this book	xi
	How to read the infographics	xiv
1	**Introduction: practice from social work theory**	**1**
	Why this book?	1
	Aims	1
	Social work practice, concepts and theory	2
	How practice, concept and theory interact	2
	Other types of theory	3
	The organization of the book	4
	Method	5
	Important features of each concept and theory	6
	Some objections and an insight	8
	Bibliography: reviews of social work concepts and theories	9
2	**First contact and engagement**	**11**
	Setting the scene	11
	Introducing first contacts and engagement	13
	Action sequence	13
	Things to think about	16
	Further resources	17
3	**Assessment**	**19**
	Setting the scene	19
	Introducing assessment	21
	Action sequence	22
	Things to think about	26
	Further resources	27
4	**Communication, advice, information**	**29**
	Setting the scene	29
	Introducing communication, advice- and information-giving	31
	Action sequence	32
	Things to think about	36
	Further resources	37

5	**Counselling**	**38**
	Setting the scene	38
	Introducing counselling	40
	Action sequence	41
	Things to think about	46
	Further resources	47
6	**Resilience, risk, safeguarding**	**48**
	Setting the scene	48
	Introducing resilience, risk, safeguarding	50
	Action sequence	51
	Things to think about	58
	Further resources	59
7	**Humanistic person-centred practice**	**60**
	Setting the scene	60
	Introducing person-centred practice	62
	Action sequence	62
	Things to think about	65
	Further resources	67
8	**Mindfulness practice**	**68**
	Setting the scene	68
	Introducing mindfulness	70
	Action sequence	71
	Things to think about	74
	Further resources	74
9	**Strengths and solution-focused practice**	**75**
	Setting the scene	75
	Introducing strengths and solution-focused practice	77
	Action sequence	78
	Things to think about	82
	Further resources	82
10	**Narrative practice**	**84**
	Setting the scene	84
	Introducing narrative practice	86
	Action sequence	86
	Things to think about	90
	Further resources	91

11	**Psychodynamic relationship-based practice**	**93**
	Setting the scene	93
	Introducing psychodynamic relationship-based practice	95
	Action sequence	96
	Things to think about	100
	Further resources	101
12	**Attachment practice**	**103**
	Setting the scene	103
	Introducing attachment	105
	Action sequence	106
	Things to think about	110
	Further resources	110
13	**Task-centred practice**	**111**
	Setting the scene	111
	Introducing task-centred practice	113
	Action sequence	114
	Things to think about	118
	Further resources	119
14	**Crisis practice**	**120**
	Setting the scene	120
	Introducing crisis practice	122
	Action sequence	123
	Things to think about	126
	Further resources	127
15	**Cognitive behavioural therapy (CBT) practice**	**128**
	Setting the scene	128
	Introducing CBT	130
	Action sequence	131
	Things to think about	135
	Further resources	136
16	**Motivational interviewing**	**137**
	Setting the scene	137
	Introducing MI	139
	Action sequence	139
	Things to think about	144
	Further resources	146

17	**Advocacy, human rights and welfare rights**	**147**
	Setting the scene	147
	Introducing advocacy and welfare rights	150
	Action sequence	151
	Things to think about	155
	Further resources	156
18	**Empowerment, anti-oppressive practice and power**	**157**
	Setting the scene	157
	Introducing empowerment and anti-oppression	159
	Action sequence	160
	Things to think about	166
	Further resources	167
19	**Groupwork**	**168**
	Setting the scene	168
	Introducing groupwork	170
	Action sequence	171
	Things to think about	174
	Further resources	175
20	**Community work and macro practice**	**176**
	Setting the scene	176
	Introducing community work	179
	Action sequence	179
	Things to think about	183
	Further resources	184
21	**Systems practice**	**185**
	Setting the scene	185
	Introducing systems interventions	187
	Action sequence	188
	Things to think about	194
	Further resources	195
22	**Critical and structural practice**	**196**
	Setting the scene	196
	Introducing critical and structural practice	198
	Action sequence	199
	Things to think about	203
	Further resources	204

23	**Feminist practice**	**205**
	Setting the scene	205
	Introducing feminist practice	207
	Action sequence	207
	Things to think about	211
	Further resources	212
24	**Ecological and green practice**	**213**
	Setting the scene	213
	Introducing ecological and green practice	215
	Action sequence	216
	Things to think about	220
	Further resources	220
25	**Ending and critical reflection**	**222**
	Setting the scene	222
	Introducing ending and critical reflection	225
	Action sequence for ending	225
	Action sequence for (critical) reflection	227
	Things to think about	232
	Further resources	233
Bibliography		235
Index		265

List of infographics

1.1	Clusters of social work concepts and theories	7
2.1	First contact and engagement	12
3.1	Assessment	20
4.1	Communication, advice, information	30
5.1	Counselling	39
6.1	Resilience, risk, safeguarding	49
7.1	Humanistic person-centred practice	61
8.1	Mindfulness practice	69
9.1	Strengths and solution-focused practice	76
10.1	Narrative practice	85
11.1	Psychodynamic relationship-based practice	94
12.1	Attachment practice	104
13.1	Task-centred practice	112
14.1	Crisis practice	121
15.1	Cognitive behavioural therapy (CBT) practice	129
16.1	Motivational interviewing	138
17.1	Advocacy, human rights and welfare rights	148
18.1	Empowerment, anti-oppressive practice and power	158
19.1	Groupwork	169
20.1	Community and macro practice	177
21.1	Systems practice	186
22.1	Critical and structural practice	197
23.1	Feminist practice	206
24.1	Ecological and green practice	214
25.1	Ending and critical reflection	223

Some of the terms that I use in this book

How people use social work terms varies around the world and I have tried to standardize the terms I use. I explain here my decisions, and hope that readers do not find these uncomfortably distracting.

Carer, caregiver

'Carer' is the term used in British social care services for people who provide practical care, for example foster carers, neighbours, relatives and people employed to provide home care. The standard term in international use is 'caregiver'. I have preferred 'carer' because it is briefer and British carers often say it is less professionalized than 'caregiver'.

Client, service user

'Client' is the most widely used term internationally for people who receive social work services. It was originally introduced to avoid terms like the medical 'patient' and to reflect the expectation that, like clients of accountants and lawyers, social work clients were supposed to have a degree of self-direction in how and whether they used social work services. Another usage of the word 'client', however, describes a subordinate relationship. Some social workers are uncomfortable with that and the fact that, in practice, social work clients often have little power of self-direction. As the service-providing element of social work became important with legislative changes in the 1990s, the term 'service user' has become pre-eminent in the UK, but it is also criticized for treating clients as without agency or control and for reducing social work to using services rather than participating in a shared helping endeavour. I have preferred 'client' because of this, because it is briefer and because of its wide use internationally.

Intellectual disabilities, learning disabilities

'Learning disabilities' is used in the UK and elsewhere to describe people without fully developed learning and thinking capacities. It is a euphemism displacing older stigmatizing terms still used in some countries, for example 'retardation', 'subnormality'. 'Intellectual disabilities', a medical and psychological usage, is preferred in international and research literature as a more accurate description of the multitude of conditions included in this administrative category. I have preferred it for this reason, even though some people find its medical and professionalized character confusing and impersonal.

Social care, social services, social work

In much of the world, a wide range of provision for helping people affected by social disadvantage is described as 'social work', a term originally introduced to distinguish practical helpers from social reformers and social researchers. The term 'social services' is sometimes used to describe services offering this kind of help but it can be confused with wider social policy and provision. The English government has preferred 'social care', mainly by analogy with, and to make a political link to, healthcare services. Its use also emphasizes that social work often 'delivers' services and seeks to distinguish current from 20th-century provision.

Since this book is about professional practice derived from theories of the international social work discipline and profession, I have mainly referred to 'social work'. Even though 'social care' is not in wide use outside the UK, I use it as an understandable way to refer to services in which social work participates, as distinct from the professional practice.

How to use this book

The aim of this book is to offer brief accounts of how to practise according to the social work professional literature about specific practice concepts and practice theories. The account of each concept or theory covered focuses on the practice requirements set out in the literature rather than the professional discourse about the concept or theory; I explain the reasons for this in the Introduction. Chapters take up each concept and theory separately, rather than exploring its intersections with other theories and ideas. Each chapter also takes the literature about that concept or theory at face value, not debating conceptual or ideological issues that arise with using that concept or theory.

The concepts or theories vary in what they offer the social work practitioner. Some are presented as a sequence of steps, while others offer more of an approach or set of values about how to practise according to their premises. So, although the chapters are in a standardized format, I have been led by the approach and emphasis of the relevant literature in presenting them.

Each chapter has two different forms of presentation:

- *The chapter's text* explains the nature of the concept or theory, its aims, how it is or might be used, the practice interventions that emerge from the literature, and some things that you should think about as you practise. You would use this to gain an overview of what the concept or theory says you should do when you practise according to its precepts.
- *The chapter's infographic* presents a summarized account of the concept or theory as a diagram, in a page or less. You would use this as a reminder of the main directions and elements of practice. I have standardized the format of the infographics, and, while I hope they are reasonably intuitive, please look at 'How to read the infographics' on p xiv to check how each element is presented. A selection of infographics may be found among the online resources (policy.bristoluniversitypress.co.uk/how-to-use-social-work-theory-in-practice/online-resources/).

Some people find purely textual or graphical presentations difficult and like to use them together to supplement their understanding, others find one or the other difficult to follow. I hope it is helpful to offer both.

These presentations of the practice elements of social work, practice concepts and theory may be helpful in various ways:

- If you are a student or are otherwise in the early stages of using social work ideas and literature, they enable you to highlight the practice implications rather than other aspects of your studies. As many students have said to me: 'What does this theory mean for practice if we strip away the debate and the jargon?'
- If you are a student or new practitioner, they offer a quick crib to help you keep on track; this may be particularly true of the infographics. You might say: 'Have I covered all the points? I'll just remind myself of what comes next.'
- If you are a more experienced practitioner, they are a quick reminder of what practice according to a particular concept or theory offers you, so that you can maintain the focus of the ideas and build your practice confidently. You might be asking yourself: 'I think I've got a grasp of this, but are there other points to pick up?'
- If you are a practitioner thinking of adopting an unfamiliar concept or theory for a particular purpose, or to incorporate it into your approach or your team's arsenal of options, they provide a succinct briefing on how to go about it. I imagine the team meeting saying: 'What does it really mean if we take that on?'
- If you are a practitioner or manager needing to explain to a client or enquirer what your approach entails, they give you a vocabulary and brief formulation of what to expect from this type of practice. You might be saying: 'This is how we expect it to go.'

To help you to take the material in this book further, the bibliography in Chapter 1, the Introduction, offers a list of texts that pursue the interactions between the concepts and theories as they may be used in practice. They also discuss complex political, social and value debates about them. Such texts enable you to build a social work practice that uses ideas combining different theories, and uses theories to critique each other. They allow you to consider issues about the validity and worth of social work concepts and theories in the social context of your agency and within the policy and social environment in which you practise.

Other chapters in this book offer suggestions for further reading about the concept or theory under consideration, to enable you to follow it up in more detail. At the beginning of most chapters, where it's relevant, I cite texts that highlight the intellectual sources and some current comprehensive presentations of the concept or theory covered that you can pursue. References to the books and articles used to write each chapter are listed in the online resources (policy.bristoluniversitypress.co.uk/how-to-use-social-work-theory-in-practice/online-resources/) and are brought together in the bibliography at the end of the book.

How to read the infographics

Most of the infographics present the practice theory or concept as a sequence of stages listing things this theory suggests you can or should do. You start from the stage at the top and work through them. An arrow takes you to the next stage in the sequence. Arrows in both directions suggest moving backwards and forwards between stages.

Other graphics lie outside the main sequence. They offer:

- **Ideas**: things to think about, in thought bubbles
- **Explainers**: points to help your understanding, with a 'bullet point' icon in the top corner
- **Questions** to ask, with a 'Q&A' icon in the top corner.

These connect with the most relevant box in the main sequence, or are left open to apply throughout.

Within the sequence there are other icons:

- **Warnings**: to remind you of things to be careful about, emphasized by an exclamation mark in a triangle.
- **Mnemonics**: letters in a white box, which help you to remember a sequence of points.

Some practice theories and concepts do not lend themselves to a sequence, but the main ideas are presented as sections alongside one another; see Infographic 18.1 on Empowerment (p 158) as an example. In this case, behind the sections you can see a 'link box' paler than the background which connects these 'ideas boxes' together. Sometimes, arrows in both directions indicate complex connections.

The infographics have been created for the book by Carly Powell Design.

KEY TO THE INFOGRAPHICS

A STAGE IN A SEQUENCE

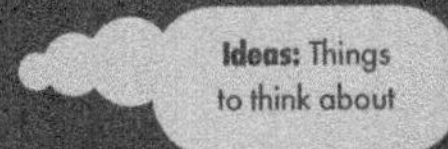

Ideas: Things to think about

Move on: from this stage to the next

SOMETIMES IN A SEQUENCE:

Warning: things to be careful about

EXPLAINER: points to understand

Interaction: move back and forth between elements in a sequence

SOMETIMES IN A SEQUENCE:

A B C D

Mnemonic: aid to memory

QUESTIONS: things to ask

1

Introduction: practice from social work theory

Why this book?

'Yes, but what does it tell you to *do*?' Ever since I started teaching about social work theory, students and practitioners have asked me this question about the ideas we have been exploring. Teaching and writing about social work concepts and theory stresses understanding their intellectual bases. You are expected to grasp the main principles of a theory, and you build on this in practice education and later experience to develop your practice. Some practitioners find it difficult to move in this way from general ideas to the practical side of social work.

Social work theories, however, are written by skilled and experienced practitioners, who have researched and experimented with their ideas in detail. They therefore often contain helpful guidance on implementing practice concepts or theories as well as their theoretical discussions. This treasure trove of detailed information about doing the job is minimized in many books that concentrate on the ideas and political and social values of social work. In this book I have concentrated on bringing this practice material forward.

Aims

My aim in this book is to pull together the actions you take when you practise, using some important practice concepts, for example assessment or safeguarding; and according to practice theories, for example psychodynamic, strengths-based or critical theory. Other books explain debates and critiques. Here, each chapter aims to help you understand how the literature on a practice concept or theory tells you to practise. In this chapter I discuss some of the distinctions I am making about social work practice concepts and theory. Then I explain how the book is organized. Finally, I outline some potential criticisms and downsides of working with concepts and theory in this way.

Social work practice, concepts and theory

I start from definitions of three aspects of social work:

- Social work **theory** is ideas that describe and explain social work and its practice in an organized way.
- Social work practice **concepts** are ideas about important practices present in all social work.
- Social work **practice** is systematic actions that practitioners take to achieve social work aims.

How practice, concept and theory interact

Theories give practitioners ideas to systematize their practice. There is no simple relationship between theory and practice. You don't just practise according to what theory tells you or look to theory for a structured account of practice. Practice, concept and theory influence each other all the time in a complex way.

This book focuses on two types of theory:

- Practice theory about changing, helping and influencing human beings, groups and communities.
  This type of theory draws on ideas from the social sciences and humanities. It looks at how and why people behave and think as they do in their relationships within their physical and social environments. This theory offers systematic prescriptions for action in social work practice. They say: 'In this situation, do this; in that situation, do the other thing.'

- Practice concepts that conceptualize general practices present in all social work.
  These concepts express ideas about significant actions that are present in all social work activity. They explain the professional aims that social workers have as they take part in the human interaction that occurs when they intervene in other people's lives. Examples include engaging, communication or safeguarding.

We are shifting away from separating practice theory from ideas about political and social thinking and social science research that informs it. Recent books on social work theory bring together ideas from a range of sources and propose that they might help us in a variety of ways, for example Beckett & Horner, 2016; Hodgson & Watts,

2017; Thompson & Stepney, 2018. They help to structure ideas and information from many sources, but they don't all set out to provide a comprehensive statement about how to practise according to a formal 'practice theory'. Instead, they often produce a variety of statements about 'what social workers think about and do'. Practice concepts, similarly, package expectations about how to carry out practice tasks that arise in many social work actions.

From this kind of writing, you gain a general idea about what is expected of you by values and understandings that circulate within social work. The legal, policy and organizational requirements of the agencies and services that employ social workers influence how you interpret and carry out these expectations. The 'practice theory' providing a package of actions in sequence therefore is less dominant in social work theory than once it was, but it still makes an important contribution to learning and developing practice because it brings clarity about how you can implement the tasks you are employed to undertake.

Other types of theory

There is, of course, lots to learn from other theoretical writing. Three other types of theory are part of the system of practice concepts and theory:

- Theory about the nature and aims of social work.
  This focuses on the overall aims and structure of practice within the intellectual and academic discipline of social work, and the policy and organization of social care services.

- Theory expressing important values in social work.
  These values express ideas about what priorities and processes are important in carrying out social work. Examples are ideas about social justice or sustainable communities which are incorporated into some practice concepts and theories.

- Knowledge and theory about the issues that clients of social work services face in their lives.
  Ideas and evidence from the humanities and social sciences about how social and psychological issues affect clients and the people around them. They say, in effect: 'The situation you are dealing with is influenced by these psychological and social factors. Understanding these factors gives you clues about what actions to take.'

These kinds of theory are all useful to understand. But, because there are many books about these kinds of theory, I have systematically cut out debate about the aims and values of social work and psychological and social information about the issues that clients face. This book, therefore, summarizes how to implement practice concepts and theories. Although it sometimes points to other types of theory, it does not go into detail about them. Each chapter, and the infographic that goes with it, starts from the assumption that you, or perhaps your team or agency, have decided to use this theory, or parts of it, and my task is to extract from writings about the theory how it says you should practise if you take it on.

The organization of the book

After this introductory chapter, each chapter in the book covers an important social work concept or theory. Each is organized as follows:

- To set the scene, brief accounts of:
  - 'What is ...?', covering the main features of the concept or theory;
  - its aims, what it seeks to achieve;
  - its uses – how you use it and when you would look elsewhere.
- An infographic setting out diagrammatically the main actions involved in an intervention in this theory or concept. This provides a very brief summary of the chapter.
- Introducing the concept or theory to clients and the people around them. This tries to put a practical slant on the main concepts that the theory uses.
- Action sequence – working your way through the interventions proposed by the theory or concept. Some theories offer us a clear sequence, for example task-centred practice; others think about practice in a different way, for example feminist practice theory identifies important areas to focus on, rather than offering a sequence of actions.
- Things to think about – other issues about the theory that might help you to use it critically.
- Further resources: references that you can use to explore the concept or theory further.

My aim is to give you brief highlights of practice according to a practice theory or concept. You can learn more from the suggested reading at the end of each chapter.

Because of this aim for brevity, I don't provide case vignettes to illustrate practice methods, but I give examples where I think it helps to explain the relevant practice better. I know that some practitioners and students like to read case studies that show how conceptual material is used in practice; and I also know that many readers simply skip them in search of the main points that they need to pick up from a book. Because this book covers a huge range of material, it would not be honest to pretend that I can produce case studies that cover every concept and theory, so I have pointed to examples that are relevant and invite you to think how you would use these ideas in similar cases that you have worked with.

Method

I have used a consistent method to create the account of practice in each chapter. I collected together accounts from journals and books about each concept or theory. Within these accounts, I searched for useful points about practice specific to the topic of each chapter. After mining the detail in books and articles about the chapter's topic, I put together my own formulation to describe a theory's main principles and then how you practise using these ideas.

Each chapter describes what writers about the approach recommend. You apply your own professional judgement and experience and your team and agency requirements to those suggestions. Where theories are clear about what to do, I use a directive style to describe the actions prescribed. Some material, however, concentrates on skills and relationships, and here I present a series of ideas or options. In each chapter, I take for granted the theory's approach, so I sidestep theoretical disagreements and debates about political and social issues. Although I introduce some technical terms, I mainly describe suggested practice actions without a lot of jargon. You can find theoretical debate and formal accounts of each theory in the 'Further resources'. The debates about validity of theories are available in reviews of social work theory; I list some recent ones at the end of this chapter.

The publishers and I have looked at how to reference the sources because almost every sentence is sourced from a different piece of writing, and often a similar point is made by several writers. Incorporating a reference for each one in the usual academic way was tiresome to read, so I have cited every reference I used in a list for each chapter published on the publisher's website, and I have only included a direct citation where I quoted a writer's point or form of words. In the bibliography at the end of the book all the citation lists have been combined so that they are all credited. But I am responsible for the formulation set out in this book.

Important features of each concept and theory

Looking at the scene-setting part of each chapter enables you to pick out distinctive features of the concepts and theories. To bring these main features together, in this chapter's Infographic 1.1, I cluster the concepts and theories into groups. A line divides some theories and concepts into two main categories according to their main focus:

- those that focus on intervention in the social;
- those that focus on the individual or psychological.

I refer here to their main focus, since of course all social work, and therefore all social work theory, seeks to respond both to the individual and psychological and to the social in our lives.

Two clusters of concepts and theories straddle the line, since they apply to both the social and the psychological in more equal measure. The first, including engagement, safeguarding, assessment and ending, cover broad elements of practice. Advocacy, empowerment and anti-oppressive practice also embrace change in both individual and social issues.

Looking at this infographic, I have formed several groupings of concepts and theories. Among the psychological theories, there is a group of broadly expressive theories, including humanistic and mindfulness practice. Another group, including strengths, solution and narrative practices, also focuses on the expressive, but in the context of positive psychologies. These are forward looking, examining mainly goals. In contrast, other groups are problem based. Psychodynamic and attachment theories originate in ideas that current personal problems derive from earlier life experiences. The next group, task-centred and crisis work, are brief, pragmatic, structured interventions, crisis practice more closely related historically to the psychodynamic, and task-centred practice more aligned with the final group, which relies on cognitive and behavioural psychologies, which are also problem based.

The theories more oriented towards the social are in two clusters. A social democratic cluster focuses on change within the present social system through group and community work and systems theory. The other, critical, cluster includes a range of critical theories aimed at social justice and structural change in society, and includes feminist and ecological practice.

CLUSTERS OF SOCIAL WORK CONCEPTS AND THEORIES 1.1

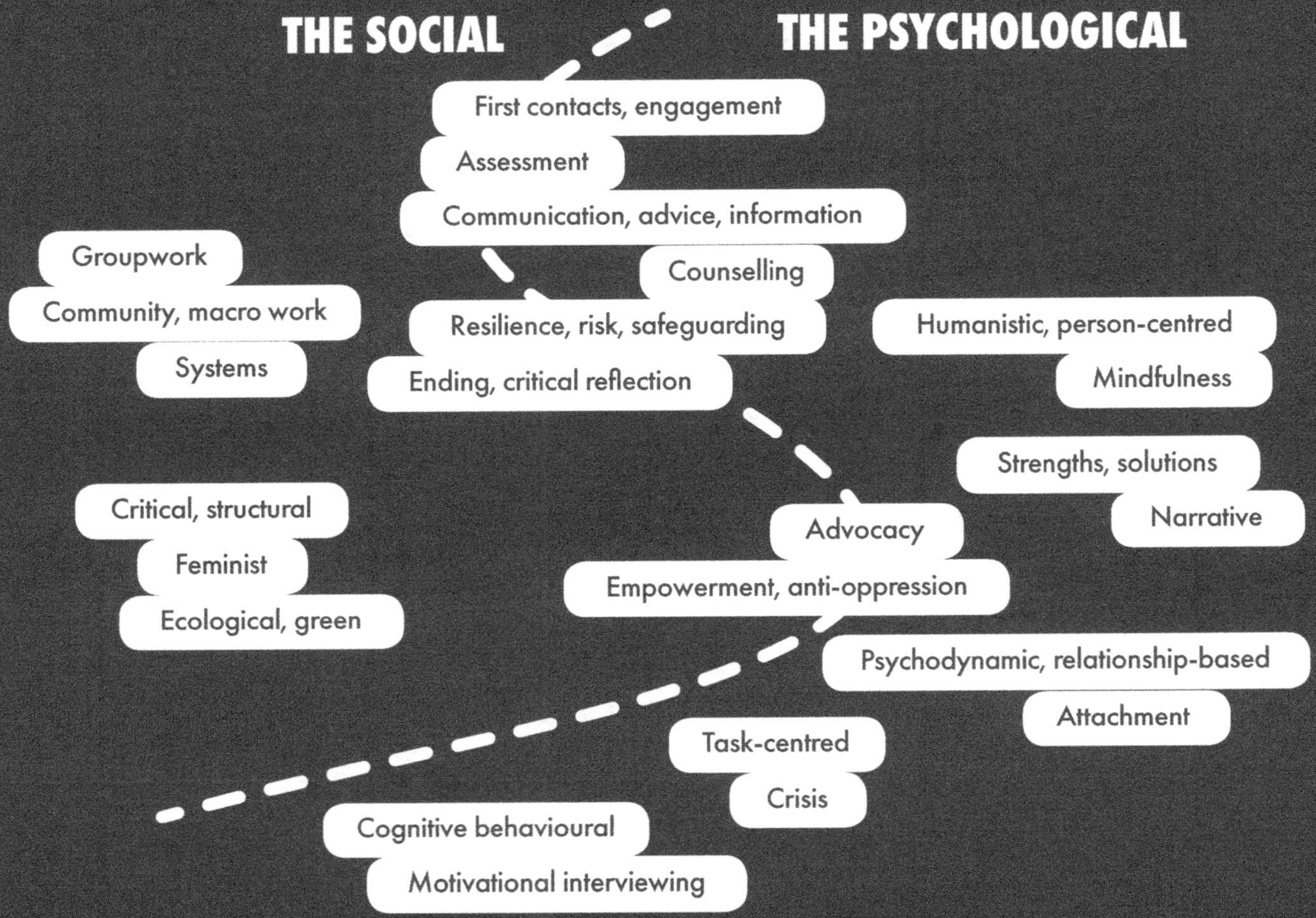

THE SOCIAL

THE PSYCHOLOGICAL

First contacts, engagement

Assessment

Communication, advice, information

Counselling

Resilience, risk, safeguarding

Ending, critical reflection

Groupwork

Community, macro work

Systems

Humanistic, person-centred

Mindfulness

Strengths, solutions

Narrative

Critical, structural

Feminist

Ecological, green

Advocacy

Empowerment, anti-oppression

Psychodynamic, relationship-based

Attachment

Task-centred

Crisis

Cognitive behavioural

Motivational interviewing

Some objections and an insight

There are five main sets of objections to my project in this book to extract the practice proposals from the social work conceptual and theoretical literature:

- Brief practice prescriptions over-simplify the complex and messy process of doing social work.
- Practice concepts and theory clash with the requirements of the law and agency policy and they don't take into account the pressures of everyday demands, including the pressures of 21st-century austerity policies, and government and managerial ideologies that don't respect the values of the social work profession.
- Separating out specific practice concepts and theories doesn't reflect the reality of practice, in which we move around among ideas from many different sources.
- The directive style of practice prescriptions misrepresents the creative and reflective style of social work's thinking and practice processes, which you need to deal with the human and social complexity that social workers face.
- The pragmatic approach of developing practice prescriptions accepts a neoliberal conceptualization of social work as a practical thing done by practical people, devoid of political and social connotations, because it doesn't explore the impact of inequality, oppression, poverty and surveillance on socially excluded people whom social workers mainly work with.

My view about these points is that you have to start somewhere. Practice concepts and theory don't tell you everything but they give you a framework, so you can get the picture of what you should be doing and be clear about things you might be able to do. The pressures or requirements may mean that you can't achieve an ideal implementation of a professional theory, but you can usually adapt them so that at least in some of your work you can achieve a good piece of practice and a satisfactory outcome. Using these conceptualizations and theories will usually give you pointers on how to enhance what you do to meet the requirements laid on you. Knowing where ideas come from helps us be clear about how to fit together the different aspects of theory that we are picking up. Being clear about how our profession says we should be practising means that we're better able to demonstrate, explain and gain respect for our achievements. Naturally, good people are dissatisfied with what they are able to do, and I have been in tears more than once during my career about the impossibility of the tasks I have been set or that I have set myself. But if we can be clear about things we can do, it is usually possible to find a way of doing at least some of them, to the improvement of humankind. Knowing about practice possibilities does not prevent you from being reflective in how you take them on. Taking them on does not prevent you from being critical of social provision and social thought or from actively pursuing social change. Social work concepts and theories give you options; without social work conceptualization and theorization presented in usable form your options are fewer.

The main aim of this book is to be practically useful by reminding you of a theory's main points as you come to try it out. As I worked on the project to create it, however, I found that it offers a different insight into these theories than you get from the more complex accounts of a theory's sources and ideas in the reviews listed in this chapter's bibliography. If you put all the chapters together, therefore, this book offers an important insight. It is this: because each theory offers a different way of 'doing' practice in social work, we can understand social work not only as a set of ideas and values pursuing political and social ends, but also as sets of distinct and distinctive practices. By extracting these practices and describing them in this book separately from theoretical debate, the particular features of these practices become the centre of a theory rather than ideals, principles or social objectives. The focus in this book on the practice elements of social work theories and concepts makes some of the practice aspects of these theories more explicit and more usable. I hope that it contributes something special to your understanding of what you can contribute to people and to humanity through your practice.

Bibliography: reviews of social work concepts and theories

This bibliography lists some recent reviews of social work theory to enable you to find academic and professional debate about the contributions of theories to social work.

Beckett, C. & Horner, N. (2016). *Essential theory for social work practice* (2nd edn). London: Sage.

Brandell, J.R. (2011). *Theory and practice in clinical social work* (2nd edn). Thousand Oaks, CA: Sage.

Deacon, L. & Macdonald, S.J. (eds) (2017). *Social work theory and practice*. London: Sage.

Hodgson, D. & Watts, L. (2017). *Key concepts and theory in social work*. London: Palgrave.

Howe, D. (2009a). *A brief introduction to social work theory*. Basingstoke: Palgrave Macmillan.

Langer, C. & Lietz, C.A. (2015). *Applying theory to generalist social work practice: A case study approach*. Hoboken, NJ: Wiley.

Payne, M. (2014). *Modern social work theory* (4th edn). Basingstoke: Palgrave Macmillan.

Payne, M. & Reith Hall, E. (eds) (2019). *Routledge handbook of social work theory*. London: Routledge.

Thompson, N. & Stepney, P. (eds) (2018). *Social work theory and methods: The essentials*. New York: Routledge.

Trevithick, P. (2012). *Social work skills and knowledge: A practice handbook* (3rd edn). Maidenhead: Open University Press.

Turner, F.J. (ed) (2018). *Social work treatment: Interlocking theoretical approaches* (6th edn). New York: Oxford University Press.

Walsh, J. (2014). *Theories for direct social work practice* (3rd edn). Belmont, CA: Wadsworth.

Webb, S. (ed) (2019). *The Routledge handbook of critical social work*. London: Routledge.

2

First contact and engagement

Setting the scene

What is first contact and engagement?

First contacts are the process of engaging 'at the agency's front door' with clients and people around them (Kirkman & Melrose, 2014). You communicate a commitment to working with them on your service's aims, and complete the formal requirements to commence the agency's responsibilities for providing social work service.

Aims

Social work practice is organized in cases, sets of human and social circumstances that meet criteria set by a social work agency for situations that it should respond to. First contacts entail two actions. *Engagement* is the human aspect, setting up an interpersonal connection with one or more of the people involved. *Intake* is the administrative aspect, identifying issues that a case will raise and defining whether they are within the responsibilities of the agency.

The main aims of engagement are:

- Understanding the reasons for this contact. These may be different from the reasons for previous contacts. If they are the same, review previous contacts to try to understand any pattern. Do so especially if you, colleagues or your agency may have misunderstood or reacted poorly to previous contacts.
- Establishing a starting relationship with clients and members of their network.
- Establishing a practical, well-organized working style.
- Engaging clients and network members in starting to take action.
- Making immediate necessary interventions, especially if safeguarding is needed.
- Collecting information for a beginning assessment.
- Collecting information to build future links with other agencies and services involved.

FIRST CONTACT AND ENGAGEMENT 2.1

PLAN GOOD ACCESS

Public information
Signage, access
Business-like, pleasant, safe
Reception, responsiveness
Feelings, privacy

What does your agency symbolize to clients and the public?

THE AGENCY FRONT DOOR

Applications from/on behalf of clients

Referrals from other agencies

RECORD THE REFERRAL

names, addresses, date of birth, consent, services, problems, risk, limits, referrer, report back

CREATE A WORKABLE WARM RELATIONSHIP

Open questions
Concerns, interests: whose?
Individuals
Networks
Relationships
Security
Sensitivity

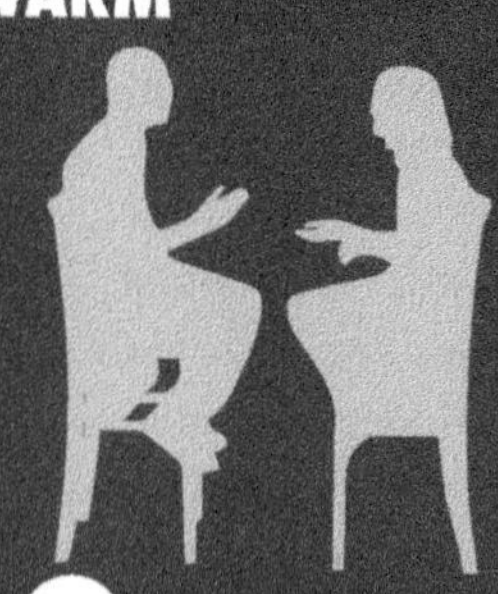

MODEL BEHAVIOUR AND PLANNING

Collaborate, join forces
Respectful
Share responses
Clarify, confirm understanding
Positive about strengths
No sugarcoating
Observe

INTAKE DECISIONS

Take it on?
Allocate

REVIEW QUESTIONS

What have we missed out?
Anything unsatisfactory?
Attitudes and approach?
What happens next?

CASE-MAKING

Case register or database
Create case record

Uses

Everything starts somewhere. Before you can start on assessment, you need to engage with clients and other people who are involved. All future actions in the case depend on doing this successfully. Your overall aim is to energize and give direction to clients' motivations to engage and work on changing things in their lives for the future. You can also try to release them from limitations, such as fears that things cannot improve or that someone important, for example their mother or husband, will get in the way of further progress. Help them express fears about you and your agency. Be up front about administrative or legal requirements of them, for example where you are investigating concerns about abuse.

Introducing first contacts and engagement

Check the information you have received and clients' views about it. Make it clear that you are now beginning your work together and you hope to sort out plans for future action. Clarify what services are requested, outline and model the agency's and social work roles, decide what needs to be done and what's most important. Explain that the agency collects information needed to do the work as well as possible. Think through possible avenues of progress and look at anything that might get in the way. Say if there is to be a decision on whether you will be able to help or how much. There may be some things you can do right away, but it may not be possible to achieve everything in one go.

Action sequence

Two types of first contact

First contacts come in two main ways. *Referrals* are requests from other agencies to work with a situation. *Applications* are requests from potential clients or on behalf of them (for example from relatives) for help from an agency. Both referrals and applications may be about an individual, a family or a group of people, for example people who have shared interests and want to be involved collectively in community work. Work at the 'front door' also involves screening to decide if immediate action is needed or if the case is not relevant to the agency's task.

Plan for your agency and team to be as accessible as possible

What does your agency, and their route to it, symbolize to potential clients? Your agency and team can prepare information for applicants and referrers about contact with and travel to the agency. Check and improve signage to help people gain access, access for disabled people, a business-like, pleasant and safe physical appearance for the service location, climate (for example not too cold or hot, not too stuffy), appropriate reception and responsiveness of staff on first contact. Consider feelings generated by making contact, for example distress, frustration, anger. Make provision for privacy and quiet space. Assure clients of your concern and engagement, and explain the realities of your agency's likely response.

Referrals

There is often a standard referral format on computer or paper for referrers. Sometimes, you extract information from a phone call, email, letter or other message. The format covers everything possible, which may not be relevant to this case, but a good basis for further contact and later decisions is:

- name, nicknames, family names, how you speak to the client;
- address, and alternatives: are they staying elsewhere or in a care home or hospital?
- date of birth to check records and make sure you are identifying the right person;
- permission from client and family for making the referral, or it may have to be refused;
- an account of the service sought, or problems identified;
- risk, time limits or urgency, in the referrer's view, and your assessment of that;
- the referrer, how to contact them, when and how they expect feedback.

Making a consistent intake process well known to colleagues assists coordination in interdisciplinary settings, such as hospitals, where professionals pass cases among them. Likely referrers need to know whom to contact or to have a contact number to refer cases. In disaster or emergency situations, for example a terrorist incident or major fire, set up a point for first contact. Collate information about people coming for help or affected by the event consistently.

Applications

If people phone or visit the office to apply for a service, they or you usually complete an application or referral form: see 'Referrals' for the minimal points to cover. The advantage of making personal contact is to start building a relationship through personal interaction. You are the human face of what working with your agency will be like.

Begin creating a workable warm relationship by putting people at their ease. Engage 'in the medium of the other' (Middleman & Goldberg Wood, 1990: 49–51) by approaching and communicating in ways that are comfortable for them, non-verbally if appropriate, for example with children or people with intellectual disabilities. Open questions help to elicit their priorities and interests. Explain rules of confidentiality to help them feel secure in talking to you and your agency. Confirm you will make notes and complete forms and check initial information at the outset, then focus on their narrative, checking back later when you make the notes. Make them aware where you may have to disclose their information.

Present your work as a collaboration, being respectful of clients' priorities and views. Emphasize how you want to enter their world, understand their concerns and join forces with them to make progress (Lee, 2001: 189–92). Share your responses, clarify and confirm your understanding regularly. Ask questions and offer options, letting clients guide the direction of discussion. Be positive about the achievements and strengths they show you. Downplay things that seem negative. Avoid sugarcoating the agency's powers and responsibilities, making your authority seem helpful when clients might find it oppressive, and be clear about likely demands on clients' behaviour, if these are issues.

Keep observing, comparing what you see with what people say. Be aware that you and your agency are a model for clients of well-planned organization and appropriate behaviour.

Issues to work on

Focus on four areas:

- What is of concern? To whom? Who is involved?
- Building appropriate relationships with clients and their network, to get enough information to decide any immediate actions or onward referral and to prepare the ground for future work.
- Identifying and establishing contact with other practitioners and services involved.

- A mutual decision: do the people involved want or need further engagement? How do we organize that?

Look for and overcome misunderstandings; relationships with clients can go wrong even before you meet. This may be because their knowledge of your agency or of social care and what it can offer may be sketchy or wrong. They may have incorrect or unhelpful beliefs about you or social work from the past experience of family, friends and neighbours. They may be misled by what they have learned from other agencies in their pathway to the doors of your agency. Being involved with social work is stigmatized as a sign of failure or dependence on others. Fear or dislike of professional or official authority may hamper cooperation, so model helpful authority.

There is no choice about making a first contact, but there are issues about how far you take it. Even if your first contact is mainly message taking, your attitude and approach will set the tone for what follows, so good further relations will build on or be set back by how you are. If you are not likely to be the long-term contact, avoid too much commitment to you personally. If direct advice or a few phone calls will resolve the issue immediately, decide and make clear the time limits before you will have to defer further action. Explain how and when you will pick things up again, especially if there is a risk to safety. Give advice or information in light bites because the situation is new to clients and the relationship is new to you and neither of you can take in too much.

Things to think about

Beginnings involve elements of the unknown: hope, excitement and the mobilization of energy. You help the client get started on working with the issues they want to focus on. It helps not to rush on, rather '*stay with the beginning and let it be a beginning*' (italics original, Smalley, 1970: 100) and build your sensitivity to what is involved in this particular beginning. Don't be in too much of a hurry to fill in the form. Make time limits clear, but otherwise be open to hearing the story in the client's or referrer's own words, gauging their attitudes and level of concern. Find out what they are bringing, be prepared to talk about what you and your agency bring, to the process (Kroll, 2010).

Social work usually involves more people than just one client. Identify and contact relevant people around clients and in other agencies early. Collect information from other agencies and past files, but critically: check correctness or relevance now. Observation in an opening interview or home, school or ward visit contributes to first decisions. Explain aims, potential and procedures to people around clients and other agencies, and secure commitment from client and others to move on to intervention.

At the end of the first contact, ask for things that have been missed or if anything has been unsatisfactory to clients or referrers. Reflect on whether you are satisfied with the client's or referrer's approach or attitude. This might simply lead to a note for the future. Or, preparing for the future, you may want to make it clear that an alternative approach would be useful in the future. Explain what will happen next, and indicate, realistically, likely timescales. Suggest things that clients or referrers could do in the meantime to make progress.

Agencies have systems for establishing clients as a 'case'. This usually involves:

- making formal decisions to 'take on' clients as cases;
- recording the decision to register clients as cases, usually generating a database entry;
- setting up a case record, which may involve a computer or paper record, or both.

The front end of computer records or cover or front sheets in case files contain basic information about the case in a structured form. They facilitate quick access to the nature of the case and useful details, such as contact details for service users, family members, agencies and others actually or potentially involved, medical diagnoses and legal matters. In first or early contacts, practitioners try to complete and check as much of this information as possible; this facilitates later work, or future contacts.

Further resources

Langer, C. & Lietz, C.A. (2015). *Applying theory to generalist social work practice: A case study approach.* Hoboken, NJ: Wiley.

Most chapters in this practical review of theories of practice have a useful section on engagement.

Dhooper, S.S. & Moore, S.E. (2001). *Social work practice with culturally diverse people.* Thousand Oaks, CA: Sage, 33–9.

The section on engagement emphasizes fully exploring clients' narratives in this phase of work, where you are working with people from a different background to yourself.

Kroll, B. (2010). Only connect ... building relationships with hard-to-reach people: Establishing rapport with drug-misusing parents and their children. In G. Ruch, D. Turney & A. Ward (eds) *Relationship-based social work: Getting to the heart of practice*. London: Jessica Kingsley, 69–84.

A chapter on working where engagement is difficult, with extensive case material.

Middleman, R. & Goldberg Wood, G. (1990). *Skills for direct practice in social work*. New York: Columbia University Press, 49–51.

Chapter 3 in this book, 'Skills for setting the stage', offers a thoughtful insight into engagement.

Rosengren, D.B. (2018). *Building motivational interviewing skills: A practitioner workbook* (2nd edn). New York: Guilford, 51–163.

A big guide to this newish model of practice focused on working with unmotivated clients has a lengthy and practical section on engagement, with practical exercises to develop skills; it merges into assessment.

Check the online resources at policy.bristoluniversitypress.co.uk/how-to-use-social-work-theory-in-practice/online-resources/chapter2 for a full list of references for this chapter.

3

Assessment

Setting the scene

What is assessment?

Assessment involves working with clients to decide on the nature, seriousness, and human and social implications of issues in a social work case. It moves on to planning appropriate actions to address those issues. Milner, Myers and O'Byrne's (2015) text provides a broad, up-to-date account of assessment. Assessing is provisional, a shared process of discovery leading to intervention based on what is known now. It may change or develop as understanding improves. Some intervention methods use specific assessment methods, outlined in the relevant chapter. Social work assessment in medical and psychiatric settings may become part of the medical diagnosis, inputting the social to the medical.

Aims

The assessment sequence is: information underpins understanding, which in turn supports appropriate decisions. Assessment expands on and clarifies the picture of the case that you gained at first contact. You, clients and the people around them are taking in and sorting information as a basis for future work together. Each person involved, not just you, uses that information to guide their responses in their later collaboration. Communication is, therefore, an important part of assessment. Unless everyone involved shares the basis for judgements and decisions, they cannot fulfil their part later.

Assessment is usually done mainly in early stages of a case. You need to get to a decision point so that you can get on with intervention. You can make interventions alongside assessment: don't let assessment delay necessary action.

Assessment is a constant of all social work intervention, not the start of a linear process leading to other things. Being provisional, it never ceases, for two reasons. First, as you work together, the people involved come to trust you more, and disclose material that they have held

ASSESSMENT 3.1

PREPARATION

Create a productive climate
Plan first interview
Aims, focus, who's involved?
Build trust and working alliance
Ask clients in advance to bring information
Safety first in emergencies
Check physical injury and risk

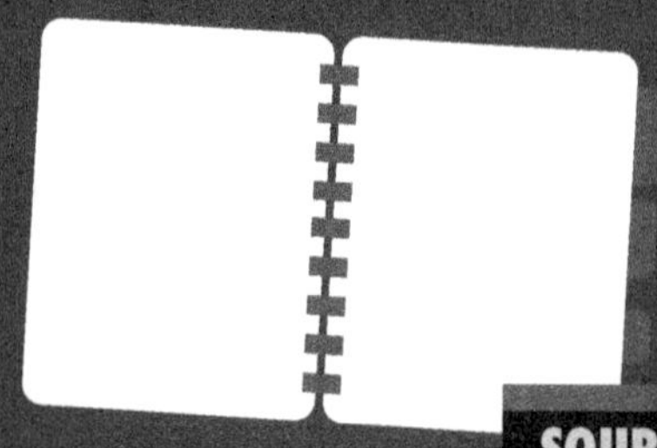

SOURCES:
Documents
Interviews
Observation

DATA COLLECTION
Explore

Experiences, feelings and relationships
Education, family, finances, health, housing
Personal material

PERSONAL MATERIAL

BASIC

Behaviours
Affective (feelings) issues
Somatic (body) issues
Interpersonal
Cognitive (perceptions, thinking)

ANALYSIS AND APPRAISAL

Expert clients, family and community
Focus on the most important issues
Query and test information
Control bias
Create and test hypotheses

Lifecourse
External factors
Power relations

ISSUES AND PROBLEMS

Safety: protection now...
...and prevent longer-term distress
Balance problems and strengths
Position clients in social structures

MOVE TO PLANNING

Make connections
Bring out alternative options
Explain agency roles
Partialize issues into smaller chunks
Balance protection and human rights
Value alternative ways of being
Link problems to strengths to aims

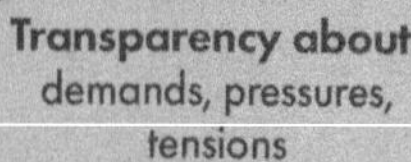

Transparency about:
demands, pressures, tensions

INTERVENTION

back at the outset. Second, you all come to understand complexities, constraints and opportunities that you could not see at the start. We adapt our planned actions when we get new information or refine our judgements.

Devote effort to the detail and implications of information and decisions. It should not be a shallow or hasty collation of half-formed judgements. Form a brief, lucid and reasoned interpretation of what is distinctive about this situation, and actions we are planning. Contrast probable outcomes if the present situation continues with aimed-for improvements.

Uses

Assessment has two uses. One is to build the basis of information and judgements that guide future interventions. The other is to meet the information and scrutiny requirements so that your agency can decide on its responsibilities and services it can or should provide.

Introducing assessment

Introducing assessment thoughtfully helps build trust to create alliances for future work.

Referrers, clients and others involved sometimes expect or require an assessment, for example when referring a child because of safeguarding concerns or older people for consideration for adult social care funding. To make an assessment may be part of the agency's responsibility, for example carers' assessments. But some people may not want or expect an assessment. Other agencies may have carried out their own assessment, and expect you to provide services accordingly, without further assessment. Clients may be applying for a service, expecting it to be provided as a right. Or they know we will carry out something called 'an assessment', but not expect the kind of information we will seek or the detail which we think necessary. For example, they may think providing family details or financial information is too intrusive. Or they may see it as collecting information, without appreciating what decisions it will inform.

Explaining what you are doing is a good start, therefore. Describe the information you will collect. Explain why this information now, how it will be used, who will see it, and how it will be recorded and kept private. If there are forms to complete, say why they are structured this way. Avoid snooping or prying into things that don't matter.

Avoid jargonizing assessment, treating it as just something we do, a task to be completed. Explain that it is provisional, to be built on, that it is shared, worked on together. Describe how it will inform plans and decisions; and what it will not be used for, especially if people might fear what we will do. People clam up if they fear that assessments for providing resources or services may lead to their not getting what they want, so be clear about decision-making processes.

Action sequence

Preparation

Establish a 'productive climate' (Compton, Galaway & Cournoyer, 2005: 207) so people feel comfortable exploring information. Agree the aims and focus of *this* assessment, distinguishing it from others in the past, and decide with clients who should contribute and how. For example, family group conferences may generate good contributions to assessments as well as to decision making (Burford, Pennell & MacLeod, 2005). Use first contact information to plan what you will cover in the first interview. Encourage clients to collect information in preparation, and to search out unknowns.

In emergencies, check for physical injury or risks and take control of safety.

Data collection

Documents, interviews and observation are the main sources of information. Start by collecting referral information, past records from your agency and other relevant agencies and online sources. Document information from agency contacts that you make, feeding back what you have recorded to check its accuracy. Record where there is no information, so you can see the gaps to be filled in later.

Collect and date precise information about people's experiences, feelings and relationships. Start from current family relationships, financial, material and housing circumstances, health and education issues. Move backward from the current situation if you are doing a social history or need more context.

Personal material to cover (the mnemonic BASIC helps):

- **B**ehaviours you are concerned about and that show how you are reacting to the issues, for example tackling them, avoiding them, being immobilized.

- **A**ffective (feeling) issues, feeling reactions you are concerned about such as anger or hostility, anxiety or fear, sadness.
- **S**omatic (body) issues, such as sleeplessness, butterflies in the stomach, injuries, disabilities.
- **I**nterpersonal issues, such as relationship problems and resources.
- **C**ognitive issues, such as how you are perceiving or thinking about the situation.

Most assessments rely on interpersonal engagement, including interviews with clients, people around them and within other relevant agencies, for example hospitals, schools, workplaces. 'Questioning' approaches to assessment rely on professionals controlling the topics covered. 'Procedural' approaches rely on your agency's functions and systems to direct what you do. 'Exchange' approaches acknowledge that clients and people around them know what information is useful and are expert in their own affairs, while you are expert in how to interpret it and use it in your intended intervention (Smale, Tuson, Biehal & Marsh, 1993). Exchange allows you to overcome your limitations and extend your agency's perspective. Reach for information in discussions and interviews. Avoid just receiving it; try for more and better detail.

Open-ended questions get more and less biased information, that is where people cannot answer with a simple 'yes' or 'no'. Practise active listening, by showing your attention to what is said by continual verbal and non-verbal responses, for example attentive posture, maintain eye contact, avoid fidgeting and distraction. Check back regularly to make sure you have understood, clarify anything you are uncertain about and make notes or complete boxes on forms to show you are retaining important information. Prefer 'what' questions (what happened? what's important?) because they are less threatening than 'why' questions. Try to overcome moves to deny or over-simplify complexities, such as the intersection of different inequalities such as class, ethnicity, gender and sexualities. Get people to be specific for example ask for a recent incident showing how an issue affects people involved.

Observation is an important alternative to and check on what people say. Find ways to observe behaviour and relationships in interview and in real life, for example by home visits.

Analysis formulating problems and strengths

Become a thinking and critical collector of information, appraising what you have found. Focus your attention on the important issues that bring the case to you and your agency. Analyse, query and test information; comparing what different sources say allows you to move towards making inferences about matters that people have not raised or that you have not yet observed. Identify and control factors that may bias definitions of problems, such as limitations in perspective. Generate hypotheses about what is happening, both about the whole case (what is going on here?) and about selected important parts of the case. Find out about others' speculations (for example colleagues, other agencies involved).

While assessment gathers and organizes information into a pattern, it also balances data with a 'narrative truth', showing how different people involved experience and interpret facts (Parton & O'Byrne, 2000: 140). While you receive descriptions of events and facts, you also get perceptions (alternative views), feelings and cognitions (alternative thoughts and evaluations) and how people reacted to and behaved as they dealt with these different interpretations of events. For example, the parties to a marriage break-up usually differ in how they see, interpret and react to events within and facts about their relationship. Their children, parents and parents-in-law also have differing narratives. Create a unified narrative of the events and interpretations from 'whys and wherefores', clients' attempts to explain behaviour. Focusing on what happened reduces emotional responses that swirl around 'why' interpretations.

The narratives enable you to move from referrals and requests for services towards agreeing on the issues that you need to work on.

Assessment tools

Most agencies have standard formats for collecting information that meet their legal and administrative requirements. Often, these require the completion of standardized risk assessments, or scales. You can also use general assessment tools such as ecograms, genograms and network diagrams, especially if you find visual presentation of information helpful and are less comfortable with lots of words.

Looking at issues or problems

In emergencies, look at factors that make people physically unsafe, vulnerable to immediate problems or unable to protect themselves. Where there is longer-term distress, look for distress signals: difficulty in managing feelings, suicidal or risky behaviour, alcohol or substance abuse, contraventions of the law or trouble with the authorities.

Identify issues that clients face or problems that the agency needs to take up. With a problem or strengths perspective, aim to define problems or strengths clearly and select focuses within that. Consider the severity, duration and frequency of problems. Balance information on problems and liabilities in clients and people around them with a strengths perspective. Cover resources and social capital people can call on, such as links to helpful people or organizations. Incorporate creative ideas from clients and people around them, capabilities for tackling issues, strengths and past successes. Positioning clients involves:

- Placing clients' and family and community members' places in important social structures such as family, school and work; think about class, religion, sex roles.
- Exploring stages of development within the lifecourse, in family development and in the development of a community's resources. An important kind of developmental assessment is a social history: looking at a client's life story through their human relationships. This is important where, for example with foster children and other long-term care, the assessment may be an information resource for clients and family members in the future.
- External factors, how social issues and resources connect with this client; how external and personal factors have affected them.

Make it clear you are respecting clients' own definitions of issues, for example by listing them on a sheet, flipchart or whiteboard separately from your notes. This is important when engaging involuntary clients (Trotter, 2006).

Consider discrepancies between different sources, resolving them if you can or at least flagging them up. Explore uncertainties and mixed feelings, conflicts between present realities and hopes and wishes, between the actual and the ideal. These can lead to fear, disappointment, sadness, hopelessness associated with anxiety or depression.

Consider power relations in the definition of problems. Think about whether class, ethnicity, gender and social power have influenced how people see problems. For example, in families, do men define difficulties differently from women? In care homes, school or work, do powerful interests, such as regulatory bodies, influence problem definition by blaming individuals for being 'difficult'? They may not recognize failings in regimes or inappropriate objectives.

Moving towards planning

Make connections between different aspects of the assessment, building on the unified narrative. Connect apparently discrete events into a full picture and recast problems and strengths to make them clear. Clarify your and your agency's roles, especially if they involve potential social control for example safeguarding action. Make clear what is negotiable and what is not and explain agency and other expectations, especially with social control responsibilities. If people resist this, maintain the authority of your protective role. With permission, share information that is only known to some. Explanation of likely future actions may contain your and their anxiety.

Partialize a complex issue, dividing it into smaller chunks. Decision trees can help make options explicit and evaluate how successful they are likely to turn out (Dalzell & Sawyer, 2016: 151–87). You identify the decision you need to make, list the options and list possible favourable and unfavourable outcomes of each one. It is possible to allocate a numerical risk to each potential outcome.

Balance protective and risk factors and people's human rights to make their own decisions, for example with older people at risk of falling in their own home. Recognize and value alternative ways of being caring, being parents, being carers of a disabled or older person. Make explicit that denial and ambivalence may be a helpful part of managing difficulties in life. For example, not talking about terminal illness helps some families cope with what everyone knows; check that some family members, especially children, are not left out of the loop.

Identify external pressures, such as the impact of poverty, oppression and bullying, that you can resolve or reduce. Be clear that this may not be enough and explain how to find and summon emergency or extra help; ensure it will respond. Recognize that emotional ill-effects persist, even if you manage to remove risks.

Bring out alternatives, perhaps from different sources, testing them out with people involved. Point out consequences of different options; listen for uncertainty or preferences for options.

Link problems and strengths to possible aims and actions. Summarize the information and analysis path that leads you to formulate immediate aims and actions, and how these form part of longer-term aims and actions. Be clear about possible barriers to achieving aims.

Things to think about

Think through your assessment model. Is it simple enough to carry in your head, adaptable to a variety of situations covering the ground that clients, you and your agency need? Is it holistic, maintaining a 360-degree perspective that includes the personal, social and economic situations of relevant individuals, families and communities? Does it consider an appropriate range of factors? Is it sensitive to power issues around, for example, gender, ethnicity? Does it evaluate cultural, economic and social blocks to meeting clients' interests? Is it flexible enough to deal with unusual or conflictual situations? Will it still be relevant later in interventions and longer-term involvements? Does the material it covers help to guide your intervention?

Try scaling different aspects of an assessment to see what you know well, and less well. You can also scale your level of certainty about aspects of information, the contribution of various people involved. These checks on what happened during an initial assessment, or as you review what you have learned from a period of working on a case, give you targets for future information gathering and for people to involve in the future.

Ideas from your peers, clients and people involved from their wider family and community add to your reflection and supervision to help you improve the process and outcomes of assessments.

Look for, make explicit and deal with potential constraints on your assessment:

- excessive and conflicting demands by agencies, referrers, clients and yourself to assess too much detail, to know everything, preventing progression towards intervention;
- pressures to think narrowly, for example only about agencies' or referrers' aims;
- tensions between respecting and valuing clients' uniqueness and putting them into categories (Meyer, 1993).

Further resources

Aspinwall-Roberts, E. (2012). *Assessments in social work with adults.* Maidenhead: Open University Press.

Dalzell, R. & Sawyer, E. (2016). *Putting analysis into child and family assessment: Undertaking assessments of need* (3rd edn). London: Jessica Kingsley.

Holland, S. (2010). *Child and family assessment in social work practice* (2nd edn). London: Sage.

Good introductions in particular areas of practice.

Milner, J., Myers, S. & O'Byrne, P. (2015). *Assessment in social work* (4th edn). London: Palgrave.

A useful comprehensive, well-established guide.

Taylor, B.J. (2017). *Decision making, assessment and risk in social work* (3rd edn). London: Sage.

Good on decision making arising from assessment.

Walker, S. & Beckett, C. (2011). *Social work assessment and intervention* (2nd edn). Lyme Regis: Russell House.

Connects assessment well with changes in UK administration and policy.

Check the online resources at policy.bristoluniversitypress.co.uk/how-to-use-social-work-theory-in-practice/online-resources/chapter3 for a full list of references for this chapter.

4

Communication, advice, information

Setting the scene

What is communication, advice and information?

Communication is the skill of imparting or exchanging information and understanding through interpersonal interaction. You do it when you take action, speak, write and when you use any medium that permits processing, storing and passing on information. Advice is helpful communication offering recommendations for prudent and wise actions. Information is communication of facts or realities. A lot of social work involves giving people information and advice in ways that they can assimilate and use.

Aims

Making an effort with communication helps to build clients' and practitioners' ability to work together. An important communication aim is to help both be aware of the importance of language and communication as a basis for helping practice and dealing with life; they need to communicate with you if you are going to be successful in helping them. Advice and information are concrete services, empowering because they provide access to opportunities for clients to resolve problems through their own actions.

Uses

Communication is a fundamental basis of human life: you communicate with others by how you present your self to them, and by everything you do and say. Professional practitioners use this universal human characteristic to perceive, receive and interpret accurately others' communications with us, and to communicate accurately with others. Among the media you use are interpersonal and written communication, and information and communication technology (ICT), such as computers, mobile phones and the internet.

STARTING

Clear, comprehensive, concise, courteous
Explain agency frame
Tune in
Create good communication environment
Seek permission for recording and technology
Offer choice
Give and take time to process understanding

COMMUNICATION BASICS

Listen actively
Model good communication
Reach for feelings
Non-spoken and spoken communication

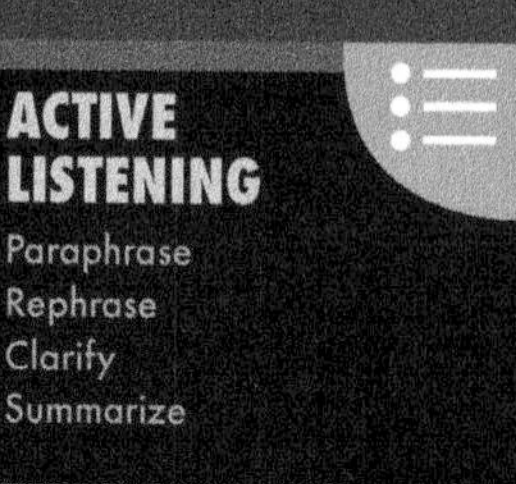

ACTIVE LISTENING

Paraphrase
Rephrase
Clarify
Summarize

EXPLORE COMMUNICATION PATTERNS

Bring communication patterns to the surface
Explore relationship communication patterns

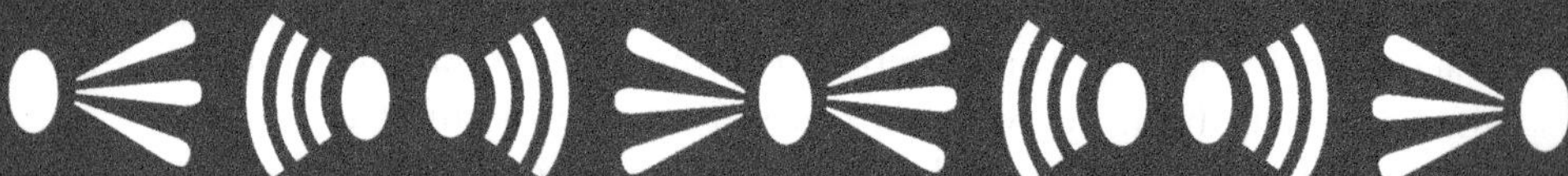

PARTICIPATION IN DECISIONS

- Clarify aims, process, possible outcomes
- Identify participants, roles
- Help clients decide, rehearse
- Separate professional and advocacy roles
- Help with documents, reports

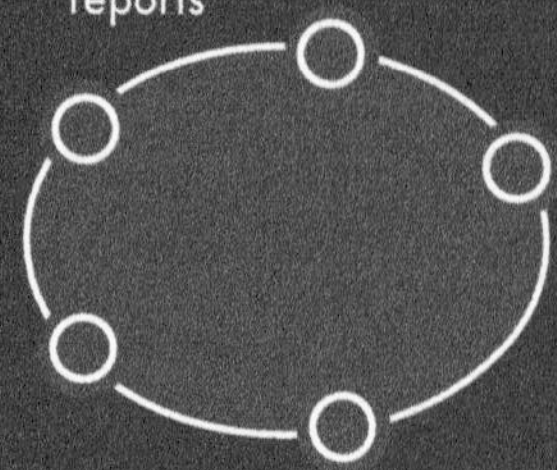

COMMUNICATION ISSUES

Difficulties: empathy, collaborate, tune in
Complexity: structure, diagrams, narratives, repetition
Relationships: balance, rivalry, dependence
Challenge: raise concerns, consequences, alternatives
Aggression: describe, discuss, offer help

INFORMATION, ADVICE

- Explain responsibilities
- Ask permission
- Clarify purpose
- Explain sources
- Explore alternatives
- Back up spoken information
- Talk about communication
- Use technology

Communication, giving advice and providing information are all basic roles of social work practitioners, informed by theory and knowledge from the humanities, the social sciences and ICT. They may be incorporated into other theoretical approaches to social work, or may be an important agency role in their own right.

Human communication theory (Hargie, 2016) is not widely used in social work as a psychotherapeutic model, so I don't explicitly cover research in this field, although it informs communication practice ideas.

Introducing communication, advice- and information-giving

Explicitly raise with the people you are involved with how you can help improve communication as you work together, and expand the focus to relationships generally if clients find communication difficult. Doing this can lead on to talking through what people may find difficult in communication. You can also explore how you plan to use communication to work with clients.

Much social work practice guidance is cautious about advice- and information giving. One reason is that the counselling style of interpersonal practice is usually non-directive, with the aim of facilitating clients to make their own decisions, rather than pushing your point of view. Giving advice, on the other hand, assumes that practitioners' views about decisions should be influential, so it can seem presumptuous. Giving information assumes that practitioners' information is more valid or worthwhile than other sources, so be clear about its sources and its importance. Another reason is the opposite: in interpersonal helping, giving advice or information may not be enough to overcome barriers in clients' emotions or thinking, or resistance to practitioners' agency and professional authority.

Nevertheless, it is a responsibility of the agency and practitioner to provide appropriate and accurate advice and information about the services they provide and other matters. Doing so may be an important part of advocacy, safeguarding and other important roles. Make your purposes clear when setting out to give advice and information, therefore, but explain alternative sources and views. Being clear with clients about how you will take up your agency and professional duties is an important area of advice- and information-giving, especially when you need to use legal powers.

Action sequence

Communication on starting: setting, environment, privacy

First impressions count: be clear, comprehensive, concise and courteous in human and written communication. Consider your backstage behaviour: if you can't say it to someone's face don't say or write it elsewhere. If you express views in a committee or a report, think about how you will communicate it to the client, carer, family or community member.

Consider and explain your agency 'frame': how do the aims, responsibilities and roles of you or your agency frame the communication you are about to engage with? For example, it might limit the issues you can deal with or, on the other hand, force you to move into areas such as safeguarding that the client is unprepared for or hostile to. Pre-plan any interaction by considering aims and exploring existing information, including existing files or reports. Aims and uses of communication often include:

- information-gathering or -giving;
- assessment and evaluation of information;
- therapeutic change in people or environments, through providing information.

Create an environment that facilitates good communication. 'Tune in' to what's important to your client and others, and how they like to communicate. Find out likes and dislikes about preferred modes of or arrangements for communication; for example, do they prefer a phone call, texting or face-to-face contact. Consider for children whether games, toys or gadgets may facilitate communication; learn, together with or from them, emojis and texting abbreviations. Using phones, consider the privacy and technical limitations. For example, in the office or visiting clients' homes, ask to turn off the television or other media, agree to turn off mobile phones, perhaps re-orientate furniture, move to another room which is more comfortable. Ensure privacy from other members of the family or from being overheard by others, particularly in institutional environments such as care homes or hospitals. Old-fashioned hospitals often have limited provision for private interviews, so ask what may be possible, and try to get improvements.

If you are going to use recording apparatus, explain why and secure the client's agreement; perhaps this will need to be a written agreement, but at least record that you have agreed. Allow a little time to demonstrate and play with the apparatus if it is unfamiliar.

Communicate respect: offer choice about communication, be comfortable with silence, giving time for people to process information, taking time to process your thinking: 'I'll just stop for a moment to think that through.'

Communication basics

From the outset, listen actively in your interactions with clients, using non-spoken and spoken communication. Travel through their story together. Continue with this; concentrate. Active listening involves:

- paraphrasing, rephrasing what the client said to show your understanding or repeating it if it was a crucial point (see Chapter 6 for more detail);
- clarifying, asking clients about meaning and importance and saying how this helps you understand;
- summarizing, picking out the important points made.

Observe, think and be explicit about communication information. Be aware of and explain the emotional climate that you observe in clients' relationships. For example, is it tense, scratchy, emotionless? Put what you see into words to check: 'I can see you feel …'; model a feeling vocabulary. Reach for feelings, particularly unarticulated ones. Ask an open question first, but follow up with how they felt then, how they feel now, how feelings changed. On the other hand, once clients have given information, confirm it using closed or narrow questions, those you can answer 'yes' or 'no' to. Model appropriate communication and help clients understand explicitly where their communication is inappropriate. For example, use an example of a client's communication to explain what is helpful and unhelpful.

Non-spoken communication involves:

- facial expression
- eye contact
- posture
- touch
- proximity

Spoken communication involves:

- register, the kind of language used and its formality
- speed

- pitch
- volume
- tone, how emotions are conveyed

Observing these helps you understand people's feelings and responses. For example, low volume, lack of eye contact and maintaining physical distance may indicate shyness and anxiety. Another example: anger or aggression may be indicated by facial expression, proximity, volume or tone.

You may want to learn one of the systems for analysing human communication, for example see Koprowska (2014).

Work on patterns of communication

For relationships to work in the long term, people establish ways of communicating with each other. They fix agreed ideas about the image that each presents to the world and in the relationship and acceptable and unacceptable topics of discussion. Observe interactions, then ask about or bring to the surface the image that clients and others present of themselves to the world. Explore these relationship patterns, by seeing how they typically talk and, on the other hand, identifying things they would never say to each other. For example, people can be unaware of how negativity, putting someone down regularly, sometimes percolates into the pattern of a relationship. That can lead to one person feeling oppressed and unable to challenge the adverse atmosphere. Another example is talking over the other, interrupting them or redirecting the conversation away from a topic that the other has started. If someone shows these communication patterns, point it out to them every time and demonstrate better patterns. Suggest that people can agree communication rules, for example one turn at a time, no complaints unless you make a positive suggestion. Similarly, aggression or anger expressed in a relationship can make the other apprehensive about communicating important things. Think through with a client or carer appropriate times, places and ways of communicating emotions such as anger or frustration that may be experienced as difficult.

Describing and exploring these patterns makes it possible to disrupt them, asking people as homework to try a different way of communicating, or a different presentation for an hour a day. They can discuss with each other and report back how this changes their relationships. There may be a chain reaction in which such changes lead on to further relationship changes.

Communication issues

Help people follow complex material, for example use clear structure, diagrams, narratives, repetition.

Help people raise communication issues in their relationships. Explore balance and fairness in communication. Help clients think through how they express blame, responsibility, rivalry, dependence or independence of the other; on the other hand, help them express positive feelings for the other person regularly and at the best times.

Challenge behaviour by feeding back your worries, asking about and then describing possible consequences. Ask how other people will be affected or feel. Offer alternatives, ask how they might be better. Explore the aims and roles of authority figures. Discuss alternative behaviour that does not impinge on those aims and roles.

Respond to aggression by clear description of behaviour that worries you, and inviting further discussion. Avoid asking lots of questions, and prefer to talk about how you can help build more positive communication behaviour.

Where making progress is difficult, give advance warning and time to tune in to the difficult issues: 'I want to raise something that is hard for us to deal with.' Ask for their views. Use collaboration: 'How can we work on this together?'

With difficult emotions, use empathy: paraphrase their account describing your understanding, ask about positives, feelings: 'You found that a frightening event, but at least you heard what he thought. How did it make you feel?'

Client participation in decision making

An important area of information sharing is facilitating clients' participation in decision-making processes, such as case conferences. The fear of adverse consequences such as, in children's services, losing parental rights or, in adult services, not achieving care funding packages, may silence people (Smithson & Gibson, 2017) or lead to other responses that obstruct communication. Prepare clients by being clear about the aims of the process, participants and their roles, and possible or likely outcomes. Help the client decide what they want to say. Rehearse or otherwise help them prepare what they are going to say and what is appropriate behaviour. If they are not going to be present, help them be clear what they want said on their behalf, whether they can or should have an advocate and who this should be. Can you advocate for them? You may be the only option if there is no advocacy or representation scheme. If so, think through what your stance about the decisions will be, bearing in mind your responsibilities. Explore with clients and families clashes between your and your agency's view and theirs. You might help them prepare documents expressing their views. Throughout the process, be clear when you are presenting agency or professional judgements and clients', carers' and other views. If there are reports or documentation, help clients, carers and others involved read and understand them. For more on advocacy, see Chapter 12.

Things to think about

Communication contains informational content, a means of communication and a relationship. How the content and the communication works is influenced by the relationship. Communications are punctuated sequences of interchange between the communicators. Conversations are broken up as the speaker and listener change roles, change subjects, and change the medium of communication. Look at these patterns if conversations don't seem to be working smoothly.

Back up or extend one form or medium of advice, communication or information by another. For example, support spoken advice by reminders such as written instructions or information leaflets. Written information can be given context and interest by a spoken interchange. Use whiteboards or flipcharts to co-construct communications, that is, work on the communication with clients and other people you are involved with.

Use appropriate assistive technology when working with people with disabilities. Choose aids that they are accustomed to, for reading and hearing. With sensory (seeing, hearing, feeling) disabilities, find out what affects clients and act accordingly, for example facing people in clear light, using gestures, to give them all the clues to meaning that you can offer. Also check whether older people fully understand how their hearing or seeing may be declining, and compensate. People with intellectual disabilities may find visual assistance, including pictures, symbols, emojis, useful.

Consider the ethics of giving or not giving advice and information. The motivational interviewing approach of asking for permission may help you to test clients' and others' perceptions. Failure to advise or inform may exclude people from the ability to act, or lead to the practitioner or agency being negligent or obstructive.

Practitioners need feedback on their communication skills, and your agency may have feedback forms that bring results you can explore.

Consider eliciting feedback from regular clients; perhaps you have taken their views for granted because you have established a pattern of communication with them. Individual practitioners can, with clients' permission, use video equipment available on phones, tablets and laptops to critically examine their approach. Teams can do this in pairs or groups.

Further resources

Koprowska, J. (2014). *Communication and interpersonal skills in social work* (4th edn). London: Sage.

Woodcock Ross, J. (2016). *Specialist communication skills for social workers: Developing professional capability* (2nd edn). London: Palgrave.

Two comprehensive and practical guides, with detailed guidance for different client groups and social work situations.

Check the online resources at policy.bristoluniversitypress.co.uk/how-to-use-social-work-theory-in-practice/online-resources/chapter4 for a full list of references for this chapter.

5

Counselling

Setting the scene

What is counselling?

Counselling is giving assistance by facilitating clients to explore and resolve personal concerns. You use your 'self' in a respectful relationship with the client. Counselling focuses on emotional, psychological or spiritual reactions to life events, transitions and interpersonal relationships (McLeod, 2013). It is a step from advice towards personal helping.

Counselling is a separate profession in many countries, but until the 1960s social work was the main source of personnel for counselling. In some countries, particularly in North America, social work remains a major mental health counselling and psychotherapy profession. International representations of social work theory, therefore, sometimes give prominence to counselling and psychotherapy, without differentiating it from counselling by accredited professionals. Elsewhere, it is a skill that social workers use as part of wider practice.

Aims

Counselling helps people think through personal and interpersonal troubles so that they can use their own human and social resources to resolve those troubles. It is related to psychotherapy, but social work's roots are wider, less concerned with treatment for behaviour disorders and mental illness. In social work, counselling focuses on clarifying people's subjective experience and the meanings they attach to events in their lives (Halmos, 1965: 3). This enables you to move on to changing clients' attitudes and skills. The aim is to improve their management of social relationships and problem solving. You do this by building up and harnessing clients' existing capacity.

APPROACH

Create a shared agenda and alliance
See yourself as a temporary resource
Help to identify and explore life problems
Work out aims for an improved life scenario
Devise steps towards the scenario
Strive to understand by stepping back

Boundaries
Professional power

USE YOUR SELF

Build integrity, empathy and acceptance through self-work and supervision

UNDERSTAND CLIENTS IN THEIR WORLD

Enact encouragement
Be non-directive and supportive
Explore individual experiences
Look for possible alternatives
Understand their view of the world
Are they in tune with it or dissonant?
Understand their drive to make progress
Offer support to motivate them
Clarify their attitude to being helped

YOUR SKILLS

Square up
Open posture
Lean forwards
Eye contact
Relaxed

INTERVENTIONS

Listen, paraphrase and mirror words
Be assertive about wanting to help
Balance helping and enabling
Be flexible about aims
Uncover events and insights into them
Evaluate personality interactions
Reveal strengths and resources
Fully explore emotions and reactions
Allow time to explore complexity
Make thin narratives thicker
Seek both maintenance and change
Search for and evaluate solutions

Uses

Counselling is an element in all helping activity. Examples are: improving people's understanding so that they can contribute to assessment; helping people make improved choices about using services. It may also assist clients and families to understand their needs and wishes so that they can participate in advocacy and policy-making. Enabling them to assess and manage risks in their lives, work together with professionals in safeguarding and service provision, and understand how they can work with agencies and other organizations are also useful. Counselling may help people respond to difficult or life-changing events. Such events generate powerful or uncommon reactions that people need help with. Where wider social work engages with intimate issues, for example sexuality, or important interpersonal relationships, for example divorce and marriage, counselling may become an important element of social work interventions.

Important aspects of counselling in social work are:

- helping clients understand, regulate and use their emotions and reactions as part of their social situations;
- your personal self as part of your professional self, its emotions and reactions to clients and their worlds;
- how clients' and your emotions and reactions in the counselling process affect the social world in which they live;
- how clients and you manage emotions and reactions better in the counselling process and in wider social relationships.

These 'wider social relationships' include the whole social work process and your counselling work as part of it. Counselling is, in this way, reflexive: it feeds into the wider social work, which in turn affects how the counselling proceeds.

Introducing counselling

Clients engage in counselling alongside other social work interventions. Agencies may not see this as a priority, but it often smoothes the path of other interventions. Sometimes, clients ask for counselling help, or it becomes obvious that they want or need it. Issues susceptible to counselling often emerge in healthcare settings, where people negotiate birth, severe illness or disability, or death and bereavement. It may also come up when important transitions affect people with mental illness or intellectual or physical disabilities, for example moving home, losing an important carer. You might be able to refer clients to a counselling service, but this is often unavailable or over-stretched, or clients cannot afford it. Sometimes befriending or volunteer support is available and that's enough to keep people on an even keel as things change around them, for example bereavement services.

If counselling help seems useful, relevant to the case plan, and needs more than brief supportive conversations, introduce it by agreeing to set aside some sessions to explore the issues of concern. Between four and six sessions of up to an hour provide a regular time-limited chance, separate from other pressures, to uncover and sift through the issues. Agreement to do this can be renewed if further time is needed.

Action sequence

Starting point and approach

All the theoretical approaches used in interpersonal social work also inform counselling approaches, with humanistic person-centred and narrative approaches currently dominant (see Chapters 7 and 10). Pursuing a theoretical approach offers the security of greater clarity in practice. Like social work, however, many counsellors are eclectic, that is, selecting aspects of different theories to use as required, or integrational, that is, building up a single perspective from elements of several theories. Egan's (2010; 2014) 'skilled helper' model fits well with social work. It assumes you help clients with identifying and exploring problems in their lives, working out their objectives into a preferred scenario for the aspects of their lives that you are working on together, and devising steps towards reaching that scenario.

Unlike social work, you step back from doing things to achieve that preferred scenario. Instead, your role as a counsellor is to facilitate clients' own exploration and action. You are a temporary supplement to their lives, helping them use their own resources, aiming to move the locus of control away from the helping process towards independent thinking and action. So, you step back.

Clients in their world

You do not, however, lean back: show that you are striving to understand and help clients understand themselves, their actions, their world. Enact encouragement, being non-directive and supportive. See them and their world from their point of view and in their social context. Explore that view: is it in tune or dissonant with other perceptions?

Focus on the client as an individual: how are they experiencing, perceiving and thinking about their social situation? Expand their perspectives as they describe what is happening, encourage them to see a wider range of issues. Can they see different ways of understanding what happened or additional possibilities? If what they are doing to tackle a problem doesn't work, could they find another way?

What is a client's drive to make progress? Participating in counselling must be voluntary, or people won't put in the emotional labour involved, that is make the effort to engage with difficult feelings. Identify and support factors that motivate them to work on the issues you jointly face in the counselling, for example making sense of a difficult situation or surprising feelings.

But even if they seek or accept counselling, clients may be reluctant to deal with the implications of the outcomes of rethinking their views of the world. Our lives are often unexamined and we cannot imagine how things may be different. Clients may fear, for example, that there will be conflicts, or they will have to reveal things that worry them or that they are ashamed of. Perhaps they see themselves as strong, and receiving help as weak. Respond to reluctance by emphasizing that they are co-producing, that is, part of deciding on and implementing, this process. Help them see that it's not being done to them, they control the agenda, even though you will help by identifying things to work on. Perhaps they have been discriminated against or treated disrespectfully in the past, or have had bad experiences of professional help. Deal with this by openly setting up regular 'share the unfair' moments as part of your time together, perhaps every half hour. If something that you are doing, or something that happens repeats a bad experience of the past, or it looks as though you're going that way, keep an eye open for rising anxiety, and spend a few minutes exploring worries. Involve friends or relatives in supporting the client to carry on.

Your 'self' and your skills as part of counselling

Be constantly aware of how you are holding yourself and reacting physically. This sharpens how you are projecting your attitude. Good communication means tuning in to clients and their concerns (the mnemonic SOLER helps):

- **S**quare up to clients, don't sit at an angle, or gaze out of the window or at your papers.

- **O**pen your posture, don't cross arms or wring hands, tighten face or leg muscles.
- **L**ean alertly towards clients.
- **E**ye contact, without glaring or staring.
- **R**elaxed and natural, polite but not formal, leave aside the red tape (Egan, 2014).

Integrity is about your genuineness as a human being in this counselling relationship. How you behave towards clients must be integrated with how you think, feel and believe about them. If it's not, you will seem false in your reactions. Confirm your reciprocal commitments to the process, sharing co-responsibility for aims and tasks, with both of you equals in working for the client's best interests. Acknowledge you both bring strengths and limitations to counselling. Acknowledge awareness of the power of your professional status and, if relevant, official role.

Are you sympathetic and caring, warm, treating the client as your equal, liking and respecting them? Make sure this comes across. Remember you are not a friend for life, but a temporary resource. To be a useful resource, you need awareness of your own responses to the issues clients are concerned with. For example, a social worker who recently miscarried felt that she could not help a widow work on her feelings about the recent death of her husband. The social worker's own loss meant that she did not have the emotional resources to help at that time; a few years later, her experience helped her be empathetic with bereaved clients.

Be wholehearted in your concern and commitment to help them. But keep a balance between helping and enabling (Jordan, 1979). Accept that while you want to be the person who is most of help, the best way of doing that is to enable people to do things for themselves. What has got in the way of dealing with this problem? What do you need to know that will help you tackle this? Emotional support and reassurance are an important part of mental health services.

Empathy for clients means engaging your emotional responses with their experiences. It builds on your striving to understand them and the issues they are trying to tackle. Show that you value their efforts. Demonstrate your commitment to a belief that understanding the client and their concerns are a valuable way of moving on in their lives, that these issues can be understood and worked on. There is more in Chapters 7 and 16 on humanistic practice and motivational interviewing.

The role of acceptance and unconditional positive regard in counselling is to separate the client's intrinsic worth from their behaviours and problems. Express and demonstrate this: 'I think we should explore how being loving to your daughter led you to ignore things that you might have helped her with.'

Ask permission to challenge clients, exercising authority to prevent them doing unwise things and motivating them when they are in the doldrums: 'I wonder if I can help you question the choice you made there?'

For clients, and sometimes for ourselves, issues that we need to take up are on the edge of awareness; we feel something is not quite right, or we do not quite understand. Explore the particularity of events. Many aspects of life are ambiguous, a balance of pluses and minuses. Look at uncertainties, unclarities, both sides. Try to clarify and understand feelings and the impacts they had on those involved. What strengths, weaknesses, risks, expectations are revealed? Did they lead to triumphs or let-downs? Did they help to sustain or damage relationships?

As your counselling moves on, try, with your supervisor, to challenge your own assumptions and recognize blocks that prevent you from listening carefully or responding appropriately.

Counselling interventions

Start by creating a shared agenda, developing an alliance to work on it. Both your client and you are creating 'a small community of diversity' (Derezotes, 2000: 9). *Diverse* because you are unique people in different social positions and roles; a *community* because you are joining together, respecting and trusting each other to work together. Emphasize flexibility in amending initial aims. Pick up concerns, issues, objectives and be assertive about wanting to help with it.

Start each session by listening: 'what's happened about … since we met?'. Aim to uncover relevant new events and insight since you last met, and rising or declining emotions and reactions. Listen for strengths, opportunities and resources to be revealed. Simply setting out on narratives of events can reveal new understanding. As the client tells you the story of what happened, they are putting their narrative together, that is, their assumptions or explanations are demonstrated by what they exclude, include or take for granted in the story. Doing this may allow you to identify unexpressed feelings about what happened. See more in Chapter 10 on narrative practice.

Make sure clients' emotions and reactions to issues and to being involved in counselling are fully explored. You may hear minimal or 'thin' accounts of clearly complex troubles. Do they fear revealing too much, uncovering unimagined traumas? Emphasize how you both share in handling what you work on, so they don't need to fear getting out of control. Particularly in the early stages, spend time listening, because people feel put down if they think you are pushing them to solutions too quickly. Allow time for their explorations of complexity and uncertainty to emerge.

When counselling is concerned with personality factors it does not judge or invade privacy. We want to understand and work on how personalities interact and especially how they interfere with social relationships, for example parents and children, marital relationships, and affect social institutions, for example community groups, schools, workplaces.

Make thin narratives thicker: ask for additional details, alternative points of view, wider thoughts. You are not just an observer, but participating in making events and experiences more understandable. What was most interesting or valuable about what she said? What did you find difficult to understand? What would help you understand it better? How did you feel when that happened?

Two important actions are:

- Paraphrasing – using your own choice of words to collect up and feed back in an organized way the importance of a series of points the client has made. You do this summarizing regularly, to check and demonstrate that you have understood.
- Mirroring – identifying and making clear how important a feeling or experience is; do this rarely. You repeat exactly what the client said about it, pointing up its significance: 'When you said "...", I thought you were making a really new point about what happened. What do you think?'.

Paraphrasing and mirroring help you to clarify and point up the important feelings and reactions that the client is experiencing, not how you think and feel. After paraphrasing and mirroring follow up with 'because ...'. For example, they are angry about what their child has done ... perhaps because it is important that the child avoids getting into trouble or upsetting the neighbours, or because they fear the child getting out of control. To get at the 'because', ask yourselves why this part of the story is important to the client and think how you can explain this to them.

Based on this greater understanding, move clients on to search for and evaluate solutions. Focus on thinking through differences in their experiences and alternative pathways of action. How was her reaction different from previous occasions? Are there other better ways he might react? How could you help her do that differently? Aim to demonstrate that you are jointly developing understanding and potential actions.

Counselling does not necessarily seek change in the person. Maintaining things as they are against pressures for things to go downhill may be worthwhile. For example, when a man had head injuries from an industrial accident, his wife decided on the priorities of keeping up mortgage payments and their daughter's revision for her examinations, before thinking about longer-term actions. Other non-change gains might include greater insight and individual enlightenment that improve problem-solving abilities and other social skills or raise new opportunities. Such successes may feel good because they are self-actualizing. Improved self-understanding brings a sense of psychological education; improved relationships with others can bring greater social acceptance. Experiences can be put together in a new way. People may be empowered to do something by new insights, or helped to see that they might try several things. Help people articulate their learning and progress.

Things to think about

Counselling does not compensate for inadequate resources in our services or for the long-lasting damage of oppression that affects some people. Look carefully, therefore, at whether a counselling intervention is appropriate and sufficient.

Boundaries are important in clients' and your own emotional management. They are about expectations. What behaviours help people feel safe with each other, even when talking about difficult personal or private matters? Is this professional relationship different from what you expect in friendships? Does a behaviour trespass into personal matters that are not appropriate in a counselling relationship? Does the response vary according to people's culture, ethnicity and gender? Are there issues about your professional power and status and clients' dependence on you in the relationship?

Using your 'self' in counselling means being aware of the constraints and possibilities offered by your identity, experience and views, both personal and professional. Understand ways in which you are already implicated in relationships of power and powerlessness with clients. Counselling makes self-work important. Self-review constantly both the fixed attributes, such as ethnicity and gender, and also the changing feelings, thoughts and behaviours typical of you in relationships. This connects with critical reflection on the intervention, which you inevitably develop both during and after interactions with clients, and through supervision. Self-work helps you include your own reactions to what clients bring into critical reflection about what may hinder or help them. See Chapter 7 on self-actualization and Chapter 25 on critical reflection.

Counselling requires supervision so that you can review your own emotional and personal reactions to what you are experiencing in working with clients.

Further resources

Miller, L. (2012). *Counselling skills for social work* (2nd edn). London: Sage.
Reviews social work applications of important counselling theories.

Riggall, S. (2012). *Using counselling skills in social work*. London: Sage.
A useful practical review of counselling practice and skills in social work settings.

Check the online resources at policy.bristoluniversitypress.co.uk/how-to-use-social-work-theory-in-practice/online-resources/chapter5 for a full list of references for this chapter.

6

Resilience, risk, safeguarding

Setting the scene

What are resilience, risk and safeguarding?

Resilience is the capacity of individuals or social groups, including families and communities, to recover from adversity and the effects of damaging actions or events (Greene, 2012a; Walsh, 2016). Risk is the likelihood of harm or disadvantage to them of adverse actions or events and is an important area of social science understanding (Webb, 2006). Safeguarding is action taken to secure wellbeing by enabling people to have good outcomes to each phase of their lives and by preventing harm from damaging actions or events (Munro, 2008).

Aims

Work on resilience seeks to prevent or right damage to human lives by people's experiences of adversity. We can make people quicker and stronger to respond to adversities and the damage that results.

Risk work centres on:

- identifying how likely harm is to self and others from actions people might take or events that might affect them;
- better managing harmful or problematic actions or events in their lives.

Safeguarding is a system of administrative and legal procedures, in which social workers play a central role. These procedures provide for investigation and planning to mitigate the impact of harmful actions and potential adversities that may interfere with people's wellbeing and security in their personal, family and social relationships.

RESILIENCE, RISK, SAFEGUARDING 6.1

PREPARATION

Legal requirements and procedures
Act on safeguarding concerns in both your work and private life
Training and development work

Types of abuse
areas of risk
'secrets & lies'

AREAS OF RESILIENCE

physical • mental • social
financial • spiritual

SAFEGUARDING

Take allegations and concerns seriously
Act at once if people are at risk
Report concerns
Check: don't rely on the system
Involve agencies and people widely
Cooperate in strategy meetings
Fit investigation into assessment
Create a timeline
Communicate best evidence
Co-evolve plans

SAFEGUARDING RIGHTS

to have basic needs met
to be safe
to be secure from danger
to be able to build connections with others
to be shown affection and love
to achieve potential

RISK

Risk and social work assessment
Define behaviour of concern
Risk to clients from themselves
Risk to clients from others
Risks to others from clients
Scale of likelihood
Scale of seriousness
Signs of safety
Consequences of risk

RISK OF

What
Where
to Whom
When
Why
How?

This person in this situation

MAKING DECISIONS

Use all evidence
Avoid first impressions
Avoid the vivid
Look at social as well as personal factors
Defend against groupthink
Best interests, not safety-first

CAPACITY?

This issue now
Assume capacity
Support decision-making
Practise decision-making

INTERVENTION

Balance clients' risks with their resources
Balance rights to safety and risk-taking
Balance risks and potential harms • Start from human rights
Look for resilience • Clients are partners in managing risk

Uses

Practice in these areas takes up professional social work and agency responsibilities for protecting both adults at risk and children from abuse, harm and neglect. It is regulated by legal provision for both groups of clients, and by local procedural guidelines. More broadly, social care provision and social work seek to counter and prevent social difficulties and pressures that generate abuse, harm and neglect. By building resilience, which unlocks people's personal, family and community resources, social care and social work can generate secure and long-lasting prevention. Resilience is, thus, not about building a 'rugged individual' but safeguarding networks of strong relationships that enable people to respond to adversity and manage risk (Walsh, 2016).

Introducing resilience, risk, safeguarding

Safeguarding is an important professional responsibility of all social workers. Enabling people to feel emotionally and physically secure and resilient in the face of adversity is part of that. Resilience and security gives people and their networks the capacity to reduce the impact of risks in their lives.

Nobody likes being insecure or at risk, and neither does anyone like being criticized or investigated. Procedures set for safeguarding investigations require openness about the fact that there are concerns about safeguarding, what the concerns are and what the duties of social workers and other professionals are. Direct questions allowing people to respond to and deny allegations and concerns are needed at some point early on, but take time to develop some rapport and understanding, ideally shared, of the situation as a whole before getting down to detail about allegations or concerns.

The social work open listening approach at first contact and assessment (see Chapters 2 and 3) gives the people involved the chance to describe their situation and reveal complexities that an allegation or expression of concern do not give you. It allows you to explore it from their starting point. It also allows you to present your responsibility: to people who may be at risk and should get services to help them build security and a sense of safety. Risk is a sign that more needs doing. Sometimes, when you look at risks, you find that you must accept some risk but can do things to control adverse possibilities. Sometimes a focus on resilience allows you to do that in a way that means **clients** can assemble the personal and social resources to deal successfully with the future.

Action sequence

Preparation

Secure your knowledge of legal requirements and procedures for safeguarding that coordinate local responses; every country and often every region has them. Some UK examples are, on children and young people, in England, *Working Together* (HM Government, 2018); in Northern Ireland, the *Procedures Manual* (Safeguarding Board for Northern Ireland, 2018); in Scotland, the *National Guidance* (Scottish Government, 2014); in Wales, the *All Wales Child Protection Procedures* (Children in Wales, 2008); on adults in England, the *Care and support statutory guidance* (Department of Health, 2014). Know and check regularly your agency's protocols for implementing them. Be aware of and act on the direct responsibilities for safeguarding included in your role. Be proactive. In your private life and in carrying out other responsibilities, watch for and raise concerns about abuse, neglect and risk appropriately with the correct authorities. Be persistent in pursuing action; have concerns formally recorded.

Be aware of the full range of types of abuse and areas of risk that may affect your clients. Think about how they might interact in this instance. Consider abuse, harm and neglect that may be less easy to articulate or observe, especially domestic abuse, economic abuse of older people and emotional abuse. Think about the 'secrets and lies' accepted in the life cultures of communities and families.

Identify areas of resilience to understand where improvement may be helpful:

- physical: health and strength to fulfil responsibilities;
- mental: emotional strength, perceptions of control and mastery of tasks required, optimism and hope;
- social: networks, support, education and leisure;
- financial: access to resources, employment, social security;
- spiritual: larger values, meaning, purpose and ways of developing in life and relationships.

Participate in organizational efforts to develop resilience in practitioners, teams and carers, good practice in managing risk, including training and supervision, peer review and support. Make sure only people and agencies that can handle a risk take it on, and ensure staff have skills and competence to handle likely risks, updating them regularly.

Safeguarding principles

All people have the right to have basic needs met: to be safe, secure from danger, able to build connections with others, and to show and be shown affection and love. More than this, people should have the chance of self-development, to build their own wellbeing and to achieve their potential.

Safeguarding stages

National and local guidance and procedures build on a widely relevant sequence of processes.

1. Alerts and reports of allegations and concerns are received and recognized from your own observations and from others' information.
   - 1.1 Reassure informants that you are taking this seriously and will decide on what action to take after you have heard all they want to say.
   - 1.2 Use open questioning: 'I wasn't there, could you … tell me more; … describe that further to me.'
   - 1.3 Explain that to make things safe for this client and others, you will have to inform other people.
   - 1.4 Explore things you don't understand in the account with only minimal interruption.
   - 1.5 Make notes at the time, writing a few phrases down. Make a full record as soon as possible afterwards.
2. Act at once if immediate protection against harm is needed.
3. Report concerns according to the protocols. Check that information has been properly shared; don't rely on the system.
4. Strategy meetings according to the protocol, often by phone, make shared decisions on action. This should cover information sharing, who is informed, who should carry out interviews and visits, what medical and other assessments should be made.
5. If this is your role, investigate within a wider enquiry. Place these events in a timeline within the context of the client's lifecourse, family and community. Investigate each specific concern. Cooperate with investigations that others carry out.
   - 5.1 Consider how the home and wider physical environment and family and community relationships contribute to risk. Particularly so where it makes access or intervention for professionals difficult.

   5.2 Look at spaces where intimate encounters in homes or institutions take place: are they suitable for the age (child or older person) and ability or disability of the client? Do they contribute to abuse, neglect or risk?
   5.3 Look at all relationships with all people present in the client's home. Identify and evaluate other important relationships, for example grandparents, for contribution to successful intervention or risk of harm.
   5.4 Make a chronology, social history or timeline focused on the main victim(s), but cover other appropriate people within family and community.
6. After the investigations, collect and communicate the best available evidence of abuse or risk. Use conferences, sometimes family group conferences (with children) or family meetings (with adults), make safeguarding plans, involving clients and people around them.

Sharing information and responsibility is important in safeguarding, therefore be consistent in cooperating with others so that colleagues and agencies are confident that you and your agency will integrate your approach with theirs. In summary, be predictably cooperative and try to ensure that your agency is similarly consistent in coordinating with other agencies. As work develops, be prepared to co-evolve your own approach with others so that your responses fit together better. Be prepared to negotiate with colleagues about shared approaches. Differentiate clearly among agency and professional responsibilities. Practise 'everyday teamwork', a continual alertness and responsiveness to colleagues' needs and concerns. Voice your own personal and professional needs, so colleagues can cooperate with you.

Risk assessment and management

Broad social work assessment runs alongside risk assessment; decision making should be informed by both. You may have to deal with:

- risk to clients from others, for example abuse or neglect by a family member living with them, and from their own behaviour, for example self-neglect among older people;
- risk from clients' behaviour to known or unknown others, for example mentally disordered offenders may harm a family member or (less likely) a member of the public.

Many safeguarding protocols focus on risk assessment, using risk assessment tools adopted by local coordinating bodies. These aim to decide resource allocation to reduce or prevent risk; risk assessment often intensifies as resources decline. Consider the present balance between risk assessment or seeking more resources. Balance professional judgements and standardized measures in risk assessment. Remember that signs of abuse and other dangers are not predictive; much, if not most, abuse is not understood at the time.

Explore what has been happening in context: what might lead to individuals or people being at risk? Take a critical open-minded approach.

- Risk of what, where, to whom, when, why, how (the mnemonic is 5WH – for another application, see Chapter 15 on cognitive behavioural therapy)?
- Define events or behaviour of concern.
- How likely is it that the risk will occur – rate 1–10 (be sure you are sharing the same rating scale, for example is 1 low and 10 high or vice versa)?
- In what situations might the risk arise?
- Impact: how serious will it be if the risk occurs?
- Consequences of the risk: who might be affected, what harms might occur?

Look for counter-evidence. Check what people say against other evidence. Never rely on memory: keep notes about important matters and include them in official records. Check through it all when making a review. Always interview the alleged victim and hear their views. Bear in mind, but don't overweight, factors that might lead them not to tell the truth, for example fear of consequences, misunderstanding. Avoid discounting the evidence of low-status or inexperienced colleagues or people in the community, because they may have seen something, or achieved a rapport with someone, that is not accessible to you.

Taking risks

People vary in their capacity to take risks. All humans are fallible so risk-taking may lead to loss. But even prudent humans take risks because they must meet needs, although some needs, for example for survival, are more important than others, for example for having fulfilling life experiences. No situation is certain, perhaps safety is desirable, sometimes risk is. Prediction is impossible: you are looking for 'signs of safety' (Turnell & Edwards, 1999) or strengths, showing that resilience and safeguarding in family and networks around a person at risk protect them. Consider clients' physical, psychological and emotional wellbeing against possible disadvantages and harms. Identify their values that will be supported by taking a risk, for example personal independence, supporting a spouse.

To take risk successfully, you and clients for example parents of children at risk, or adults at risk and their carers, need conscious awareness and clarity that something is at stake. Listen carefully to the narrative: how is the perception of risk influenced by potential rewards and by experience of accidents or losses, their own and others'? Assess clients' wishes and feelings about taking a risk. Be precise about what they perceive as risky. Balance this with clients' and families' capabilities and coping resources. Balance clients' and families' rights to protect against risks: don't force carers to take on clients' risks, or parents to risk children's safety, which they can't accept, but don't swaddle clients against reasonable risks because of carers' or other professionals' anxieties. Evaluate the consequences of not going ahead with a risky activity. How can people take control of their own choices? Restrict rights only where there is impaired capacity to resist or avoid abuse. Explore what contributes to security and wellbeing in this situation.

Making decisions

To increase your resilience in dealing with difficult issues, regularly build your training and expertise. Ensure emotional support and supervision. Note who has responsibility for your professional growth and wellbeing in the agency; in UK official social care, this is often a 'principal social worker'.

How can you make communication and conversations effective in enabling people to raise concerns and take up opportunities (see Chapter 4 on communication)? What situations enable them to contribute, for example advocates, preparation and rehearsal for participation in decision making?

Use all the evidence available, not only vivid, concrete, emotion-laden and recent events. Avoid getting stuck on first impressions. After a few contacts with a client or family, explicitly review how your picture of them has changed since the first contact.

Defend against attribution errors. These explain behaviour by referring to character traits, rather than the circumstances that form their behaviour, for example poverty, poor housing, poor family and community support. Find out the context in which worrying behaviour occurs, for example when and where it happens, and who else is present. Look for exceptions to abuse, neglect or other concerns (see Chapter 9 on solution-focused work to understand 'exceptions'). Can you reproduce the circumstances in which things go well, and stop events that go badly?

Defend against groupthink by questioning too much agreement. Members of a decision-making group may feel invulnerable to mistake because they have taken time and trouble in the group, and not question the ethics of their actions because they are pursing good outcomes. Warnings of information from outsiders may be rationalized or discounted. Stereotypes of professions or of particular grades of staff may lead to their being discounted or devalued. People may feel pressure to agree or keep quiet so that there is an illusion of unanimity. Develop a culture of dissent and criticism; try to express criticisms of your own thoughts and decisions. Group leaders should express views at the end of discussion; low-ranking members should speak first. Use other groups or regular review to find ways to critique decisions.

'Best interests' decisions are formally where decisions have to be made on behalf of people who lack the capacity (usually mental capacity) to make their own decisions, for example people with intellectual disabilities, people with dementia. Other social work situations arise where you must consider someone's best interests before taking some action, or before helping them decide best course of action. Look at what people can do and avoid too much 'safety-first' emphasis on what the person can't do, your or other professionals' fears of danger or need for control. The process is broadly the same:

- Define the decision clearly, and its boundaries.
- Identify relevant law.
- Create balance sheets of positives and negatives for each option.
- Favour the least restrictive way of achieving desired outcomes.
- Make and record decisions, involving colleagues and people around the client.
- Identify ways of reducing risk and planning for contingencies.

If you are dealing with someone who may not have the mental capacity to make decisions for themselves, legal duty in many countries and professional responsibility implies that you must:

- assume that people have capacity, even if they propose doing something unwise;

- encourage them to develop decision-making skills by making everyday decisions;
- provide practical support to make their own decisions.

People have good and bad days, so capacity varies. Assess capacity on this issue at this time, for example everyone knows what marriage entails, so people must be very incapacitated not to be able to consent to it, whereas consent to financial investments is complex and requires more capacity.

Intervention

Focus on risk where concerns are raised about possible harms. Examine the options: the choices people have made to modify the harms. What courses of action might reduce risk, make no difference or increase it? Did circumstances force them to act the way they did, or could they have chosen a different course? Don't hold them responsible for changes they could not have made. How can you help them use this experience to improve their choices in the future? Set goals.

Start from people's human rights. What human rights may be engaged by your intended actions? Consider what resilience may come from fulfilling social welfare service responsibilities: education, housing, social care and social security. Is mental health legislation engaged by any of the client's circumstances? Does the client have mental capacity to make decisions? If not, are there plans for decisions to be taken in their best interests or are there guardians or others who can and should take decisions for them.

Help people become partners in managing the risk in their lives. Ask: what is important to you? What is working well, what is difficult? What risks do you see? Could things be done differently? Who is it important to you that we involve? Look for ways to prevent difficulties. Protect people from the consequences if risk-taking goes wrong. Be transparent about what you and others see the risks are, and open about measures to protect those involved, for example be clear about how you are taking responsibility if a carer or parent is worried they will be blamed or feel guilty when something goes wrong. Look for conflicting interests: with carers, community concerns, colleagues at work. Focusing on accountability reduces anxiety: who is responsible for what? If there are differences of opinion, what could I do to support you?

Engage others around the client in supporting or helping. Referrers have expressed concerns: does this mean they have responsibilities or willingness to help?

Think about various levels of legal duties: most officials and professionals have a general responsibility to act lawfully, proportionately, reasonably and fairly. Part of this is communication: notifying clients and people round them, and other agencies of your intended actions and their responsibilities. Who (individuals or agencies) have duties of care, statutory responsibilities and may fear criticism or legal action for negligence, or must meet administrative or political pressures to be involved? Advocate for them to meet responsibilities to the client and others.

Legal bases for professional action vary. Does this situation engage your legal responsibility to coordinate with others, enquire or assess needs?

Things to think about

Make it personal. Think about *this* person in *this* situation (Lawson, 2018; Local Government Association, 2013). Use your personal relationship with them to achieve security in their best interests.

Be clear what your agency and you think about risk, and constantly review it. Consider local, national and international policy and social constraints, developments and pressures that may alleviate or heighten risks. Among these may be personal, family and community resilience.

Keep a balance between intuition and rationality. Intuitive thinking, in risk and safeguarding issues, means judgements are speedy and reflect broad understanding of the situation and its background, but the factors involved may not be clearly articulated and you may not generate and use evidence appropriately. Rationality means that research and evidence are more fully included, but decisions may be slower and more plodding. There may be poor research findings about this situation, so you rely more on intuitive understanding.

Ethical reflection is crucial to work on risk and safeguarding. Perceptions of risk are socially constructed. As a result, cultural anxiety about the hazards of complex societies may make public perception and official decision making over-anxious about taking risks. You aim to minimize risk, respect rights and secure people. Make sure in doing so you are not just regulating or surveilling their environment and behaviour to avoid blame for problems falling on you or your agency. When social provision is residual rather than universal, risk rises because people may not ask for help, and services may respond less comprehensively. Resilience may improve because people realize they must cope with troubles. But without help building their resilience, they may struggle on inadequately, producing bigger problems later.

Then we start to judge people: how careful or 'prudential' have they been? Help then becomes compulsory, to avoid risk, or conditional, to avoid people being careless. Is that just or appropriate in this instance?

Think about the continuum from normal behaviour to risky or abusive behaviour. Test out judgements with others when you think some aspect of behaviour has crossed that normality line. Consider the possibility of both abuse and neglect, including self-neglect.

Further resources

Kemshall, H., Wilkinson, B. & Baker, K. (2013). *Working with risk: Skills for contemporary social work*. Cambridge: Polity.

A good general book on social work risk practice.

Ferguson, H. (2011). *Child protection practice*. London: Palgrave Macmillan.

MacIntyre, G., Stewart, A. & McCusker, P. (2018). *Safeguarding adults: Key themes and issues*. London: Palgrave.

Two good, practical books on important areas of safeguarding with a good understanding of social work practice.

Walsh, F. (2016). *Strengthening family resilience* (3rd edn). New York: Guilford.

A thoughtful and positive text.

Check the online resources at policy.bristoluniversitypress.co.uk/how-to-use-social-work-theory-in-practice/online-resources/chapter6 for a full list of references for this chapter.

7

Humanistic person-centred practice

Setting the scene

What is person-centred practice?

In person-centred practice, you build genuine and empathetic relationships with clients to enable them to identify directions and opportunities in their lives that will help them find fulfilment in their social relationships. This practice also reduces the impact of debilitating negative feelings and experiences. It connects with and uses counselling skills.

Aims

Person-centred practice aims to empower people to feel liberated from the limits and burdens of their lives. By concentrating on the individual's potential, you try to rise above the relationships and practicalities that hedge them in. Think of yourself as flying a drone up over their social locality and look for ways up the peaks they want to climb.

Uses

Person-centred practice offers interpersonal help so that people can achieve in their lives a sense of liberation and human achievement, self-actualization. Person-centredness is based on developments of the work of Carl Rogers (1951), an American psychotherapist, and self-actualization by Abraham Maslow (1971; 1999), a psychologist. The ideas connect with existentialism and humanism. These systems of philosophy ask: what's important in our lives? Why do human beings exist? What do they contribute to the world? Most of us are troubled by doubts about our own value as human beings, and at times dread what's going on in the world. Such concerns can be a factor in depression, anxiety and relationship difficulties.

'Person-centred planning' and 'person-centred care' are practised as part of personalization in UK adult social care, respectively in

STARTING POINTS

Aim for a 'step up' in people's lives
Attend to clients' beliefs and feelings
Explore responses to current life events
Connect with clients' lines of thought
The *here-and-now* not the *there-and-then*
Physical health, the body
Motivating needs, not *deficiency* needs
Find resources and peer support
Co-production, work on actions with clients

Holistic, unite ambiguities into a full picture

GO

INTERVENTIONS

Enter and explore clients' worlds
Increase depth of understanding
Help clients open up to positives
Identify choices and options
Work on complex judgements
Avoid idealizing end-states
Focus on concrete steps
Explore wow moments
Experience taking on responsibilities
Counter hindering attitudes and people
Counter hindering lack of resources
Balance own and others' expectations
Balance needs and wishes
Encourage creativity

Motivation towards social and emotional growth

CORE CONDITIONS

Communicate them in your relationship with clients
Be genuine and congruent – behave consistently with your beliefs and feelings
Unconditional positive regard – accept clients' value as human beings
Empathy – connect emotionally to clients' frames of reference

domiciliary and institutional care settings. They emphasize that care services should centre on the assessed needs of service users and their caregivers. This avoids providing services according to in-built assumptions of the agencies involved. You treat service users' needs holistically to include physical, psychological and social provision. Person-centred care and planning calls on and integrates a range of services from diverse sources of provision (private, public and voluntary sector organizations). Unlike humanistic person-centred practice, this does not aim for personal and social liberation, but at freedom from the agency and policy assumptions about needs. Within this limited context of service provision, however, the importance given to service users' and carers' wishes, human needs, holistic integration, and user co-creation and co-production of care reflects some of the ideals of person-centred practice.

Introducing person-centred practice

Person-centred practice is introduced in a similar way to counselling. Emphasize explicit agreement on plans. Ensure that clients are clear that they want to expand and understand better their life and experience.

Action sequence

Starting points

Unlike relationship-based social work (see Chapter 11), person-centred practice attends primarily to clients' beliefs, feelings and responses about their life and the world, rather than to their relationships. Inevitably, though, some of those responses are about relationships, and the most important issues may be about the most intimate or troubled parts of life.

Concentrate on the 'here-and-now' not the 'there-and-then'. Future planning or finding solutions to problems is also unnecessary. By increasing awareness and understanding of the present, clients strengthen their capacity to deal with past difficulties and the future. Begin by asking about what is currently important to them in their life and relationships. Focus on what animates people's existence in the personal and social aspects of their lives.

One important starting point may be physical health, feelings about the body and the natural world affecting the client. People may express how they feel ugly, tired and weak, wanting to give up the struggle, everything seems grey. Explore specifically what aspects of their lives are generating these feelings. When are these feelings at their strongest?

Needs offer another starting point. Clients' concerns about their needs may be expressed as deficiency needs, what they don't have, or have lost. Respond to this by looking at motivating needs: what people want to achieve. The social work approach to such issues, as opposed to a counselling approach, is to find resources, peer support or co-production opportunities, that is situations where they can work with others, to begin to meet some of the needs. Find a starting point to take a step upwards, then build on this to take another step.

Person-centred practice, like counselling, emphasizes genuineness and integrity in relationships with clients (see Chapter 5); you model appropriate relationships with others. Focus on everything that clients say, and ensure your comments connect with their line of thought. Hear their expectations. If they are appropriate, model how you respond to them; if inappropriate, model alternatives. In either case, clarify their expectation and be explicit about your response. For example, with worries about children, do they want to manage behaviour better, or understand children's experiences? What would be appropriate in the client's situation? How would they move from one to the other?

Focuses and possibilities for interventions

Person-centred practice assumes that we all have an innate motivation to grow, emotionally and in social relationships. People who do not have the words to express what they want, or have been ground down by constant adversity, need to have opportunities to describe what might be improved in their lives. Put aside evaluating their troubles; instead, enter and explore their perception of the world. Clients can open themselves to looking for positives. Become absorbed in one or a few important issues, try to identify choices that clients can make. Nobody is a blank slate, so look for things that have been successful that you can build on. Help clients to express more complex judgements on their experiences; not 'it went wrong', but what aspects of it worked, at what stages did it work, what affected events, who and what was helpful. Model being honest about issues, about what happened, so that plans can be based on accurate understanding of the past. Listen to the internal voices about uncertainties and ambiguities, not external voices of criticism. Avoid thinking about ideal end-states, but concrete steps that will be a plus. Try to identify even occasional or fleeting 'wow' experiences. Look for ways in which the present is different and offers more opportunities than in the past. Help clients to have experiences of accepting and fulfilling responsibilities and exploring alternatives and opportunities. In both cases, it improves self-confidence to be able to take on opportunities for growth in the future.

A useful focus is what hinders growth. Two main sources of hindering are people and resources. People may devalue clients, and this attacks their feelings of self-worth. For example, perhaps carers do too much for a disabled family member, fearing various risks. What do the disabled person, the carer and others say about this? How specific are the risks? Can easy steps lead on to greater freedom? Hindering may also come from lack of capacity, resources or skills. Identifying opportunities for learning, grants for equipment or participation in support groups can help people move on. You can also raise confidence by demonstrating readiness and security yourself that, if an experiment does not work out, you can work with them to find a way back. And express the confidence that they can try something else.

Expectations from others, or expectations of oneself are often among the interpersonal issues that people want to work on. Being congruent is not only for the practitioner. Feeling incongruent places everyone, including clients, at odds with themselves (Howe, 2009a: 162) and with others in their social environment. People have expectations and make demands. A husband expects his wife to be agreeable all the time, never angry, never stressed; an older person expects her children to be caring and respectful whatever the pressures on them. Helping clients to explore the appropriateness and reality of demands and expectations, their own and others', enables them to work out where they stand. When they are clear, it's easier for them to be firm with other people, but without expressing anger, coldness or hostility. They are more able to set boundaries, and to balance their own needs, emotional and practical, with others' wishes.

Developing creativity is an important self-actualizing objective. Involvement in art, music, writing, physical and group activities individually and collectively can give people positive experiences. It may include hobbies such as dressmaking, gardening or physical activity such as running, walking or birdwatching. This allows them to feel more positive about themselves. This can be started as a 'Sunday activity' separate from formal helping, then moved onwards into groupwork activity and shared with the practitioner or family members. It may be the basis of better communication with family and friends. Encourage spontaneity, receptivity and responsiveness to the outside world; discourage striving for perfection or achievement of outcomes. Focus on the experience of being creative. Progress in creativity inhabits our whole life and can allow us to be more spontaneous and creative in relationships and responses to life difficulties.

Things to think about

Critical reflection

To be critical about and guide how we use person-centred theory, we constantly think through important ideas about what it means to be human; this can be an important aspect of the critical reflection discussed in Chapter 25. These ideas come from the philosophy of humanism, and humanistic psychology and psychotherapy. Counselling is also strongly influenced by them (see Chapter 5).

The main humanistic practice ideals about human beings are as follows:

- Human beings use their brainpower to manage their lives and the environment through rational thinking and planning. How does your intervention stimulate clients to plan and think through their aims and options?
- Human beings seek to meet their practical, psychological and social needs, aspiring to achieve the highest possible level of thinking and self-expression, self-actualization. How can you motivate people to aim higher?
- Human capabilities achieve their highest fulfilment in an integrated society in which human beings care about and help each other in human relationships. How can you help clients and carers find relationships that will strengthen them?
- Humanity endows everyone with human rights to equality, freedom and social support to achieve the highest possible expression of their humanity. Human actions may be tested against the human rights expressed in various official charters. How can you enhance clients' and carers' rights to self-expression?

An important way of thinking critically about our practice is to evaluate the extent to which and the ways in which we are achieving these ideals. Are we moving people towards achieving equality, freedom and self-actualization? Success leads to changes in clients' self-perception and evaluation: clients see more positives and fewer negatives in their lives and selves and find it easier to talk about achievements.

An important aspect of person-centred practice is the 'core conditions' of the practitioner's relationship with clients. Early research found that these were necessary and sufficient to achieve good outcomes in interpersonal practice. More recent research suggests that this overstates their importance (Munro, 1998). But they remain a valuable source of ideas about practice, helping us to think critically about our relationships with clients. The core conditions are as follows:

- Practitioners should be 'genuine and congruent' in their relationships. Our behaviour towards clients is consistent with our beliefs and feelings about them. We don't hide doubts and challenges.
- Practitioners treat clients with 'unconditional positive regard', accepting that they are valuable people, with rights to receive help, services and support, despite failings and weaknesses in their behaviour, personality and social relationships.
- Practitioners demonstrate 'empathy' in their understanding of the client's attitudes and thinking; sometimes people refer to 'accurate empathy'. This means understanding the client's frame of reference accurately, with the emotional connections to the things that they see as important, trying to perceive their reasoning. To be accurate, you use your observation, but you also need to ask, sometimes in detail, about things that join with their concerns. Look for resonances with your own experience. Express double-sided reflections: 'I see you are troubled by this, but you seem also to feel there are some positives.' They need to feel that you are really working at connecting with their complex of feeling and analysis around the issue; really dancing with them.

It is important that people can see you communicating these behavioural elements in your relationships. Constantly test out with yourself and with the client how well you are doing this. 'I've not got that quite right, let's think it through again.' Summarize the points you have shared.

Compassion (the word translates as 'with-strong feeling') is an important aspect of humanistic helping relationships. Clients should experience you as being passionate about being alongside them in their attempts to understand and help themselves. Help them remember important aspects of their being, personal identity and relationships, reconcile different aspects of their feelings, uncertainties or ambiguities into a holistic understanding of themselves and their relationships.

Your practice works to reunite the forgotten or excluded, oppositions and conflicts into a full picture of their lives.

An important aim is to increase clients' depth of understanding and experience of their lives. But they may start from different capacities to do so. The stages of development towards greater depth of understanding are:

- communication in a detached way about external events;
- expression of feelings and attitudes about non-self topics;
- discussing personal reactions to external events;
- describing feelings and personal experiences;
- expressing and owning present feelings;
- awareness and expression of continuing flows of feelings within themselves;
- understanding of a diversity of personal emotional reactions to different aspects of an issue, awareness of inner debates and ambiguities.

Further resources

McLeod, J. (2013). *An introduction to counselling* (5th edn). Maidenhead: Open University Press, 165–201.

Chapter 7 is a good general introduction to person-centred practice for counsellors, applicable to social work and making connections with other psychological approaches also used in social work.

Rogers, C.R. (1951). *Client-centered therapy: Its current practice, implications and theory*. London: Constable.

A classic account by the originator of these ideas.

Check the online resources at policy.bristoluniversitypress.co.uk/how-to-use-social-work-theory-in-practice/online-resources/chapter7 for a full list of references for this chapter.

8

Mindfulness practice

Setting the scene

What is mindfulness?

Mindfulness is a practice of cultivating people's capacity to pay attention to important aspects of their body, environment, mind and spirit. This is used to strengthen their ability to manage their emotions, thoughts and relationships. Hick (2009a) is an important source for the application of mindfulness to social work.

Aims

The main aim of mindfulness practice is to enable people to feel more in control of their personal responses to life events and their environment. Part of this is to feel more secure in the appropriateness of their behaviours and emotions, and more comfortable, stress free and tranquil in their engagement with daily life.

Uses

Some formal psychotherapeutic techniques use mindfulness ideas combined with other clinical psychology practice: mindfulness-based cognitive therapy (MBCT) and mindfulness-based stress-reduction (MBSR). If they are included in your agency's provision, you need specific training and supervision.

Used more generally, mindfulness techniques can enable people to work on emotional concerns that are affecting their capacity to live a satisfying life. They can also build permanent resilience and stability in their behaviours and emotions.

This may be a useful part of working with difficulties in reacting to the stresses of daily life as a carer, in intellectual or physical disability, in loss and bereavement, and with mental health problems. It may also help people manage their reactions to difficult experiences, for example bullying or coping with organizations they must engage with, such as care homes, hospitals, school, work.

MINDFULNESS PRACTICE 8.1

A MINDFUL ATTITUDE

Intentionally observing and describing to yourself...
...important aspects of your life...
...so that you are fully aware of their nature...
...and how they affect you.
Take time and thought before reacting to your inner experiences

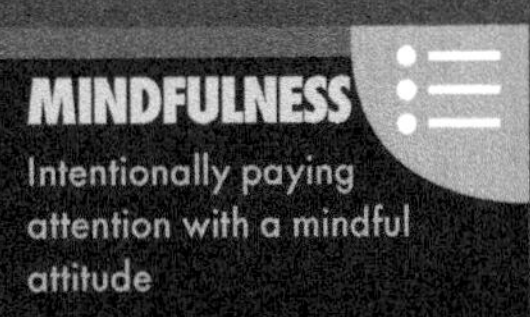

PREPARATION

Gain confidence through experience using mindfulness techniques
Clarify that mindfulness involves taking planned time
Awareness of breathing

INTERVENTIONS

Set up a group, or make time in a regular interview
Use appropriate techniques
Navigate barriers by 'exoticizing the average'
Become aware of flows of ideas and energy
Become aware of repetitive elements in relationships
Become aware of oppositions in organizations
Explore surprises
Be playful
Encourage helpfulness

Introducing mindfulness

Many people are aware of mindfulness as a personal therapy, like yoga, often done in groups for relaxation and personal and social development. As a result of this, proposing mindfulness as a response to, say, problems of oppression or poverty, or as part of a response to safeguarding issues can seem insubstantial to clients. While it does not help people resolve broader social or relationship issues, you can present it to clients as a useful way of coping with changes or difficulties that are forced on them, and being more flexible in how you deal with difficulties.

Explain that mindfulness has three main elements:

- intentionally...
- ... paying attention ...
- ... with a mindful attitude.

To explain further, a mindful attitude involves observing and describing to yourself important factors in your life, going into detail about them, so that you are fully aware of their nature and how they affect you. You are non-judgemental about those inner thoughts and you take time and thought before you react to them. Accepting your experiences, you are curious about what they might mean to you, and open to further observations of how they and future experiences affect you.

The aim of using this technique as a social work intervention is to practise and build up the skill of sustaining attention on what is important to you, getting rid of flitting from one issue to another. On the other hand, you also avoid over-elaborating problems. Discourage people from extending a current experience into a fearful spiral of possibilities; they need to see what happened for what it is.

A helpful way of explaining why this is useful is to talk about musicians or sportspeople. Prowess depends on a moment-by-moment awareness of how they are holding themselves and how their bodies are responding to messages from the brain. Mindfulness applies that kind of awareness to our skills in living everyday life, particularly if our life is troubled by our caring responsibilities or powerful emotions. Neurobiological evidence suggests that practising mindfulness techniques might generate physical and mental capacity to maintain attention and regulate emotional and physical reactions to stresses.

People often express doubts: the answer is 'give it a try'. Help them look for space and time in their lives to practise and work out where they may be safe and uninterrupted to spend time on their own awareness. Encourage regular practice for a few weeks to see if this instils a useful habit. Be a model of curiosity and positivity.

Action sequence

Preparation

Identify and experience a small number of basic techniques that you are confident in using, either in a class or with an individual. Draw them from experiences you have had so that they connect with your experience, for example as a musician or in sport.

Be clear with yourself and clients that mindfulness requires taking specific, planned time and applying yourself patiently for that period. Demonstrate that in an introductory session, taking time away from the other things that you are dealing with as social worker and client.

As with all meditation-based techniques, awareness of breathing is basic. Sit or lie comfortably and breathe slowly, for a planned period. Notice how your body moves and reacts to the breath, attending to changes in your nose, mouth, chest, diaphragm and upper body. Experience how each breath is different, and how your whole body and mind changes as you continue focusing on breathing. Tense? Or more relaxed? As your mind moves away to other things, consciously bring it back. Where did it go? How do you experience that process of paying attention only to breathing?

Intervention

Mindfulness is often done in groups at a planned daily or weekly time. Six to eight sessions is typical. Participants learn techniques that they can practise on their own between sessions. An example is the MBCT 'three-minute breathing space'. Stop what you're doing and pay attention to your experience now. What can you hear, see, feel? What emotions and ideas does this produce?

If a group is not desirable or possible, make a space for learning and practising a mindfulness technique as part of a regular session. At the session's beginning, this can cut you and clients off from everyday stresses and make other transactions more constructive. At the end, it can help you return to steadiness after a difficult session. This might help a session focused on other matters, even if clients do not learn or practise the technique elsewhere.

Techniques people use include the following; you can devise many more:

- Body scan: focus on sensations, or lack of them, in each part of the body in turn. This raises thoughts and feelings about each part of the body; issues might be pain, relaxed feelings, tensions.
- Body stretching: scan each part of the body while stretching it, to be aware of thoughts and feelings about movement or lack of it.
- Breathing: becoming aware of the sensation of breathing, short or long, shallow or deep, sounds, strains.
- Conscious walking: climbing the stairs or travelling during your day, especially when you are hurried or restless, pay attention to your movements and the experience of your surroundings.
- Daily activities: concentrate mindfully on stacking the dishwasher, cleaning the car. Pay attention to the detail and sequence of your activity. What emerges in your emotions and mind? Boredom, appreciation of sparkling results …?
- Emotional/feeling observation: remaining still for a time, pay attention to feelings and emotions that emerge. How can you describe it, is it pleasant, worrying, positive? How does it change, how does it settle, how powerful is it, is it fleeting or persistent? Move on to accepting that emotion – what does that mean for you?
- Music or poetry: what ideas and feelings develop as music is heard or a poem or story is read? Use brief examples.
- Self-care: if you are part of stressful transactions, take a set time, even just a few moments, to explore your reactions to a question or reaction that stresses you, before you react. What feelings welled up? How did your body change?
- Standing meditation: stand for a set while. How is your body changing, stretching differently?
- Thought experience: remaining still and silent, what ideas, stories and thoughts come forward in your mind? What can you remember has drifted or moved away? Follow a thought, be curious about it and what it is like, what it means.

An important aspect of each of these techniques is that you are not trying to intellectualize about or interpret the experiences; your intention is to be aware of them. Later, if you want, you can think about how to react in human transactions to your awareness.

Options for awareness

Mindful awareness helps people navigate barriers in their lives, or cope with averageness by 'exoticizing the domestic' (Paré, Richardson &

Tarrgona, 2009) or 'making the familiar visible' (Chambon, 2007). This enables people to manage their emotional reactions and regulate their changed consciousness and that of others. Part of doing so may be to 'let go' of our feelings and reactions, having become aware of them.

In transactions, help people be aware of flows of energy and ideas, moving between people as part of the process of the transaction. Look for aspects of situations as they emerge and transmute.

For example, clients can learn awareness of and reflection on the human transactions they are involved with. In transactions with others, become aware of repetitive elements of the discourse, and positions within it. Ask yourself what a speaker's intention is in each remark; how are they trying to affect the dialogue? Then, what responses are available? How will each response affect the dialogue? What knowledge underlies a statement? Is it explicit? Why or why not? How does the discourse flow? What disrupts it? What have you and others learned from an exchange? Apply this to a grumpy grandma or a demanding child.

A useful technique may be to develop awareness of oppositions in organizations clients are part of and in human transactions. Examples are: between the present and the past, between organization and disorganization, between rigidity and flexibility, between separation and connectedness. How is school, or the day centre, or the care home: rigid or flexible?

Explore the unexpected and surprising. That was a shock; take time: what was it that made it surprising to me in this context?

Try being playful. Jump: what was it like? In a group, what were the different ways people jumped? Throw a ball: what happened? How is it different each time? In a group, what are the variety of ways people catch?

Encourage people to be helpful to one another, in daily life or in a group. How did it feel? How did you experience people's reactions?

In group and community interventions, mindfulness enables you to focus on the process of interactions you are engaged in. What emotions are generated by people's political and social experience, what passions for change are expressed and how do they motivate? What alternative experiences and passions are available in the group? Awareness of conflict or stability, of what we value and dislike, what energizes, engages or enrages people, can help to define alternative directions for the flow of activity or articulate barriers to moving forward.

Things to think about

See mindfulness as a way of managing the pressures of your practice and professional life; experiencing it helps you to enable others to take it on. It always focuses on the present, exploring it and squaring it away; shifting you from 'acting', 'doing' 'reacting' towards 'being' and 'feeling'. Treat it as a way of being familiar with your mind and how it functions, open to doing things in a new way, alert to change and difference in your experiences, sensitive to different contexts that affect you, being aware of alternative perspectives and other people's perspectives.

Restrain your desire to take action. Mindfulness does not seek to build up creativity or imagination, or develop critical analysis of actions, patterns of behaviour, or thoughts. Neither does it aim to stop what are perceived as negative thoughts or aim at some ideal state of emotion or behaviour, such as being calm. Do not move on from awareness to getting clients to plan actions or carry out changes in their lives. That may come about, because of the agency, strength in their ability to change things, that people gain from awareness. But it is not part of mindfulness. If you need to act, or clients want to make changes, make that explicitly a non-mindfulness part of the social work process. Action will probably be enhanced, however, because people are more aware of transactions they take part in.

Further resources

Hick, S.F. (ed) (2009). *Mindfulness and social work*. Chicago, IL: Lyceum.

Northcut, T.B. (ed) (2017). *Cultivating mindfulness in clinical social work: Narratives from practice*. Cham: Springer.

Both books are useful and detailed explorations of mindfulness concepts and examples from practice.

Check the online resources at policy.bristoluniversitypress.co.uk/how-to-use-social-work-theory-in-practice/online-resources/chapter8 for a full list of references for this chapter.

9

Strengths and solution-focused practice

Setting the scene

What are strengths and solution-focused practice?

Strengths practice identifies capacity, potential and resources in clients, families and communities for taking up opportunities hidden within troubles that afflict them. It collaborates caringly to enable people to move towards achieving their aspirations within their social context. Saleebey (2013) is a significant originator of the idea. It has influenced community mental health practice because of its emphasis on using community resources; Rapp and Goscha (2012) are significant researchers. The approach has connections with ideas about resilience (see Chapter 6).

In solution-focused practice, you work with clients to open ways of moving towards solutions to difficulties. You do this by extracting fruitful ideas for progress from unconsidered past accomplishments. The founders of these ideas are the psychologists, Steve de Shazer and Insoo Kim Berg, but there are now widespread interpretations including some for social work for example Shennan (2014).

Aims

Strengths and solution-focused practice adopt similar 'positive psychologies', an idea associated with the psychologist, Martin E. P. Seligman (2018). They say that we focus too much on problems. Useful experiences (called 'exceptions') are hidden by difficulties and offer us openings to create new strategies for moving forward. Forget the past and the problems, focus on the future and the answers.

These social construction theories emphasize that how we think and talk 'constructs' how we behave. Avoid 'past-talk' and 'problem-talk' and spotlight 'future-talk' and 'solution-talk'.

Co-construct solution-talk and action, that is, build collaboration between you and the client to talk and think about finding solutions

STRENGTHS AND SOLUTION-FOCUSED PRACTICE 9.1

START CO-CONSTRUCTION

Clients' account of the problem
Assertively reach out
Explore recent change
Identify problem patterns
Solutions, exceptions, strengths
Select best options
Exceptions give direction

PRINCIPLES

Expert client, collaborating worker
We've got what it takes
Do what you can do ● Build on success
Take the first step ● Leave failure behind

STRENGTHS

Why not? ● Hopeful ● Assets and skills
Collaborate ● Plan A & plan B
Small steps ● Rallying round

BRIDGING STATEMENT

Provides summary plan leading to

TASK DEFINITION

Solution-focused
e.g. observe and describe

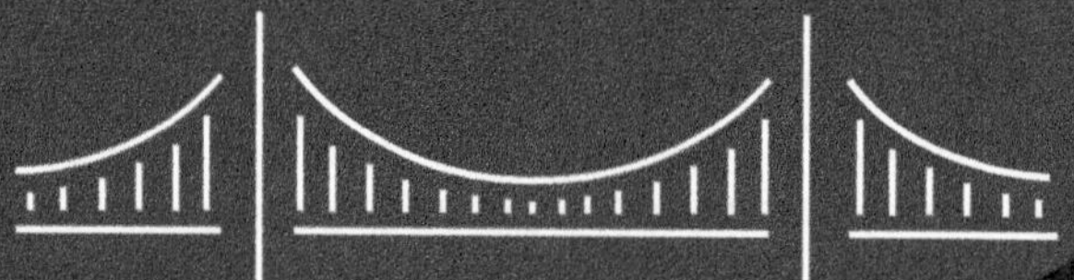

USE RESPECTFUL CURIOSITY

Miracle questions set goals
Time machine questions define motivation
Outcome questions define behaviours
Follow-up questions set steps on the way
Relationship questions link with solutions
Difference: positives & strengths
Coping questions offer interim strategies
Scaling questions allow self-evaluation

CONTINUING SESSIONS

How did you do that?
Emphasize choices made
Detailed questions
Disrupt problem patterns
When was the problem absent?
Surprise task

BUILD STRENGTHS

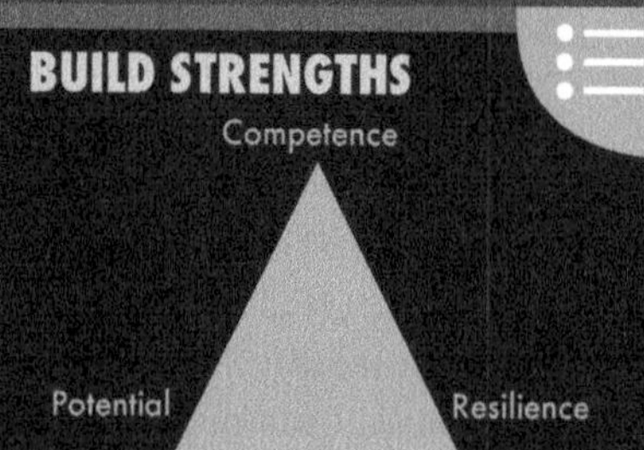

ENDING

Achieved enough?
How to maintain progress?

and acting on them. Encourage clients to feel responsible for turning options for solutions that arise in your joint work into reality.

Uses

Strengths approaches can be helpful where clients are often devalued or stigmatized, for example families in poverty, homeless people, or people with intellectual disabilities, a mental illness or physical disability. Avoid language that focuses on their problems. Pay attention instead to things that they can do, have achieved or their unrealized potential, for example a seriously disabled woman always has a cheerful demeanour and makes people admire her enjoyment of life, so build on her positivity. Include community and family support. Build opportunities for choice in their environment, and emotional and psychological strength and relationship and social resources to be able to act on them. Membership and participation are important parts of creating citizenship for people, and avoiding de-citizening (Payne, 2017), processes which take away freedom of action from people

Strengths and solution-focused practice influenced the 'signs of safety' approach to safeguarding (see Chapter 6). This is an adaptation because in this area of practice we can't just accept clients' goals as the direction for our solutions. Instead, solutions must build on signs of safety within the situation.

Introducing strengths and solution-focused practice

Clients often arrive at your agency with things that are not going well. To demonstrate that you value their starting point, listen to and acknowledge their experiences and feelings about them. But everyone has things that have gone well, and they have the ability to achieve a lot in their lives. Rather than concentrate on what went wrong, solution-focused practice builds on what went right, and while you don't devalue their troubles, you say you want to emphasize the scope for positives. The main principles, coming from strengths practice but relevant to solution thinking, are:

- We've all got what it takes: start by focusing on strengths we already have to solve our problems.
- Focus on what you can do, not what you can't; help people to build on these with new skills.
- Clients are the experts in their own goals; the practitioner focuses on collaboration.

- Build on success. Change is constant: we build on changes where things went well. These are called 'exceptions' to problem patterns, where things went exceptionally well, even if the outcome was not good.
- Take the first step on the journey. Small changes lead to bigger changes, so we can build up from good beginnings. Use naturally occurring resources in the client's family and community, not formal services.
- Focus on the future, looking for where we want to go, so we can choose beginnings that lead in the direction of our goal.
- When something hasn't worked, leave it behind and do something different.

Action sequence

Start co-construction

In the first session, help clients give a clear and explicit account of the problem. Explain this is so that you can both work on finding a helpful approach to dealing with it. Although great importance is given to building on the client's priorities, reach out assertively to motivate clients and families who have difficulty in engaging (Rapp & Goscha, 2012).

Explore how the situation has changed since the client was referred or decided to approach your agency. How has it changed? If it is for the better, what happened that led to the improvement? This allows you to start right away on thinking about change and strengths that may become solutions.

The co-construction process starts with this account.

- Listen so that you can jointly explore the problem patterns:
  - Pick out potential solutions that are important to the client.
  - Identify exceptions to the problem patterns, resources and strengths.
- Select the best options for action.
- Build on exceptions to identify directions and first steps.

Pay attention to the client's language. Assume they have tried to deal with the problem. Find out what they found helpful. Affirm strengths. Reinforce motivations.

To concentrate on strengths:

- Start from 'why not?'; avoid 'it's difficult'.
- Remain hopeful.
- Look for helpful assets, attitudes and skills.
- Collaborate in co-constructing a positive view of what may be possible; do not dismiss optimism as impracticable.
- Use 'plan A' and 'plan B': take the most hopeful option, but have a good fall-back position.
- Take small steps towards empowerment.
- Encourage others to rally round and be a community of encouragement.

Respectful curiosity with the miracle and other questions

The solution-focused approach uses questions to get clients to reconstruct their ideas creatively. Encourage clients to develop ideas that will move on to solutions. Your approach is being respectfully curious: 'I wonder what it would be like if …?'

The miracle question is an appropriate variation of: 'imagine going to sleep tonight, and while you were asleep a miracle occurred, and this problem was solved. How would you know things were different?' What would the client be doing? What would be happening?

> Answers suggest the goal, potential first steps and the direction of travel.

The time machine: if a time machine took you into the future, when the problem was solved, what would be better for you? What would people say had changed in you?

> Answers suggest gains that would motivate the client.

Outcome questions: if I met you three months after our final session, what would I notice about you that was different?

> Answers suggest precise behaviours you are aiming for.

Follow-up questions: what would show the change has started?

> Answers clarify possible steps on the way.

Relationship questions: who would be the first to notice the change? What would they see?

Answers connect the solution with relationships and help to identify people who may support the process.

Difference questions: how was it different when this was not a problem? What made things change?

Answers help people identify positives and strengths.

Coping questions: what keeps you going? How do you manage?

Answers help people find interim strategies for managing.

Scaling questions: on a scale of one to ten, with ten the most …, how would you rate how you felt … how successful that was …?

Answers encourage self-evaluation.

Make a bridging statement

Summarize the first session by sharing your understanding of the issues that are important to the client, the strengths that clients have demonstrated and resources they have managed to get hold of and use. Check the extent to which the client accepts this view, and modify it accordingly.

Agree a solution-focused task

From your bridging summary, work together to create a task that will move towards the solution. A common option is to ask clients to observe things happening that they want to continue, and be able to describe them in the next session.

Later sessions

In later sessions, review the task and concentrate on detailing successes. Strengths work values ability, effort and hard work. Ask 'how did you do that?' questions which can highlight the client's agency for both of you: they did something and it had effects. Emphasize the choices made, to confirm agency, strength and resources drawn in. Scaling questions generate self-evaluation, confidence and motivation. Difference questions check how things have changed. Feed back on actions that have been successful; look at how clients can put aside actions that were unhelpful.

Encourage clients to pay attention to the times when the problem was absent. When was that? Who was there? What was happening? What did you do?

Make your questions as detailed as possible, so that clients analyse behaviour and actions precisely. For example, after 'I was anxious', ask: 'how did the anxiety reveal itself?' 'What did you do to overcome it?' 'Looking back, was there something else you could have tried?' 'Did someone else do something that helped you?' 'How could you get someone else to help if it happened again?'

Understand problem patterns. What happened just before? What happened afterwards? Who is usually present … absent?

Aim to disrupt problem patterns. Set tasks that encourage clients to test out behaving differently for a short period and observe the outcomes. For example, plan not to argue with your husband before he goes to work and observe what happens. If the client can't think how to observe events, give some examples. Did your plan affect how you behaved? How did you both behave differently? How did you feel? If, in spite of your plan, you argued, how did it start … continue … end?

A common option is a 'surprise' task. Do something positive with someone who is relevant to the problem that will surprise them, and observe. Talk about what clients will do, and their expectations. This discussion helps you both understand what the usual pattern is, and what might disrupt that pattern. In the later session, review and scale success and how the people involved felt.

Avoid stereotyping and labelling people with the problem; instead work together on seeing how they can master the problem.

Groupwork

Solution-focused groupwork takes the same approach, emphasizing cooperation and collaboration among group members. You take a 'one-down' position, not questioning clients from an expert position. Instead, avoid confrontation, affecting confusion or uncertainty if you see inconsistencies in the client's narrative. Encourage the group to use humour and creativity in sharing experiences, for example 'the way the policeman treated me made me feel small'; 'Were you a mouse looking for a hole?' Or 'did it remind you of being a child sent to bed?' Get the group to produce ideas for solutions. Encourage group support by getting the group to discuss how it could help members who raise issues to find solutions.

Endings

Check regularly if clients think they have achieved enough. Ask detailed questions about how they have arrived at that view. Then ask them to reconfirm their judgement; perhaps on looking at the detail they can nuance how they think about what has happened.

When you come to the end, work on follow-up actions that will maintain progress. How confident do you feel about being able to make progress? Who could help you when there are difficulties? What's going to be most difficult? What might the obstacles be? Is there one lesson you want to remember if things get tough? What will the benefits be if you keep going on this track?

Things to think about

Strengths are an interaction of

- **C**ompetence, capacities and courage
- **P**romise, possibility, positive expectations, potential
- **R**esilience, reserves, resources, resourcefulness (Saleebey, 2009a: 10).

While solution-focused practice is primarily a psychological intervention, strengths-based practice has an emphasis on community and family resources, and building on agency and legal responsibilities in helping people make the best of their own resources. In many ways that connects well with social work roles. Developing resource knowledge in a team and adapting models of practice dominant in agencies therefore make this model easy to integrate into agency practice requirements.

Further resources

Greene, G.J. & Lee, M.Y. (2011). *Solution-oriented social work practice: An integrative approach to working with client strengths.* New York: Oxford University Press.

A good general guide to solution, narrative and related theories of practice drawn together in a comprehensive practice guide.

Rapp, C.A. & Goscha, R.J. (2012). *The strengths model: A recovery-oriented approach to mental health services* (3rd edn). New York: Oxford University Press.

A good research-based account of strengths practice in the mental health field.

Check the online resources at policy.bristoluniversitypress.co.uk/how-to-use-social-work-theory-in-practice/online-resources/chapter9 for a full list of references for this chapter.

10

Narrative practice

Setting the scene

What is narrative practice?

Narrative practice explores how clients have resolved ambiguities and challenges in their lives by constructing a continuing story of the events of their lives that are affecting them. It then restructures narratives about how best to respond to future challenges. Like strengths and solution-focused practice, it draws on the ideas of Seligman's (2018) 'positive psychologies' (see Chapter 9). The originators of this practice are the Australian psychologists, White and Epston (1990), and narrative ideas are part of Parton and O'Byrne's (2000) 'constructive' practice, which introduced a variety of social construction ideas into UK social work practice. The emphasis of this practice remains psychological adjustment to personal and practical difficulties, often following distressing events.

Aims

Narrative practice enables clients to examine and deconstruct stories about their lives and their challenges. They created these stories about the experiences and values of their family and community. Based on understanding gained from looking at their stories, they reconstruct, re-author or re-story their narrative in ways that:

- awaken them from ways of living that they see as problematic;
- liberate them from externally imposed constraints;
- identify and author stories of their achievement, competence and self-respect;
- recruit others who support them in their new life story.

Uses

This approach is particularly useful for people who have survived traumatic experiences and major life transitions. It is also useful with people who are challenged by being part of marginalized or oppressed

NARRATIVE PRACTICE 10.1

PREPARATION

Witness clients' experience through narrative
Deep listening: creative, open, attentive to detail
Info first, build-up, event, reaction, then analysis

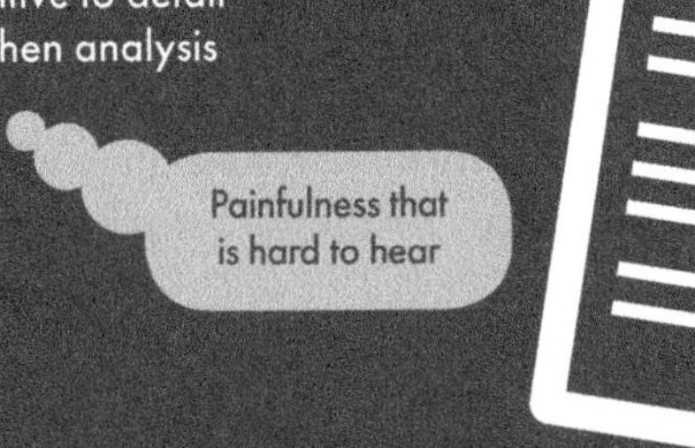

DECONSTRUCTION AND EXTERNALIZATION

Separate people from problems and practicalities
What happened? Not 'why'
Map issues
Evaluate what happened, explore social issues
Externalize the problem, label it
Notes for discussion, e.g. flipchart

Rights to express ourselves

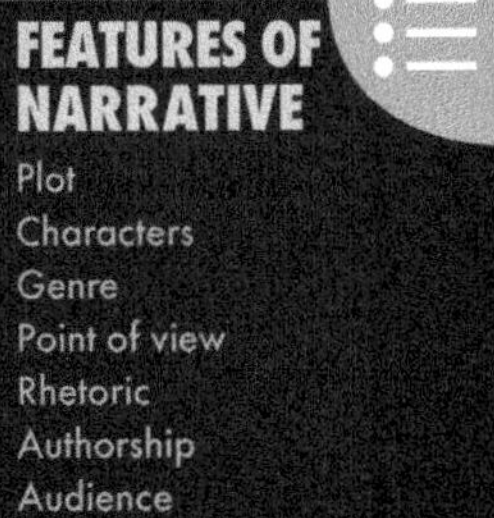

RECONSTRUCTION AND RESTORYING

Exceptions, achievements, good things
Write client into the story
Possibilities in exceptions lead to change
New identity contesting the old
Try new things, people, ceremonies
Emplotment and re-emplotment
Poetry and music
'Planning letter', homework

ENDING

Decentralize practitioner
Achievement ceremony

groups, who have issues with their personal identity and want, for some other reason, to review their life, for example children leaving or thinking through their experience of foster or residential care, people recovering from mental illness, or people approaching death.

Listening to stories is also important where clients do not have the dominant voice in the situation, for example where other people make decisions affecting them, or they are stigmatized or excluded.

Introducing narrative practice

'Listening to' people is a vogueish demand of managers and politicians faced by criticism that they disregarded unheeded issues and people. Narrative practice requires more than inviting people to tell their story. You might have done this at first contact or assessment: how do you go further? And how do you introduce 'telling your story' to clients so that they understand you're going beyond listening?

Explain that your approach is to explore 'things that happened' that led to the issue that worries the client or your agency. This is motivating because people often want to understand better why things happened. Usually, there are so many things going on in our lives that we emphasize only some of them and create a line of thinking about what happened. But if we concentrate on other things, we can often find alternative ways of doing things or looking at the phase of life that is troubling. As you look together at the sequence of events, you will be looking for occasions that might have gone differently. Looking back, we can usually all see things we might have done differently. Our aim is to explore those and see if we can use them to improve how we do things in the future.

Narrative theory starts from the position that people have many stories, each with many potential plot lines. Nobody is stuck, there is always another road onwards or a change you can make. Help clients become privileged or 'lead' authors, co-construct a new route alongside them. They are privileged by their own perceptions and understandings. Some, perhaps many, things in their lives work; don't change these. If things worked once, do those things again.

Action sequence

Preparation

Start as a witness to the client's experience. Hear and acknowledge their perception of the story. Practice 'deep listening'. This means being clear that you are open to, really want to, listen to specific details. Wind yourself up to be creative. No narrative is 'true'; there are many ways of looking at each event. Could you have felt differently? Might someone in the story have reacted in another way? Is what the people involved did typical of their personalities? What responses did you make? Might other people have responded differently? Could you have reacted differently too, and what might have happened as a result?

In narrative practice, you both explore and understand how the situation you both are dealing with fits into clients' lives and their family relationships. What is its impact on clients, their family and community now and in the future?

There is no assessment 'stage'. Do not set a timetable, or a number of sessions, but limit the process. As you progress through the story, you will find opportunities to identify the beginnings of multiple stories within its narrative.

As the narrative starts, always ask for information first, and then work towards analysis of feeling, thinking and interrelationships. Especially you want to hear about the build-up to a situation, who was affected, how, what were their feelings? How did people react, how were relationships affected? What happened afterwards? What are the consequences now? Future options and fears need to be explored.

Narrative intervention – deconstruction and externalization

Help people separate from problems. Deal separately with, or make referrals to, other services on practical issues, so that they can concentrate on their self-efficacy in resolving more complex situations.

Focus on what happened. Avoid 'why' questions, do not seek explanations, because this ends up in people trying to justify themselves, instead of looking at what might have been different. If you respect and value your client, they will have things in their lives that allow you to respect them more. Look for them. As clients tell their story, look for strengths, things they coped with, positives, potential opportunities, chances to find more resources. Look for changes in perception: when did these events come to seem traumatic, or less significant?

Map the issues that narratives bring up. Look at the seven features of narratives (in 'Things to think about' towards the end of this chapter): what can we discover about the important features of this narrative? For example, how have events been defined to see parents' behaviour as a narrative of child abuse? How has mental illness become disabling and stigmatizing for a family or community member? You could draw diagrams of links between occurrences, and between people involved. Are there people in the family or friendship network or group living together who don't get involved? Look for intersections: how and when different factors affected the narrator or the event. Build timelines, so that you can see the story clearly.

Invite clients to evaluate what happened; what about other possibilities? What could the client have done to achieve more favourable outcomes?

Identify social issues that have a bearing on reactions to the issues you're working on. For example, do gender assumptions mean that family members assume women cook the meals and do the cleaning? Or does cultural ignorance lead to racism at school or work? Is stammering assumed to be about low confidence, or is there a family history of speech problems? What was stigmatizing and can people's preconceptions be changed?

Use narratives to externalize problems, putting the problem outside yourself, so that you can see and attack it as a separate issue. Get clients to describe what happened and pick up on the images or metaphors they use to create new stories. For example, 'I feel like a square peg' might lead you to ask: 'how can you change the shape of the hole?' Avoid fear, fighting and overcoming metaphors, pick up or redirect stories towards development, education, training: how to train your dragon. Label the issue you're working on: the British politician Churchill called depression 'the black dog'. Your depression lies in wait for you: how can you see it in advance?

Make notes in the session, but use them openly as part of the discussion. Read back what people said, so that you can both see how it might have been different. Share diagrams on paper or flipchart.

Narrative intervention – reconstruction, re-storying

During the deconstruction, you start to co-construct (work together to build) a new version of the story: this reconstruction becomes a new narrative, with the client as the privileged narrator.

Exceptions, as in solution-focused work (see Chapter 9), give you a picture of what might be possible. Pick up recent achievements or good things, go into them in detail, work out what happened. What did the client do that made the good thing happen? Can you do that again? More of that? Adapt it to work in other situations? If there really are no recent achievements go back to a better time. If there really are no good things, suggest that they look out for one in the next week, and come prepared to talk about it.

What happened next? What did the client do that helped? Many people find it difficult to write themselves into a story: it's about what their child or persecutor did. If the answer is 'don't know', try waiting for more, giving people more time to remember or think through things that happened. Go into a detailed story of what happened to reveal what more of what they know or did. Ask about what another person involved would have seen; would they think about it differently?

Re-storying means seeing the possibilities in exceptions that might lead to change. Are memories reconsidered, reinterpreted, renewed? For example, a survivor of mental illness might remember her one visit to a day centre as embarrassing when they could not talk with others or take part in activities. You could encourage them to try again, just once to start with, and practise one or two gambits for talking with others. Then review afterwards how it went, to see if a new story can be built up. Through firming up a new set of stories, clients come to believe in one or more of them. This helps to build an investment in success in trying them out. Plan to get others to cooperate in a new pattern, so that the client's change is reinforced by others.

People's identities are often bound up in their stories about themselves. How does the new narrative create a new identity or contest the old? Gaining new competencies, receiving some education or training may help them towards a new identity. People who are overprotected, for example with physical or intellectual disabilities, or with a history of failing at relationships because of anxiety or depression, benefit from new experiences of success; tell stories about it. Others around them can help to create experience that gives them new stories of success, and help them to manage downsides. For example, an adult with intellectual disabilities was included in church activities. As she gained experience, church members offered her new contributions to make, for example training her in flower arranging, and then giving her a specific location for her weekly arrangement.

Suggest things in their lives that they might play about with, to try new things. Couples or families might have (fairly formal) meetings to plan changes, and then review how the change went. Look for people in their lives who have power to engage them in new activities and support them in carrying them out successfully. Such 'characters' in the new story can help to redefine them so that others in the family, social group or community who may not have noticed their achievements can see them as successful.

Try ceremonies. You might give an accolade of 'hero' in your joint sessions with a client when they help a disabled person in their day centre. The award helps your client gain confidence in themselves and begin to accept their capacity to build a new life. The explicit recognition helps them to feel more in control of what is happening. If an overactive child goes to bed without fuss, all gather round the calendar tomorrow to stick on a gold star. If a couple in conflict get through the evening without an argument, each gives the other a breakfast treat. There may also be ways of expressing the injustice entombed in the old narrative, and the social justice highlighted by the new.

Consider poetry and music because they express things in new and concise ways, encourage creativity, enable the evaluation of emotion. This presents narratives that are hard to express in rational language and plots.

Sometimes the plot resolution must be acceptance, and finding conditions for that, for example only drinking at weekends, so that family can be sure the wage for the working week will still be secure.

At the end of a session, ask if clients want to return, when and what they will focus on. Jointly write a 'planning letter', noting positive things you have learned in the session and things that they are going to try before their next session.

As clients become secure in their new story, practitioners are decentralized, less important. When this occurs, a ceremony of achievement and a closure of involvement can boost their future self-confidence.

Things to think about

Many people are in situations where it's too painful for others to work with them to think through their story and the future. This is true for people whose behaviour is routinely condemned; it is a routine that social work rejects. Working in end-of-life care, I know it is commonplace for people to repeat the story of the death. Families and friends are warned to be ready to listen again and again to the story of the accident or illness and its progression towards death. But the story changes in little ways each time. Deep listening requires hearing about ambiguities in the relationships, uncertainties about responsibility, responses to changed situations and futures. Listening in this way helps you underline the complexity and colour of the whole picture.

Narrative practice, like all social work, makes us aware of the power of language, how we speak about events in our lives. It also explores thinking, how we link events together into a story that makes sense to us. Our coherence as a human being comes from our analysis of what is important in events in our lives and the impact they have on us. That analysis structures stories that appear to be just accounts of what happened. But in choosing events to include and putting them together, we reveal our analysis of what's important.

People's rights to express themselves in a story may be denied. For example, the children of older people may not want to lose an inheritance by incurring care costs and so might deny a story of the older relative being increasingly unable to manage at home. Parents or neighbours may not accept the ability of an intellectually handicapped adult to create the freedom of greater independence.

The features of narratives may help us understand the aspects of stories that clients present:

- plot, the sequence of events and its underlying explanation of failure, motivation or success;
- characterization, the way people within a narrative are seen;
- genre, the general kind of story presented, perhaps love, conflict, a detective story;
- point of view, is the story about me, or am I a neutral observer, or excluded?
- rhetoric, the way a narrator makes a story convincing;
- authorship, did I tell this story, or has someone else influenced it or taken over?
- audience, who is presenting the story, to whom and with what end?

People make choices in how they present their stories. Perhaps the story seems chaotic: emplotment, giving a narrative a clear sequence and explanations, imposes a form on it. Life is chaotic. Whose emplotment has been selected? What gave them that influence on the client's life?

Further resources

Greene, G.J. & Lee, M.Y. (2011). *Solution-oriented social work practice.* New York: Oxford University Press.

Parton, N. & O'Byrne, P. (2000). *Constructive social work: Towards a new practice.* Basingstoke: Macmillan.

These two books merge narrative with solution-focused practice, connecting them because of their social construction theory base, but contain useful accounts of narrative practice.

White, M. & Epston, D. (1990). *Narrative means to therapeutic ends.* New York: Norton.

The classic text, with a psychology emphasis.

Check the online resources at policy.bristoluniversitypress.co.uk/how-to-use-social-work-theory-in-practice/online-resources/chapter10 for a full list of references for this chapter.

11

Psychodynamic relationship-based practice

Setting the scene

Definition

In psychodynamic practice, you build interpersonal relationships with clients and people around them to support their psychological capacity and reduce psychological impediments to making progress with problems that affect them. This generates social skills and resilience in managing their lives and relationships. Historically, it was called psychosocial or ego-related practice; current terminology emphasizes relationship-based practice; all are based on psychodynamic ideas originating in the work of the creator of psychoanalysis, Freud (1974), and his followers and detractors. Psychodynamic sources influenced counselling and person-centred practice (see Chapters 5 and 7). Important modern formulations of these ideas are books, in the UK, by Ruch, Turney and Ward (2018) and, in the US, by Goldstein, Miehls and Ringel (2009).

Aims

This approach to social work focuses on people with wide-ranging problems in their lives that stem from psychological difficulties in fulfilling important social relationships and responsibilities. The aim is to improve their capacity and skill in negotiating important relationships. This, in turn, helps them to take on important responsibilities such as bringing up children, caring for others and dealing with practical problems in life.

Uses

Psychodynamic practice is one of the basic models of social work practice. Its assumptions underlie everyday approaches to interacting with clients and others and solving problems arising from the personal

PSYCHODYNAMIC RELATIONSHIP-BASED PRACTICE 11.1

APPROACH AND PREPARATION

Build an alliance to tackle problems
Practice is about both the client and about events
Disentangle and tackle complications
Explain your practice approach
Gain clients' **informed** consent

WORK ON PERSON-IN-SITUATION OR PERSON-IN-ENVIRONMENT

Explore

Problems
Places where problems arise
People involved
Processes that repeat

Observe

How people *interact*
Patterns of behaviour

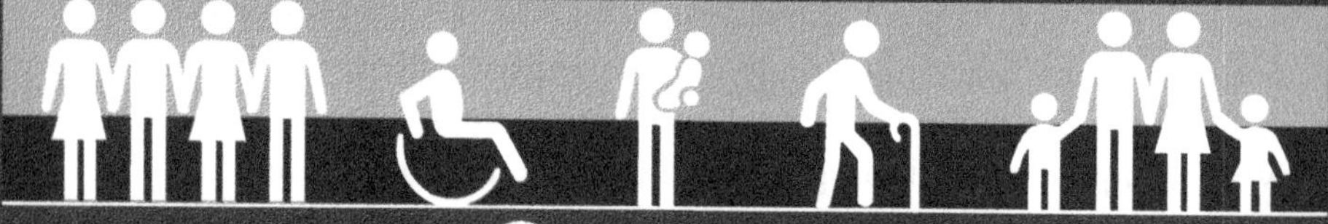

PSYCHOSOCIAL ASSESSMENT

Assess facets of problems

Bio-psychosocial development stages
Physical or medical conditions
Psychological problems
Personal responses to events
Interpersonal issues
Social factors
Resource problems
Disasters

Dynamics – how the facets interact
Etiology – source of the problems
Classification – aspects of clients' lives affected

INTERVENTIONS

Create 'secure home' as a 'holding environment'
Model effective behaviour to clients
Sustainment: providing a secure, confiding relationship
Head off adverse events
Share understanding and options
Encourage coping, finding workable options
Accept ambiguity and uncertainty
Offer experience of cooperation as part of your work

Improve clients' relationships with other organizations
Develop clients' insight into feelings and thinking
Tease out what works and what doesn't
Look for irrational defences
Validate clients' successes
Challenge repeated unhelpful behaviours
Bite off workable chunks of problems

impact on clients of social problems. It also informs the open, responsive engagement and assessment processes explored in Chapters 2 and 3. Borden (2009) provides a broad summary of various schools of psychodynamic thought and their influence on social work.

This practice is used in cases that require relationships to be maintained between practitioners and clients lasting for months or years, often backed by statutory responsibilities or other ways of imposing social work help involuntarily. Such cases involve problem-solving and support for clients managing their lives in challenging circumstances, where mental disorders, poverty and stress affect them, their families and their community.

Psychodynamic practice is also relevant in long-term relationships with foster carers and carers of older people, people with intellectual or physical disabilities or mental health problems. It can be adapted to short-term interventions, where relationships and personal history are more important than practical problem solving.

Introducing psychodynamic relationship-based practice

Because relationship-based work follows naturally from engagement and assessment processes, it is easy to carry on from referral or an existing relationship without explaining what you are doing and why. But clients are entitled to know and give informed consent for your approach and interventions. We often use this kind of work with clients who have complex and interacting problems, so it's easy to lose track of the direction of travel.

Pause for overview, therefore, at suitable events in the life of a case. At the beginning, explain that relationship-based practice involves:

- forming an alliance to tackle the problems identified in assessment and any that come up later;
- working on a fusion of 'things that happen to you (the client)' and 'things about you and your family';
- disentangling the complications of this mix and tackling them in as cool a way as we can: 'we're going to be keeping calm and sorting out.'

You need to find or make occasions in the future, perhaps agency case reviews, or crucial events, to reinforce these three aspects of intervention.

Action sequence

Assessment and study

Assessment is crucial to understanding how the 'person' and the 'situation' have interacted to create the problems. You draw out this understanding from agency or other initial assessment. When you do assessments, if you think longer-term intervention or feeling, behaviour and relationship issues are going to be important, add psychodynamic factors to otherwise prosaic agency assessments. This helps later relationship-based practice. It also means that your psychodynamic assessment relates strongly to the agency's function. This can focus your efforts, and set a timeline and priorities when issues are complex.

Create a picture of multifaceted problems faced by individuals, families or communities that arise from the impacts on relationships of different facets of people's lives:

- bio-psychosocial developmental stages, for example childhood, youth, ageing;
- physical or medical conditions, for example disabilities, surgery;
- psychological problems, for example mental illness, substance misuse;
- personal responses to events, for example school or work problems;
- interpersonal issues, for example abuse, marriage, parenting, sexuality, victims of crime;
- social factors, for example class, ethnicity, gender conflicts, migration, sexuality, spirituality;
- resource problems, for example poverty, homelessness;
- disasters, for example fire, train or car crashes.

An example of how different facets interact: an intelligent young man who finds it hard to take on responsibility for managing adult life (developmental stage) because poverty in childhood (resource factor) meant that his family gave him few opportunities for exploring different educational options (social factor), and he finds uncertainty (personal response) about his sexual identity (interpersonal) generates anxiety (psychological) about the risk of oppression in work relationships (social factor).

Problems are usually also multidetermined, having different sources. Exploring three main issues helps you to maintain focus:

- Dynamics – how interactions between different issues heightens their impact.
- Etiology – sources of problems.
- Classification – different aspects of clients' lives affected by problems, for example their parenting, school, social or work lives (Hollis, 1970: 52). You usually find some aspects of life working well.

Psychodynamic thinking on etiology focuses on problems that stem from important relationships in clients' past lives, especially childhood. Their conception of their self, where that view has come from and who influenced it, are important. For example, do they feel weak in dealing with aggression because parents expected them to be submissive? Did a previous spouse make them feel incompetent in relationships with their children?

Another aspect of etiology is mental energy. What gives the behaviour or problem relationship its legs to keep on running? Why doesn't it wither away, especially if it leads to problems? Why does it seem so important to those who are involved? This theory is about how mental factors are *dynamic*, pushing issues to the fore in people's lives.

Observation helps you to understand how clients connect with other people, or whether their relationships are not working out in some way. This is particularly useful with children and their play. Seeing people within their home or other everyday settings, such as day centres, gives you a cogent view of their relationships. Identify patterns of behaviour or repeated features of life experience. Often, the same problems recur, in the same places, with the same people and as similar social processes take place. Exploring, in interviews, problem, place, people and the process of interactions between them may help each of you to understand better and find alternative ways of responding.

Intervention

Your role in relationship-based practice is to create a 'holding environment' or 'secure haven' so that other issues can be explored; this idea has been strongly developed in attachment practice (see Chapter 12). The mutual client–worker, two-person relationship is the safe forum for tackling other outside issues. Sustainment means providing a secure confiding relationship, instilling a sense that you care, maintaining morale, and persistence and expressing everyone's entitlement to help. This supportive atmosphere makes it possible to confront difficulties in clients' lives.

Use your relationships with clients to repair difficulties that come from past injurious relationships. Other relationships, perhaps from the past, can be compared with how your client–practitioner relationship is enacted. Modelling effective ways of relating to others helps clients get in touch with inner strengths for managing their lives better (Bower, 2005: 13). Contain the complexity they face by helping them sort out priorities, divide problems into manageable chunks (partialization). Working with colleagues and other members of the family, head off potentially adverse events until troubled clients gain the strength to manage them.

Person-situation reflection involves sharing comments on what is happening in the client's life, asking questions about it and suggesting possible explanations. This influences clients' understanding directly, through giving them new insights into their lives and thinking. It helps because people value gaining understanding of adverse events. Your shared reflection includes looking at pros and cons of possible actions, encouraging planning and action, but confronting possibly unwise proposals.

Coping is an important objective (more in Chapter 14 on crisis practice). Your alliance does not aim at perfect functioning for clients in all situations, but at improving existing ways of dealing with specific problems that you are focusing on. Can clients perceive the problem differently, or define parts of it that they can cope with to reduce its impact? Can they identify some workable options? This reduces pressures from other aspects of the problem.

Psychodynamic thinking values awareness and exploration of ambiguity and uncertainty; avoid a rush to certainty. Ethnic, gender and social difference often throws up ambiguities in people's minds about their relationships: for example gender conflicts in their or their parents' marriage, race conflicts in their community, school or workplace. Exploring these is an opportunity to examine important influences on people's thinking or pressures on their social relationships. In your holding environment, people can think through and find things to value in diversity, uncertainty and conflict rather than seeking to control other people and situations to avoid it.

Seeking to control other people and events to avoid conflicts that make clients anxious or angry can thus be talked through, but action helps too. Experience of working cooperatively with others, in groups, or on small projects or activities, enables people to experience supportive relationships, helps them feel an identity with others in the community and validates their personal identity as being valuable to others.

Looking at how clients deal with outside agencies, with other people and with problems enables you to understand patterns of behaviour which get in the way of effective 'object relations' (how people deal with other people or organizations they encounter). Mediation, by preparing the way with other people and agencies, by being alongside them preparing, rehearsing and guiding them as they deal with others and by using advocacy in decision-making processes, can help them learn better skills. It releases clients' capacities and self-confidence to give them practice in trying out different strategies.

Helping clients gain insight about their feelings and thinking aims to give them back control over their lives. It helps them realize that their lives and relationships are social, and that this influences their self-development. Provide a secure non-judgemental space to talk about their reactions and get over anxiety, distress or anger. Help people work out what their model of thinking about a problem or social situation is, how they make sense of it.

One way of gaining insight is 'transference'. Watch for and discuss how clients transfer repeated ways of reacting into their relationship with you. This gives you evidence, which you can both see, to explore how clients learned patterns of behaviour in past relationships. They can practise making changes with you before trying them out on others. Also point to any counter-transference that you experience. For example, people troubled by over-controlling parents often act in ways that get other authority figures, such as teachers, or bosses at work, or you, to become controlling even though they and you don't want to be that way. Again, it provides evidence you can both see to work with.

'Working through' experiences and relationships involves teasing out in detail how clients reacted to specific events, what worked, and didn't, in responding, thinking about alternative ways of doing it and trying out different options in a controlled way, not every challenge at once. Clients can rehearse their options with you.

Irrational reactions or over-reactions to problems often reveal anxieties about a significant personal experience in the past. People build up defences that ward off pain experienced in relationships. Most defences involve burying psychologically difficult issues away from our conscious awareness. These leak out when people have to deal with an apparently insurmountable problem. By looking at problems that make them anxious, you can often explore with them ways in which their defences against the impact of past troubles stop them from dealing effectively with present difficulties. You can validate their successes and respectfully challenge repeated behaviours that are unhelpful.

Encourage them to develop an identity as someone who can bite off workable parts of the problems they face and make steady progress in relationships and with problems.

Things to think about

Psychodynamic practice works on problems identified by clients or agencies that refer clients to a social work agency. But this is a foundation for planning, not a judgement on clients. Clients may have problems, but *they* are not problems. They may be referred to social work agencies or have to accept social work interventions because of problems that others have identified. A social housing provider, for example, may see rent arrears or poor maintenance of property as arising from psychological or social inadequacies in a tenant. A court may see domestic violence or child abuse as caused by psychological or relationship problems in a family. But these specific, and possibly stigmatizing, problems do not define clients. Problem perceptions may overwhelm awareness of a client or family's skills and strengths; social workers try to keep a balanced perception of the pluses and minuses of their clients' way of dealing with their problems. Practical, psychological and relationship difficulties may result from long-term oppression or poverty, and constant support to mitigate its impact is justified. Problems may be crushing, say for someone with a mental illness, or appear insoluble to an observer, such as a neighbour, an official or a relative. But a steadfast approach to finding resolutions in small things can lead to progress and change in both perceptions of, and reality for, social work clients.

Psychodynamic practice starts from a view that people's mental processes are dynamic: they can influence the whole person and the surrounding environment. Social circumstances and relationships influence people's psychological responses, and people's internal psychological processes have an impact on their social environment. Some of these may be unconscious. The unconscious can be a powerful influence on action, and not all thinking is in the rational mind. However, social work does not emphasize this, but finds ways of helping people keep in control of their own behaviour and social relationships. Important problems may arise because of conflicts between both hidden and rational psychologies and their interaction with the social. 'Relationship-based' refers to interpersonal and social relationships as the source of people's problems, and also as the foundation of interpersonal and social help with those problems.

The historical term for this practice, 'psychosocial', aptly referred to its focus on how the psychological and social interact. Social workers assess and intervene with 'the person-in-situation' or 'the person-in-environment'. Neither the person nor the social is ever the sole explanation or the sole target for intervention. Always consider whether we are focusing too much on the person and their psychology and not enough on the situation or environment, or vice versa. Always look for the interaction of *both* factors.

Working on long-term cases can seem never ending. Making progress in dealing with life problems is, however, not all or nothing. Most people can take steps towards improvements in their lives, even though there are setbacks. This model of practice enables you to maintain a constant involvement, while picking up issues as they arise and trying to resolve that facet of the interlocking problems. The relationship keeps the 'holding environment' steady, while dealing with sometimes disturbing or destructive events. Call on your agency's function and the role it gives you to retain your focus on where you are trying to go.

Because the relationship is so important in this approach to social work, it can seem undisciplined – but it's not enough just to maintain a good relationship. There is also the risk of interminable repetitions of anger or anxiety, which never get dealt with. The response to this is to confront the evidence of repetitive behaviour calmly and constructively – how can we break out of this pattern? What is so difficult about this issue for a client's psychological make-up?

Another issue for relationship-based work is to balance your power and your clients' relative powerlessness. You have the resources of the agency and your professional role, giving you the ability to get things done. The perception that they can never achieve as much can immobilise clients and carers. Show that you understand how their troubles may place them in a difficult position. Value and contribute to their struggle to make progress.

Further resources

McColgan, M. & McMullin, C. (eds) (2017). *Doing relationship-based social work: A practical guide to building relationships and enabling change*. London: Jessica Kingsley.

Ruch, G., Turney, D. & Ward, A. (eds) (2018). *Relationship-based social work: Getting to the heart of practice* (2nd edn). London: Jessica Kingsley.

These are two recent and excellent practice guides to a range of relationship-based work, both well informed theoretically.

Check the online resources at policy.bristoluniversitypress.co.uk/how-to-use-social-work-theory-in-practice/online-resources/chapter11 for a full list of references for this chapter.

12

Attachment practice

Setting the scene

How does attachment theory contribute to practice?

Social work practice using attachment concepts involves working with people to identify and repair harmful impacts of disrupted or lost attachments to important people in their lives. An important source of the ideas is the work of the psychoanalyst, John Bowlby. His accessible late contribution, republished in 2005 with an update, is a good starting point to his work. Current research adds standardized techniques to the initial ideas. A comprehensive recent general guide is Cassidy and Shaver (2016); a collection using modern attachment ideas in social work practice is edited by Shemmings and Shemmings (2014). You use current attachment theory techniques mainly as part of multi-professional agency teams, with the advanced training and support that your agency provides.

The two most significant social work practices using attachment theory are:

- work with children and their carers to help them secure stable and long-lasting relationships with adults throughout their lives;
- loss situations, to help people overcome their reactions to the loss of one or more important attachments in their lives.

Increasingly, work in adult mental health also uses attachment ideas.

Aims

The aims of attachment practice are to give children restorative attachment experiences that will offset previous damaging experiences. Another aim is helping carers to improve their interactions with children. Adults can improve their wellbeing by managing attachment and loss effectively and regulating their emotions.

ATTACHMENT PRACTICE 12.1

EXPLAIN ATTACHMENT

How people connect with others
Closeness to a small number of carers
A 'secure base'

Attachments to extended family and community are important in some cultures

ATTACHMENT STYLES: CHILDREN

Insecure avoidant
Secure
Insecure-ambivalent
Disorganized

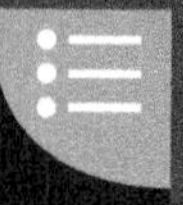

Attachments in early childhood are a template for later relationships

ATTACHMENT STYLES: ADULTS

High avoidance and low anxiety
Secure-autonomous, low avoidance and anxiety
Entangled, low avoidance, high anxiety
Unresolved, high avoidance and anxiety

INTERVENTIONS WITH YOUNG PEOPLE

Incorporate other child development ideas
Find protective factors in the child's environment
Support parents to be better attachment figures
Encourage restorative experiences
Help substitute carers maintain consistency
Be a champion to children
Help children to express feelings
Prepare children for changes
Review experiences of successful living
Life story, ecograms etc. to explore attachment
Encourage adventuring with children
Activities to balance relationship insecurity
Help teenagers build peer relationships

INTERVENTIONS WITH ADULTS

Encourage protective factors
Provide social support
Support new ways of relating
In loss and bereavement, encourage people to remember attachments
Use creative arts

Mentalization is the process by which early childhood attachments create a mental image of how people behave towards us. This affects how we behave towards others

INTERVENTIONS WITH CARERS

Help carers believe in restoration
Help carers stick with difficult behaviour
Consistency and warmth
Attunement to the child's thinking and relationships
Encourage talk about positive caring experiences
Encourage protective factors
Provide social support

Uses

Attachment is a technical intervention theory. If you're using it with children, you're probably part of a multi-professional agency, for example a child and adolescent mental health service, with standardized programmes of interventions to follow. The theory is informed by complex research and at present is constantly developing, so you need specific and up-to-date training to use it and the programmes offered in your locality.

Some attachment work with adults and carers also uses technical interventions, often based on the findings of the Adult Attachment Interview, which asks about how attachment experiences as a child and in other relationships connect with adult thinking. Other measures are also used, for example the attachment story completion task and other story stem methods, where children complete a story that is begun for them. Adults may use other measures to identify particular aspects of attachment behaviour, for example the Dissociative Experiences Scale, Working Model of the Child Interview. All these require training before use.

More broadly, you can use attachment ideas to help people understand their anxieties and difficulties in relationships with others, particularly around emotional closeness in relationships. People can work out how their insecurities come from the ways in which they process their experience of how others behave. Their working model about relationships becomes clearer to them. By seeing how these ideas were formed in childhood attachments to important people in their lives, and in other important relationships, they can manage emotions and relationship difficulties better. This can be useful for adults as well as young people.

Understanding attachment behaviour may also help you make decisions about children's futures.

Introducing attachment

Introducing attachment interventions involves understanding attachment ideas. Attachment is about how people connect with carers, often parents, in childhood, and important figures in adulthood. Human children, like all animals, instinctively seek relationships with a single person or small number of people who care about them and for them, care providers. They want to feel safe by being physically close to those carers. This enables them to feel secure about adventures to explore the world, without experiencing fearful reactions. How the carers react to them affects how secure they feel. Attachment is not just about children feeling good: they need a 'secure base' from which to have experiences of the world from which they can develop.

Attachment relationships in the first months and years of life form a template for later attachments and affect many other aspects of our mental health and social functioning. So, childhood experience influences later life experience through intersubjectivity, that is, experiencing in our own minds how others' minds seem to be reacting to us. We 'mentalize' the other's response to us, and this affects how we think about other relationships. The good news is that people can learn to overcome early difficulties with attachment, and interventions are designed to help with this.

Mentalization is an important process in attachment. It is about building an internal model in our heads of how people behave towards us and helps people regulate how they behave towards others. It gives clients a picture which enables them to understand other people's treatment of them. A useful starting point is to get clients to talk about how they see other people to build a picture of how they mentalize important relationships and how this affects their view of other people.

Action sequence

Identifying different attachment styles

Most children build secure attachments with one or a few carers, and this pattern continues through life. Some carers do not give consistent messages that help the child feel secure, and they consequently feel insecure and anxious about how carers are going to treat them. Children's reactions to this insecurity vary, and these patterns also persist. Some avoid attachments and keep themselves to themselves. Some are ambivalent, so sometimes they approach carers and sometimes shy away, depending on how they interpret the carer's behaviour or attitude. Some experience relationships as disorganized and unpredictable, so are equally unpredictable in response. A few people develop a pattern of avoiding attachments. These reactions are tested in clinic settings by the 'strange situation procedure', in which you watch how children react to the introduction of strangers into the room when a known carer is present or absent.

Being aware of the four types of attachment style in children may help you see how attachment styles in important adults have affected them:

- insecure-avoidant styles: children who feel unloved but are self-reliant, and see other people as rejecting and intrusive;
- secure styles: children feel loved and are competent, and see others as dependable;
- insecure-ambivalent styles: children feel unvalued and are dependent, and see others as unpredictable;
- disorganized styles: children feel unloved and isolated, and see others as frightening and unavailable.

Most children are secure, and have a secure base for further development. Insecurely attached children may manage life adequately, behaving consistently and coping with change. A disorganized attachment style may lead to inconsistent behaviour that adults and schools find difficult to manage.

Helpful interventions for young people

Look for protective factors in the child's environment, for example extended family, neighbours who provide support. Practical economic and social support reduces stress and gives time for activities that stimulate better attachment, for example regular social work visits, help with shopping and cooking, reducing conflict between parents, increasing support for anxious or depressed parents, help with social security benefits.

Help carers restore young people's wellbeing by organizing good attachment experiences at home or in placements. Support parents, foster carers and other substitute carers, for example grandparents, so that they understand better the behaviour they are seeing and stick with trying to overcome difficult behaviour because they can see its origins.

By how you behave towards children, you can help them feel valued, and that you are their champion and supporter. Make sure children know they can express their feelings about losses and changes, before and after they happen and while they are in process. Be clear that you want to hear about their views on adults' trustworthiness.

Prepare them for changes in their care arrangements. Try to ensure that these will produce positive experiences to counterbalance difficult experiences in the past. Use life-story work, ecograms, ecomaps and genograms to help children understand their links in the past and the future. After periods of successful living, encourage children and young people to review what has helped them to be more secure. This demonstrates and reminds them of successful change. Even if a placement doesn't work out, help children review positive points about it.

Help to ensure that caring staff in residential, day care, and youth work can build positive relationships with children who feel anxious and insecure about exploring new life opportunities. Encourage 'going with' young people as they approach new experiences so that they can feel safe as they start to explore the adventures of life. This does not deal with attachment problems, although it may help in the long run if consistently applied, but it supports children in their personal development.

An important opportunity occurs as children develop to have wider experiences of relationships. This includes members of their extended families and figures such as social workers, teachers and youth workers. In adolescence, young people can also gain experience of reciprocal caring with peers.

Building a wider range of links with people in a network of leisure activities, school and extended family and community contacts can counterbalance feelings of insecurity in important relationships. If there are no central caring figures, compensate by providing other contacts, and making exploratory behaviour safe for example through 'adventure pedagogy' (see Chapter 24) and other well-managed youth work.

Helpful interventions for carers

Working with carers, make it clear that by their behaviour they can replace past bad experiences with good experiences. But the anxiety and insecurity from difficult attachment experiences means that children are often untrusting and volatile in their reactions. Consistency and emotional warmth in relationships with children can re-establish a greater sense of security.

Encourage an important caring skill of 'tuning in' to what the child is thinking about their relationships and surroundings. Standard measures use sentence completion, and you might borrow from these to get children telling stories about their attachment and caring experiences. It can help you and adults around them become 'attuned' to their feelings about caring figures and what gives them increased security to explore their world.

Listen to adults talk about attachment and caring experiences to gauge how far challenging or distant behaviour comes from these, for example people with intellectual disabilities, mental illness or experiencing loss in adult and later life. Better understanding may help carers accept challenging and difficult behaviour. As with young people, build protective factors into the family support.

Helpful interventions for adults

Four types of attachment style may be recognized from the Adult Attachment Interview (a psychological proforma). Various self-report measures identify a similar range of attachment styles, emphasizing the balance between avoidance and anxiety. These four styles relate to the four children's styles. An important aspect of helping adults to explore their style is to get a picture of how these styles apply to them:

- Secure autonomous adults (low avoidance, low anxiety) value attachment, can appraise relationships with others and their own emotional style accurately.
- Dismissing adults (high avoidance, low anxiety) downplay emotional or attachment experience.
- Entangled adults (low avoidance, high anxiety) are preoccupied with confused or emotional responses to attachment experiences.
- Unresolved adults (high avoidance, high anxiety) are caught up in past attachment and loss experiences and cannot regulate confused experiences about them if they surface.

These attachment styles to some extent affect how adults will be as carers of children: secure adults mostly reproduce secure attachment in children.

Looking for protective factors in family and community, and providing practical and social support, is a good strategy for reducing the impact of anxiety in relationships and because of loss of important attachment figures in adulthood, as with children. Where relationship difficulties arise from avoidant behaviours, provide encouragement and support to try new ways of relating to important family members and romantic partners.

Seeing bereavement as coming from the loss of attachment figures such as children, parents and romantic partners is an important way of helping people understand important emotional experiences during adulthood. Help people think through ways in which they may be able to adapt to anxiety and insecurity about attachment for example by moving to new environments, renewing their activities and having good experiences. Using the creative arts, for example craft, creative writing, music, painting, sculpture, can help memorialize lost attachment figures, stimulate new interests and provide a medium for social relationships.

Things to think about

Building security and attachment is consistent across the world but cultures and ethnic groups vary in their preferences. In some, caregiving is widely spread within extended families or communities. Consider the usual way clients' families organize caregiving and community lifestyles. The diversity or limitations of people's experience affects how comfortable they feel about patterns of caregiving that you or other services are offering them. Aim to adapt how carers or services offer new attachments to clients' cultural expectations.

Although attachment is an important mechanism, other theories of child development and adult loss also contribute to our understanding, for example ideas about development stages throughout the lifecourse, theories of the stages or tasks people work through in dying or bereavement.

Further resources

Howe, D. (2011). *Attachment across the lifecourse: A brief introduction.* Basingstoke: Palgrave Macmillan.

Shemmings, D. & Shemmings, Y. (2011). *Understanding disorganized attachment: Theory and practice for working with children and adults.* London: Jessica Kingsley.

These books provide good modern accounts of attachment ideas and some information about intervention.

Check the online resources at policy.bristoluniversitypress.co.uk/how-to-use-social-work-theory-in-practice/online-resources/chapter12 for a full list of references for this chapter.

13

Task-centred practice

Setting the scene

What is task-centred practice?

In task-centred practice, you work with clients to identify a limited number of high-priority problems in their lives. You jointly devise and carry out a brief sequence of tasks that form steps towards resolving the high-priority problems. Doing this builds their skills and activates their motivation to respond to later problems.

The approach developed through a series of research projects initially in Chicago, with the model developed by Reid and Epstein (1972); research carried out across the globe supported the model of practice. Both authors continued to develop the ideas during their lifetimes and the most recent comprehensive iteration to involve Reid is Tolson, Reid and Garvin (2003). The most recent comprehensive British account is Marsh and Doel's (2005) handbook.

Aims

Getting people moving on something that is important to them is the main aim. The assumptions are that if you provide opportunities for change, action on tasks is a good strategy for achieving it.

Activation as a social policy, widely used to combat unemployment, refers to services that energize people or increase participation, particularly in employment. Sometimes, these are policy interventions, for example rules to make seeking or staying in employment a condition of receiving disability or unemployment benefits. Other activation policies may use social interventions to remove barriers, such as care responsibilities, to employment. Alternatives involve increasing employment-related skills, for example volunteering to improve work habits or participation in groups to improve social skills. Other programmes aim to motivate people who feel depressed or excluded to seek jobs. Some of these methods of social activation employ tactics that are like task-centred practice, for example setting people a series of tasks to complete to improve skills or seek work. In activation practice,

TASK-CENTRED PRACTICE 13.1

EXPLORE OR SCAN PROBLEMS

Client lists problems they want to deal with
Describe > specify > name each problem
Don't jump to solutions
Avoid 'why' questions
Are the listed problems suitable?

Should you freeze these problems to make them actionable?

PRIORITIZE GOALS AND PROBLEMS

Choose up to three problems
Balance the important against the urgent
What is the main priority and why?
Be clear about your client's motivation
Be clear about agency requirements.
Extract and agree goals for each problem

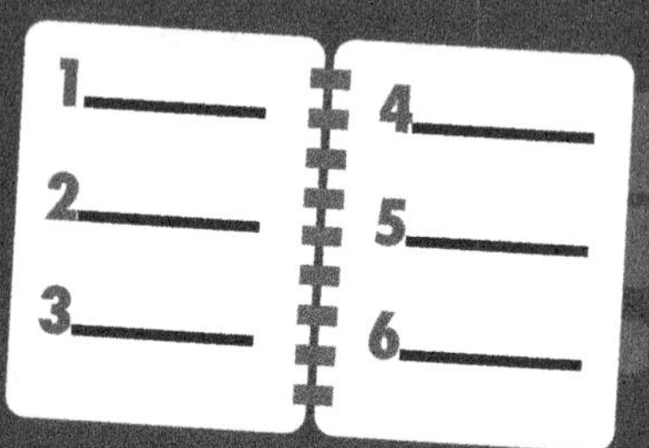

MAKE AN AGREEMENT

Agree to take on up to three priority problems
Define each problem and its goals
Identify tasks to achieve the outcomes
State or write the agreement

GOALS SHOULD BE:

- **S**pecific
- **M**easurable
- **A**ttainable
- **R**elevant
- **T**ime-bound

DECIDE AND PLAN TASKS

Identify tasks
Build motivation
Work out details and skills needed
Devise a programme
Identify and remove obstacles

TASKS SHOULD BE:

motivating
feasible
desirable
problem-focused

MIDDLE PHASE CYCLE

Timetable for task completion
Client and worker both involved in tasks

Agree, record tasks
Prepare, rehearse
Carry out tasks
Report back, log
Review: aims achieved?

DEFINING TASKS:

What to do?
Who will do it?
How?
New skills needed?
Why it will help?

ENDING PHASE REVIEW

Repeat for each problem.

How did it go?
How did it feel?
What did you learn?
What did you achieve?

these are allied to administrative sanctions or psychological and social pressures towards conformity, which run counter to the philosophy of task-centred social work practice.

Uses

Task-centred work allows you and clients to clarify problems, cut away complications. You also refine and agree goals, things that the client and you want to achieve.

The initial research (Reid & Epstein, 1972) identified problem areas to use task-centred practice with:

- interpersonal conflict;
- problems with social relationships;
- dealings with formal organizations, for example landlords, schools, work;
- problems in role performance, for example parental responsibilities;
- social transitions, for example moving to a new area, retiring;
- reactive emotional distress, for example bereavement;
- inadequate resources.

These later expanded, and task-centred practice is also used as an insert into longer-term help using other models of practice. Task-centred practice gives structure to one-to-one helping. It has also been successfully used in family, group and community interventions. For example, a group of people, often peers facing similar situations, can support each other in a programme of tasks that will resolve their personal problems. Families and community groups can plan a project using programmes of tasks shared among them.

Task-centred practice can be used on a broad range of issues, particularly everyday practical problems, that social workers tackle. So, it is a good basis for intake and general work in agencies. Because it focuses on clients' priorities and identifiable problems, even where client engagement with agencies is involuntary, it is respectful and responsive when providing service, especially to people from minority groups.

Introducing task-centred practice

Two different contexts for task-centred practice require related but different approaches to introducing it. Both emphasize that this is brief, systematic, immediate and can be learned and applied to other problems in the future. People often find this empowering.

One context is where clients are referred or apply for help with a problem that is amenable to this approach. Here, you suggest that a recognized way of dealing with issues like this is for both you and the client to form an alliance to work together through a series of steps to deal with it. You and the client each take on some of the tasks involved. When you have finished the sequence, you agree to end their involvement with you or your agency.

The other context is where you are in a continuing relationship with a client, or providing long-term services. When problems amenable to task-centred work emerge, you propose to the client a shift in focus to this model of practice. You may need to agree to warn others around them that you are changing how you work together for a while. After completing the sequence of tasks, you explicitly terminate the use of the model, and just as clearly move back to other ways of working, again letting other people involved know about the change in approach.

Action sequence

Initial phase 1: explore or scan problems

Start by getting the client to list problems they want to deal with. Describe, then specify, then name, each problem. Look for patterns. Put in your ideas, to see if clients are prepared to take these on. Your suggestions develop from your agency's and the referrer's priorities, so they may differ from what clients see as important. Focus on problems of living, how people manage themselves in the relationships and social situations they are regularly involved with. Draw on other relevant people's views, for example parents, spouse. Create a list on a computer screen, flipchart, sticky note, whiteboard in writing, so that you can both have input and it is clear that all contributions are taken into the process. Solutions are not problems; it's easy to jump immediately to answers before you've asked the question. For example, 'I need to get a job' is a solution, but problems such as 'I've no money', 'I'm unemployed' or 'my mum complains I laze around all day at home' might lead you eventually to that solution. List the problems because there might be a variety of things you could do to resolve each of these.

Avoid 'why' questions because trying to explain why things happened distracts you from planning for the future. Instead, focus on how people solved problems in the past and what that suggests about better problem solving in the future.

Think through whether problems are suitable for working on. Factors may be urgency, pressures from others, consequences of not resolving the problem, chances of success, whether there is support.

Initial phase 2: prioritize problems and extract goals

Choose no more than three problems as priorities. Think about which problem on your joint list is most important. It's a different issue to think also about which you should tackle first. Discuss links between importance and urgency. Think whether some problems are sub-problems, parts of bigger problems, rather than something that should be your main focus. Ideally, you might start on the most important, but this might be difficult or complicated. Accept the reality that you or the client are not, yet, able to work on a more complex problem, however much you would both like to, and move to another as a starting point. Also, sorting out one problem might make it easier to solve another connected to it. Securing an easy win improves motivation and builds your relationship. Talk about why you are choosing one problem as the main priority. Be clear about the arguments for the choices you are making, balancing different concerns and views.

Identify the problem you are going to start with but be clear that you can move on later to others that are also important. Talk about how strong the client's motivation is to act on this problem. Draw on other's people's views in case they might help to push forward or stymie something the client thinks is important. But if the client is not motivated, task-centred practice is impossible. Ideally, therefore, pick a problem where motivation is strong. If it's something you must insist on, like not leaving children alone at home, you may have to work first on helping clients understand why this is important to them, and not just you.

Extract goals from the problems. What will your programme of action achieve – for you, your agency, the client, others around the client? Which goals can you agree on? Which can you and the client accept, even if you don't agree? In contrast with solution-focused practice, task-centred work accepts that goals may not be a complete answer to a problem. Seeing what people want to achieve, however, can help you identify motivating factors and tasks that might help.

Task-centred practice is a brief method of intervention, so don't choose a long-term issue, or break it down into manageable lumps or clear stages.

Initial phase 3: make or write an explicit agreement

The acronym SMART helps to check that the problems, goals and tasks are specified well enough. The plans must be:

- **S**pecific
- **M**easurable
- **A**ttainable
- **R**elevant
- **T**ime-bound, that is timely and with timescale tightly managed (Doran, 1981)

An example problem is a depressing home environment. The motivation is that the unpleasant home environment discourages children in the family from staying home, putting them at risk of getting in trouble on the streets. A useful intermediate goal might be keeping the kitchen clean and tidy so that the table can be used for other activities such as children's homework (relevance). This might mean family members following a rota for washing up dirty crockery, wiping the table and vacuuming dropped food (measurable, attainable), within 15 minutes of family members finishing eating (time limit). Having achieved this, hoping that it's an easy win, you can see future similar goals that clients might value, for example tidying the living room and bedrooms, and moving on to redecoration.

You can devise tasks to achieve these outcomes. You might specify them as part of the agreement, or work them up as you go through the intervention.

The agreement might be written down as a contract, or put headings of the agreement on an email, flipchart sheet or text message. You both need a copy to refer to.

Initial phase 4: decide on and plan tasks to resolve the problem

Tasks are a series of steps leading to resolution of the problem. Everyone involved in taking the steps should be part of deciding on tasks and be involved in making an agreement. Both client and practitioner should have tasks, which ideally depend on or interact with each other.

Undertake a series of sessions, each with a similar format: review, clarify, plan, prepare, summarize. Generate a list of possible tasks for each problem aiming at the goal. Follow Reid's (1975) task implementation sequence. As you identify a target goal and tasks that will meet it, build motivation for taking action on it. Work out details, with skills needed and practicability of each task. Pare them down to a shortlist or a programme. Identify obstacles and find ways of removing them. Devise ways to guide, model and practise the tasks.

Avoid small or trivial tasks: combine these into a worthwhile step. Also, break up too-big tasks. Tasks should be motivating, feasible, desirable, and alleviate an important aspect of the problem. As you devise them, it should be clear what is to be done, who is to do it, how they should do it (including developing the skills) and why it will help.

Back to the tidy kitchen example. Leading up to this might involve discussing the rota, the worker taking the lead in a family discussion. Perhaps an obstacle was that the mother did not usually have this kind of planning discussion with family members, so one of the tasks might be for you to model and later on support her in doing this. The discussion might involve thinking about future steps after this one, so that everyone can see where this is leading; another possible obstacle if people think they're having a meeting to no purpose. After the meeting, agree who can do which tasks. The mother makes and pins a written rota on the cupboard door. Both worker and mother take a hand in training family members to do unfamiliar tasks. The tasks include collecting crockery and cutlery, washing up, drying up, vacuuming, taking turns to check the clock, check each other's contributions, issuing reminders. The worker supports the family activity by checking on the state of the kitchen on a regular visit, reporting back to the family.

Middle phase (repeated): carry out and achieve the programme of tasks

Agree a timetable for task completion in stages. Rehearse what to do. Work on tasks for the client and the worker at the same time or make it clear how they are alternating in making a contribution. The process starts: at a meeting, agree the tasks and perhaps record them. Then prepare for and carry out the tasks. At your next meeting, report back and perhaps make a log of what happened. After that, review the tasks, that is, evaluate whether they achieved your intentions. Then start again.

So to summarize: meet to agree and prepare. Carry out the tasks. Meet to log what happened, review what you achieved. Then agree and prepare the next tasks.

The kitchen example: rehearse in the office with the mother how to raise the idea of the meeting and its aims with family members. Perhaps role-play how to deal with protests, run through likely objections or non-cooperation. The mother does that; the practitioner agrees to be available on the phone to advise if there are problems and to check what happened at their next meeting. Then the worker conducts the family meeting. They share views about what happened, jointly review successes and any issues that came up at their next meeting. Then they plan and record their next tasks. They both take part in training family members, inform each other what happened and review whether the rota should be amended. If so, this time the mother conducts the meeting, with the worker present to consult. Then the family tries it out, the worker being available to consult about problems. The worker does a visit to check. Report back, and review again at the office. Another week, another check, another review.

Terminal phase: final review, future tasks

At the end, review how it went, how it felt, outcomes. Identify successful learning, particularly problem-solving strategies for another time. Then the same thing for the next task, if any. If this is the end of involvement, be clear about termination; if you are shifting back to more generalized working, be clear what this phase has achieved. Celebrate.

Things to think about

Focus on the model's underlying assumption that action, doing something, is a good basis for achieving change or resolution in a problem. This approach solidifies problems, not allowing for complexity and a range of views about the problem; think about whether freezing problems in this way is helpful. Make a problem less diffuse, more actionable, but don't deny its complexity; perhaps you're only dealing with some of the implications, but at least you're making progress. What actions are helpful and can offer broader learning as well as a solution for this problem?

Work at obstacles and barriers. Think about narratives: what might happen if we did this? How can we avoid that? Also, build up narratives of what has been successful and how it can be generalized to other situations. For example, if you have rehearsed how to deal with obstacles, talk through how clients can find other people to rehearse with in the future.

An important part of the model is being clear about what's involved in a task, communicating well about it by reporting back what you've done and evaluating achievements and failings. This helps to find ways of building on and celebrating what went right and not being overwhelmed by things that went wrong.

You may need to overcome obstacles to using task-centred work in the way practice is organized. Bureaucratized practice may limit time beyond even the briefest of interventions, and require the use of standardized procedures for assessment and risk management that do not permit the openness and flexibility of relationship required by task-centred practice. Identify and make space for clients who may benefit from this cooperative approach, perhaps where more routinized approaches have not worked or led to hostility from clients or carers.

Also, focus with clients on the importance of empowering cooperation as a way of building future strengths.

Further resources

Marsh, P. & Doel, M. (2005). *The task-centred book*. Abingdon: Routledge.

A comprehensive practical guide to task-centred practice.

Tolson, E.R., Reid W.J. & Garvin, C.D. (2003). *Generalist practice: A task-centered approach*. New York: Columbia University Press.

Highly detailed practical guidance for using task-centred practice in a wide range of situations.

Check the online resources at policy.bristoluniversitypress.co.uk/how-to-use-social-work-theory-in-practice/online-resources/chapter13 for a full list of references for this chapter.

14

Crisis practice

Setting the scene

What is crisis practice?

Using crisis theory, you intervene briefly in a sequence of events or social transitions in clients' lives that have led to tension and disorganization in their usual ways of coping with the impact of social change on them and people around them. You help them to manage their emotional responses to the events and find personal and social resources to establish strength to cope with future difficulties.

The theory originated in community psychiatry, formulated by Caplan (1965) and a group of associates, including Parad (1965), who promoted the ideas within a social work context. Theoretical development continues in US psychiatry and community emergency services, particularly concerned with suicide prevention and treatment and responses to rape (James and Gilliland, 2017).

Aims

The three main ways of looking at crisis see it as:

- losing your equilibrium, knocking you off balance, turning from harmony to dissonance;
- seeing or thinking about events in a faulty way; cognitive disruption;
- going through an important psychological or social transition in your life.

In the equilibrium model, your aim is to return people to balance, or the steady state in which they can manage their lives with their usual coping mechanisms; you try to enhance these by your intervention. In the cognitive model, your aim is to get people to perceive or think about the events in an organized way to create a new path forward. In the transition model, you aim to explore ways of re-establishing their coping mechanisms in their new situation. Aspects of all of these models may be relevant to your clients.

CRISIS PRACTICE 14.1

THE CRISIS SEQUENCE

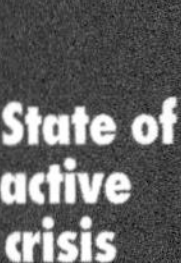

Steady state
Managing pressures successfully

Hazardous event
Sets up risky situation

Vulnerable state
How the client is at risk

Precipitating event

State of active crisis
Tension, immobilization

Improved steady state
Resumed steady state
Decreased steady state

REACTIONS

A Affective
B Behavioural
C Cognitive

CRISES

Turning points in people's lives

IMPROVED STEADY STATE =

improved coping and resilience

ASSESSING RESPONSES TO MAJOR PROBLEMS

Problems → Actions taken → Outcomes of action → Coping mechanisms and style →

INTERVENTIONS

Release emotion to generate helpful action and thinking
Maintain sense of security
Support maintaining relationships
Live in the moment, but plan for the future
Affirm and support development of strengths
Work systematically on clients' priorities
Develop options for action
Find resources and support networks
Make plans, defining goals, solutions and time limits
Increase coping skills
Identify and balance barriers with motivations for action
Check-in regularly with clients

COPING

continuing efforts to manage taxing demands

REINTEGRATION, RESOLUTION

Help clients take over control of actions
Identify problem-solving methods mastered
Review coping mechanisms learned

Uses

You can use the crisis model to work with virtually any immediate problem, but it is valuable in healthcare settings such as accident and emergency care, maternity and end-of-life care, where people must deal quickly with important or sudden events. You might also consider it as a brief intervention with people recovering from mental illness and their carers, because of its emphasis on coping skills.

Crisis models are particularly used in agencies that deal with people who have had traumatic events in their lives. There are two types. Sudden events are one, for example accidents, homicide, natural disasters, rape, serious injury, victims of crime. Work after disasters has been neglected in the mainstream social work literature because it is dealt with by specialist agencies, but there is rising interest. Any social worker may become part of outreach to help with a local disaster. There are three stages:

- a period of impact, for example the storm floods the house;
- a period of recoil, for example clients rescue their pets and important property, find somewhere to stay;
- a period of recovery, for example claiming insurance, cleaning up, re-establishing the home, flood protection.

Multiple, repetitive events are the second type of traumatic event: experiences of violence over a period, such as domestic violence, political persecution, war. This may arise when you are working with migrants. Some people experience post-traumatic stress disorder after traumatic events in their lives; this requires longer-term mental health care.

According to this theory, a crisis is over quickly, in four to eight weeks. People and families are not in constant or continuing crises. Think about chaos or complexity (see Chapter 21) in such cases.

Introducing crisis practice

Crises are presented as a sudden onset of tension, disorganization and immobilization, or inability to overcome a barrier to an important life goal. Sometimes people are driven into a spiral in which a crisis in one aspect of life invades all parts of their lives. The 'state of active crisis' usually lasts a few weeks. During that time, people are more open than usual to making changes in their lives. Clients sometimes come to agencies with a crisis or continuing clients may enter crisis periods.

It is important for people to understand that you recognize that this is a difficult and important issue for them. Would they agree to take quick action to tackle it? If we work hard to sort out this issue, it will help deal with other things better in your life too. Although the theory focuses on the technical definition of 'coping', avoid using this word, which people can see as demeaning, it implies that you think they are on the edge.

Action sequence

Establish relationship, assess lethality and emotional expression

With crises, you don't get time to prepare, but spend effort keeping calm, expressing concern for and interest in the client. Find out if they see the issues they present as a crisis or whether someone else does; what do they understand by this? Check 'lethality' (Yeager & Roberts, 2015c) and react accordingly: is there risk to safety for the client or others, or of self-harm and suicide? Allow people to express immediate emotions; let it all out and listen. It will help with assessment of reactions, and release what is tethering them to the crisis. As the whirl of emotions becomes repetitive, summarize the reactions. Then ask for permission to move on to thinking things through and planning how to respond.

Assessment: the sequence, the reactions and the major problems

Crises occur in sequences, so get people to tell their story. The theory says that people normally operate in a 'steady state', managing the pressures on them. They have their ups and downs, nobody is well balanced all the time. Ask them to look back and identify a time when things were going well for them. Explore what that looked like and factors that achieved this. To understand the crisis, identify:

- The hazardous event. This set up in the past the situation that put the client at risk of landing in a crisis, for example moving from a home town that has led to isolation from sources of support.
- The vulnerable state. Pull out details of how the hazardous event has left the client at risk, for example look at ways in which leaving the home town increased the client's isolation and reduced support.
- The precipitating event, connected with the hazardous event and vulnerable state, which tipped the client into the state of active crisis. This may appear minor but it has the crisis effect because they

are already vulnerable and at hazard, for example injury at work leaves the client off sick, losing income and possibly the job, and without support to manage the injury in their new town.

Try setting out a diagram of these stages on flipchart, paper, tablet or phone. Check them with the client.

Assess the interaction and severity of three types of reaction to crises:

- Affective reactions: anger, hostility, for example 'it's not fair'; anxiety, fear, for example 'what's going to happen now?'; sadness, for example 'I'm never going to get back my strength'.
- Behavioural reactions: immobilization, for example 'I don't know where to start'; avoidance, for example 'I was hoping it wouldn't happen'; or approach, for example 'I tried, but it didn't work'.
- Cognitive reactions: transgression, for example 'why is this happening to me?'; threat, for example 'what am I going to do?'; loss, for example 'it won't be the same now she has gone'.

Compare these reactions with the 'steady state' discussion. Are they usually anxious, angry or practical? Is the reaction to this issue untypical? What is it about this crisis that has changed their 'reaction style'?

Ask what the major problems are now; compare these with the sequence to look for anything important that the client may not have thought of. Take it for granted that there are problems in life that we usually overcome. Clients will have tried their usual 'coping mechanisms'. Structure the discussion of problems, therefore, as another sequence: problem > actions taken > outcomes of action > check on coping mechanisms and style. Some of the actions taken may have been successful, or partially successful, so affirm successes. List outcomes achieved, and 'things to do'. Look back to the discussion about their 'steady state'; test whether this action is typical of how they would react to difficulties: that's their 'coping style'.

Interventions

Where there has been a disaster or traumatic incident, focus on creating a sense of security. Maintain relationships with family and friends, build relationships with other people affected. Ensure that systematic records of problems, actions and referrals are kept and used to maintain the security that there will be continuity. Spend time on building and sustaining your relationship. Raise confidence that you and your agency will be responsive. Engage seriously with all the concerns raised, however minor; respond to as many as possible and check back regularly with longer-term issues. Encourage living in the moment, for example maintaining work, study or leisure interests, valuing contact with friends and relatives. Be with the client, or find other support, when the problem forces them to push their comfort zone; check back to see how tough actions went. Affirm their strengths when they reacted to the problem.

Respond to clients' reactions to the crisis; an ABC mnemonic:

- **A**ffective reactions: release of emotion, empathetic support
- **B**ehavioural reactions: information, protection to keep people safe and mobilize resources to help
- **C**ognitive reactions: order people's thoughts, clarify what's happened, limit the idea that the crisis will engulf everything.

Help clients be systematic; to order their mind. Taking each problem in turn, clarify the precise issue. Focus first on things that clients are most emotional about and most committed to: these form their current priorities. Confirm what's been achieved and what's still to do. Look at alternative options for action. Identify resources, especially support networks used in the past, or unused but available. Work out how to engage them and plan to do that. Look for strengths that can help coping. Work out a clear plan and set goals, with short-term time limits. Seek out skills that can be learned to increase coping, and practise them. Talk through barriers that are getting in the way of knocking this problem off the list. Use solution-focused ideas (see Chapter 20) to concentrate on potential achievements.

Where problems seem intractable, create a balance sheet. List on one side the barriers to acting, and on the other side things that will balance them. Often small things will make clients feel better about something, for example giving the children special time each day, so that their feelings are not neglected, and part of the family show is kept on the road even though there's lots of scrabbling around dealing with practical problems. It doesn't deal with the barriers, but it balances them with positives.

Think about conflicting loyalties, which often immobilize people in a crisis. Get clients to list people that they need to pay attention to, and work out ways of dividing time to make sure each is considered, for example between a couple or within the family. Think through ways of promising them time in the future, even if you can't do it now, for example a couple going through a divorce had to divide property and find new housing, so offered special time to their ageing parents in bank holiday weeks.

Plan regular check-ins; if necessary, contact people daily, by email, phone, text, or they can visit you, to get the plans under way. Be clear on each occasion what you are going to follow up. Do so every time you see them. Chalk up the successes.

Reintegration, crisis resolution

This is the final stage. Clients need to take control of their thinking about the problem, integrate the new methods of problem solving that they have mastered into their normal patterns of coping, and establish new directions. A positive review of how they have coped motivates them to manage better in future. Also, emphasize coping mechanisms learned and think through similar situations they might be used for in the future.

Things to think about

'Coping' is an important concept in crisis work: it involves continuing efforts to manage demands that you feel are taxing or exceeding your capacity. Reflect on this in relation to resilience, where you are coming back from adversity (see Chapter 4). Look at perceptions of the situation, the demands made, what is making it taxing and what capacities clients are using, missing out on or could develop.

Crises are turning points in people's lives. They are both barriers to change, because people are immobilized by them, but also provide opportunities for change. Crisis practice requires looking at options for change: think about who and what needs to change and how this may be done. But also, change to what? And in what direction? Change may not be complete by the end of your contact, but you may want to work through with clients the direction of travel.

There are many other short-term models of intervention, which inform each other and share many practice features. Two others, solution-focused and task-centred practice are common alternatives in social work. Think about the right model for the situation your client faces. Also, are you forced to use short-term models because of shortage of resources or lack of commitment to appropriate care in your services? Because you're hard-pressed and can't work with people in the long term, it doesn't mean you should treat clients' needs as a crisis, or label them as 'in crisis'.

Be relevant to the cultural, ethnic and religious views of clients, but do not make assumptions about what will be acceptable. For example, many Roman Catholics resist abortion as a reaction to a problematic pregnancy for religious reasons. In some cases, however, there may be community or family support, or non-family resources that allow this as an option, or the circumstances of the pregnancy may overcome religious concerns, for example if it occurs due to rape.

Further resources

Cavaiola, A.A. & Colford, J.E. (2018). *Crisis intervention: A practical guide*. Thousand Oaks, CA: Sage.

James, R.K. & Gilliland, B.E. (2017). *Crisis intervention strategies* (8th edn). Belmont, CA: Brooks/Cole.

The best of the American comprehensive, multidisciplinary texts covering a wide range of crises and disasters.

Loughran, H. (2011). *Understanding crisis therapies: An integrative approach to crisis intervention and post traumatic stress*. London: Jessica Kingsley.

A good European introduction to the basic theory, with interpretations according to a range of other social work theories.

Check the online resources at policy.bristoluniversitypress.co.uk/how-to-use-social-work-theory-in-practice/online-resources/chapter14 for a full list of references for this chapter.

15

Cognitive behavioural therapy (CBT) practice

Setting the scene

What is CBT?

Cognitive behavioural therapy (CBT) involves specifying behaviours and cognitions (thinking) that cause problems for clients and people around them. Through carrying out a sequence of procedures, you enable people to expunge, limit or manage the impact of those behaviours and thinking on their lives.

The main sources are in psychology and psychotherapy: modern CBT combines decades of research into learning theory, social learning theory and cognitive therapies. An important cognitive psychologist, Beck (1976), has been influential. Thoughtful collections of social work interpretations are, in the UK, Cigno and Bourn (1998) and in the US, Ronen and Freeman (2007).

Aims

There are three connected aims:

- to change entrenched behaviour that clients want to change but are finding difficult to achieve;
- to change ways of thinking that are making life tasks and relationships difficult to manage;
- to help people improve how they feel, think, motivate themselves and behave in dealing with social situations.

Uses

Agencies using CBT are usually in the fields of child and adolescent or adult psychiatry, but many other applications are possible. To use CBT fully, you need specialist supervision and training, usually as part of a programme of provision in your agency. Some agencies train

COGNITIVE BEHAVIOURAL THERAPY (CBT) PRACTICE 15.1

PROBLEM AND ABC ANALYSIS

Define the problem to work on
Explore ABC
Baseline levels and scaling

Formulation

ABC ANALYSIS

- **A** Antecedents: schemas and core beliefs
- **B** Behaviour or distorted thinking
- **C** Consequences

DEFINING A PROBLEM

5 W H

- What happens?
- Who is involved?
- When does it happen?
- Where does it happen?
- Why is it a problem?
- How does it affect people?

INTERVENTIONS

Work out a programme
Build understanding and commitment
Devise homework for each step

SYSTEMATIC DESENSITIZATION

Graded exposure to problem
Counter-conditioning technique
Sympathetic supporter

OPERANT EXTINCTION

Ignore unwanted behaviour
Support participants
Teach and reinforce new behaviour
Check for safety

SKILLS TRAINING

Social learning
Model desired behaviour
Showing works better than telling
Rehearse in private
Then real-life tryouts

MODELLING

- Describe behaviour
- Pay attention to the model
- Practise the task
- Reinforce performance

POSITIVE REINFORCEMENT

Define specific behaviours to reward
Social rewards are best
Tokens adding up to a reward
Start with immediate rewards every time
Move on to intermittent rewards
Chain sequences of behaviour
Shape complex behaviour

COGNITIVE RESTRUCTURING

Train clients to observe thinking
Use a diary of behaviour
Encourage scaling
Use Socratic questioning

ENDING

Evaluate, reinforce achievements
Help to maintain the change

staff on brief courses to use aspects of CBT for specific problems that commonly arise in their work, for example anxiety and depression in end-of-life care; school phobia. Where you want to use CBT, but specialized social work supervision is not available, clinical psychologists can sometimes provide supervision.

Using CBT principles brings clarity to wider social work practice, a step onwards from task-centred practice. Many clients and their families appreciate the way it helps them tackle specific troubles in their lives. It spells out accountability to them and the agency for tackling specific behaviours.

A common application is the social skills training aspect of social learning theory. Again, some agencies have 'manualized' programmes for doing this relevant to their client group, providing detailed guidelines. You follow a set of training activities from the manual, for example with young offenders, people with intellectual disabilities. You can select from these easy-to-understand techniques with other clients.

Introducing CBT

CBT is like physiotherapy for the mind and relationships. When you break a leg, you exercise to build up strength in the repaired limb – CBT does this for psychological and social problems.

The pure form of CBT is one of the 'talking therapies' that health services use to reduce hospitalization and medication for mental ill-health. Many people are, therefore, familiar with the term, without knowing what it involves. Because it's an identifiable psychotherapy, once you've agreed a plan, explain formally what you're going to do and get explicit 'informed consent' in writing. Agencies using CBT have standard documents for this.

Using it more generally, explain that you're going to use a set of techniques called cognitive behavioural therapy or CBT, which the client may have heard of. They are designed to target identifiable types of behaviour that are hard to change because they have become ingrained in people's lives. They also help with specific types of problem, such as anxiety or depression, that arise because of things that are going on in people's lives. The aim is to change behaviour that people don't want without interfering with other parts of their lives. The techniques rely on research about the ways people's minds work. CBT involves learning and practising new skills and new ways of thinking about things. It usually works quickly. If it doesn't work, we try something else.

Action sequence

ABC analysis, problem definition, assessment

As with any social work, build a relationship through assessment. If first contact and agency assessment leads to using CBT, a more detailed assessment focuses on defining the problem to work on. As the client describes the problem, get them to explain in increasing detail 5WH: **w**hat is difficult, **w**hen it happens, **w**here it happens, **w**ho is involved, **w**hy it's problematic (but not how or why it became a problem) and **h**ow it affects them and people around them. We met this mnemonic in thinking about risk in Chapter 6. This should give you a good basis for defining the problem.

You will be able to describe the ABC of the problem:

- **A**ntecedents – the patterns of assumptions, behaviour, perception and thinking that trigger the problem behaviour. Look for 'schemas', internal representations of the world controlling information processing and understanding, or 'core beliefs' about ourselves or our situation, for example a child who was abandoned by her parents fears she is unlovable. She is very susceptible to distant or unsympathetic behaviour, even though she knows she is being oversensitive.
- **B**ehaviour – precisely what behaviour is problematic, and the feelings and thinking that make it so. Are these feelings and thoughts appropriate, or are they distorted in some way? How have clients tried to deal with it or manage it? For example, the adult unloved in childhood avoids or reacts angrily to people who seem rejecting. How has she tried to approach people like this that she needs to work with?
- **C**onsequences – the social reactions to the behaviour that mean that the client or people around them think it needs to be changed. Examine the patterns of behaviour that the client and others display in coping with the problematic behaviour. Do they try to avoid the problem, or tackle it directly? How do their strategies work? For example, managers in work see the adult unloved in childhood as over-demanding of praise and support. Some react by giving inappropriate support, so she does not learn from mistakes, others avoid her out of irritation, so she does not learn from them either. See Chapter 14 (on crisis practice) for more on coping.

Set a baseline level which shows how often the problem behaviour occurs or how serious it is. Work this out by observing or getting a client, parent or carer to count how often the behaviour happens and when. If this is not possible, use a report form for the client or carer to complete, or a rating scale. There are some commonly used scales, such as the Beck Depression Inventory, and many for young people. These are nothing sophisticated, often like the personality quizzes in popular magazines, tested on a big (usually American) population.

Create a formulation, which describes how thinking processes and behaviour interact in response to situations that clients face. In real-life situations, behaviour is not just on its own, it goes alongside physical reactions and symptoms, emotions and thinking. A difficult experience, for example being abused as a child, leads to changes in all the factors, which affect each other. For example, inappropriate fear in particular situations, poor communication and relationship building, physical shakiness, and then avoidance of such situations.

The next stage of assessment is to look in the arsenal of change: what will help us make changes? Are there people who will provide social support or help with behaviour change? Are there skills and knowledge that may be taught and rehearsed?

Interventions

All CBT interventions involve setting up a clear programme in early sessions to tackle the problem behaviour or thinking. Get the understanding and commitment of clients and the people around them to carrying it out. Train them in necessary skills, then get them to carry out the programme in real life. Establish a series of follow-up sessions to iron out difficulties and reinforce their success. On a school analogy, have a class, set homework, check they do the homework and give feedback regularly. Use graphs, scales and tables so that people can check their own progress.

Positive reinforcement is rewarding behaviour or thinking that the client wants to encourage. The best rewards are social, getting approval from loved or valued people; that's why you assessed what social support is available. Social rewards are sometimes supported by tokens, for example chocolate buttons, stars on a chart or ticks on a calendar, which over time add up to a more substantial reward, for example money to buy something often works for young people. Ideally, at least at the start, rewards are immediate and given every time the behaviour occurs. Later, you reward less often, which means new behaviour sticks better. Negotiate specific behaviours to aim towards, for example 'coming home from school by 4pm' is better than 'coming home at a reasonable time'. Get everyone involved to agree their part. Write out the agreement, and get everyone to own their contributions, perhaps by signing.

Chaining positive reinforcement helps with complex tasks, for example someone with intellectual disabilities getting ready for work. Work out a sequence of actions. You, or a carer, start off by doing most of it, with the client doing the last task; train, encourage and congratulate them. When they do that satisfactorily, they take on the next-but-one task as well. Repeat until they do everything with only occasional reminders.

Shaping is used for a complex unitary task, for example a client with intellectual disabilities being able to socialize with work colleagues. Work out a hierarchy of skills. Teach some skills and encourage the client. Reward some successful interaction at coffee breaks (observe or get feedback from colleagues), then set the requirement higher, until good socializing is achieved all the time. Get everyone involved; carers and colleagues can feel part of it, are usually encouraging and can see steady progress.

Operant extinction gets rid of inappropriate reinforcement of inappropriate behaviour, for example temper tantrums to get people to notice you, sympathize and try to soothe you. Get people around the client to ignore the behaviour, rather than reinforcing it by being nice. This is tough, so give them lots of support and encouragement. At the same time, reinforce positively other suitable behaviour, for example teach relaxation, shutting your eyes and counting to ten. Check for safety considerations, for example if you're ignoring someone's temper tantrums, make sure they can't injure themselves.

Systematic desensitization is another common technique, for example with agoraphobia, fear of insects, school phobia. Introduce knowledge of reality, for example with fear of stinging insects, teach the difference between bees, mosquitoes and wasps; show how pollinating insects are more interested in flowers than you if you don't disturb them. Work out a graded hierarchy of contact, for example with agoraphobia, thinking about going out, going to the exit door, opening the door, looking out, going outside, going to the roadway, going to the end of the street. Teach a counter-conditioning technique for example you can't be anxious if you're relaxed, so teach relaxation and breathing control. Work through the hierarchy, stopping and using the relaxation when you get anxious. Do it with a sympathetic supporter, then without. Once they can do the first thing on their own without anxiety, move on to the next level. Graded exposure does the same thing, reintroduction to something feared, but starts from higher up the hierarchy if they can cope with some of it or are feeling stronger at this moment. A common technique to control bed wetting is to put a moisture-sensitive pad in the bed, attached to an alarm which wakes the person at the first dribble of wee, so they can go to the toilet. Their muscles tighten up and their brain learns what a full bladder feels like; soon they don't need the pad.

Skills training and modelling are at the heart of social learning. Showing works better than telling in learning practical things. The slogan is: practice enhances advances.

Modelling works like this:

- The client pays attention to a person (the model) that they like or value doing the task. A model that is like the client means that the task is less likely to be thought out of reach. If necessary, train and reinforce the model so that they offer good demonstrations, particularly if there are repetitions.
- The client describes carefully the elements of the task that they have seen; this gets it into an organized form in their head.
- As soon as possible after a demonstration, get the client to practise the task. Again, this helps to get it into their repertoire.
- Reinforce positively successful performance in the rehearsal, and again in appropriate situations in real life. Observe, get feedback from the client and from others.

Social skills training, often done in groups, enables clients to act as models for each other. Start with someone who is confident and competent; less competent group members can follow on. Arrange for real-life try-outs after success in the group. This is good for becoming more assertive, improving communication, managing aggression, over-confidence or timidity and relationship problems, for example greeting and talking to school or work mates, managing a critical relative, raising health problems with a doctor. With communication problems, get the group to discuss a topic. Use the discussion to highlight problems in communication, for example ignoring people's feelings, interruption, negativity. Rerun the discussion, stopping it as problems happen. Practise alternative ways of dealing with the issue.

Cognitive restructuring helps people adopt different modes of thinking through self-review. Our schemas, that is, our thinking patterns, can affect many different types of situation provoking problem reactions, for example anger, aggression, lack of assertiveness. There is another ABC sequence. Identify difficult situations (**a**ctivating events); train clients to observe their thinking. Look for dysfunctional **b**eliefs about themselves and their emotional **c**onsequences. Homework involves clients keeping a diary of events and troubling thoughts and behaviours, for example anxiety, anger, compulsive rituals. Scale how severe each thought was, how problematic the reaction. Learn to recognize irrational thoughts, seek alternatives and contradictory evidence. Practise thinking how trusted others handle themselves in that situation, for example close friends, parents, siblings. Take apart a small number of situations so that the client can identify patterns of thinking. Use Socratic questioning to encourage self-review: ask what was learned, experiment with alternative ways of behaving, offer information, summarize, what would happen if ... Using such techniques, clients often identify faulty thinking, for example overstating responsibility or risk. Facing a difficult situation, clients can practise WASP: **w**ait, **a**bsorb, **s**lowly **p**roceed. This helps manage their feelings and inject more rational thinking.

Ending: maintain the change

When you come to the end of the programme, evaluate progress and reinforce achievements. Identify the specific cognitive and learning achievements and techniques used, so that people can keep them going or pick them up again if things start to go off course. Suggest they maintain records of progress and scores of problem behaviour and thinking. If the problem recurs, start up some of the things they worked through again. Encourage them to use the same systematic approach with other similar problems. Schedule a follow-up appointment in a few weeks to reinforce progress or pick up problems. Invite them to come back with other problems that they can't handle.

Things to think about

CBT assumes all patterns of behaviour and thinking are learned, and we can find ways within ourselves of tackling it. Explaining 'why' this behaviour occurred, or working on the history of why it developed, is unnecessary in this model. It tends to lead us to blame ourselves or others for something going wrong. CBT is practical: it argues that because we learned this behaviour and thinking, we can unlearn it, replacing it with alternatives. As you work with clients, avoid trying to say 'why?' For example, someone fears mice and rats because of an early childhood experience. Understanding this may help appreciate the causes of their irrational behaviour but raises the original trauma again. Desensitizing them to rodents deals with the problem and avoids the angst. Stick with what's difficult and how it can be changed. It's motivating to focus on consequences: what clients and other people find most difficult to cope with because of the behaviour.

Thinking about consequences also reminds us of the social in CBT; empowering people to manage problematic behaviour helps social institutions and relationships work better.

Further resources

Eamon, M.K. (2008). *Empowering vulnerable populations: Cognitive-behavioral interventions*. Chicago, IL: Lyceum.

Excellent guide with many examples of using CBT with excluded client groups.

Kennerley, H., Kirk, J. & Westbrook, D. (2017). *An introduction to cognitive behaviour therapy: Skills and applications* (3rd edn). London: Sage.

A highly regarded clinical psychology text from British sources, very comprehensive and practical.

Check the online resources at policy.bristoluniversitypress.co.uk/how-to-use-social-work-theory-in-practice/online-resources/chapter15 for a full list of references for this chapter.

16

Motivational interviewing

Setting the scene

What is motivational interviewing?

Motivational interviewing (MI) is a collaborative practice working on aspects of people's lifestyles that they can see are destructive. You focus on possibilities for making changes in their lives. Then, you explore these as a motivation for keeping going through various stages of making, then maintaining, the change.

The originators of these techniques are the clinical psychologists Miller and Rollnick (2013), whose manual, in the third edition at the time of writing, is the primary source. A 'transtheoretical' model of (behaviour) change informs it, derived from the work of Prochaska, Norcross & DiClemente (1994). This, as its name suggests, applies to any situation where people are changing their behaviour, whatever theory of change is being used. It proposes that they need to go through a series of stages, perhaps talking about change before hardening their resolve. MI is focused on hard-to-engage clients, such as alcoholics and drug abusers, who, because they are engaged in a particular lifestyle, find it difficult to motivate themselves to change behaviour. Interpretations of the method devised specifically for social workers are also available; see the 'further resources' at the end of the chapter.

Aims

The main aim is to engage with clients in a cooperative venture for lifestyle change. You activate their motivation to use their emotional strengths and intellectual, practical and social skills to shift their lifestyle. It is a positive psychology approach, not problem based but forward focused. Unlike other positive psychology approaches, however, for example strengths, solution practice (see Chapter 9), it leans towards broad lifestyle changes rather than defined and limited goals, which those models focus on. It is this feature that makes it attractive to social workers, with their broad social responsibilities.

MOTIVATIONAL INTERVIEWING 16.1

ENGAGING AND FOCUSING ON CHANGE

Find out what clients expect from the helping process
Demonstrate alliance with clients and others involved
Aim to build pre-contemplation 'change talk'
Move towards agreed goals with smaller choices
MI aims to help people stick to their choices
Clarify moves from talking towards acting
Map out an agenda, zig-zagging among options

This

TRANSTHEORETICAL MODEL OF CHANGE

Pre-contemplation
Contemplation
Preparation to change
Action to make change
Learning from relapse
Maintaining the change

CHANGE TALK

- **D** desires
- **A** abilities
- **R** reasons
- **N** needs

EVOKING IN THE CONTEMPLATION STAGE

As change talk increases, clients become ready to plan
Recap 'change talk', comment, then pause
Envision improvements
Discuss discrepancy between now and a better future
Review past achievements that can be repeated

EVOKING

drawing out and articulating future possibilities

GUIDING AND TROUBLESHOOTING PLANS

Guiding involves focusing on needs and desires
Elicit wishes
Ask permission to give advice and information
Move clients onto 'sustain talk'
Ease off when there's conflict
Evoke and strengthen confidence

MI spirit

- **P** partnership
- **A** acceptance
- **C** compassion
- **E** evocation

COMMUNICATION

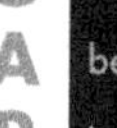

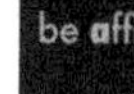

- **O** use **o**pen questions
- **A** be **a**ffirming
- **R** be **r**eflective
- **S** use **s**ummarizing
  - **S** – **s**imple
  - **A** – **a**mplified
  - **D** – **d**ouble-sided

MOVING TO CHANGE

Mobilize towards action by evoking 'activation talk'
Look for 'commitment talk'
Explore reluctance, evoking solutions
'Roll with resistance'
Help clients build self-efficacy support persistence
Revisit high-risk plans to avoid things going wrong
Keep reminding people about their plans
Reinforce discrepancy

ROLLING WITH RESISTANCE

- **S** **s**hift focus
- **C** **c**ome alongside
- **A** **a**gree with a twist
- **R** **r**eframe
- **E** **e**mphasize personal control
- **D** **d**isclose personal reactions

MI, as the technique's name implies, is about the conversations you have with clients, not social care service provision. You may need to make it explicit when you are fulfilling other kinds of social work responsibilities, and when you are concentrating on MI conversations. This aspect of practice is missing from the office-based clinical psychology emphasis of the original text. The approach is manualized, in a 'do this, then that' formula, with mnemonics as reminders.

Uses

MI is a clinical psychology method, devised for offenders and people with substance abuse problems who were not motivated to make changes in their lives and were therefore hard for practitioners to engage with and help. It may be useful for anyone who seems to be stuck in a cycle of destructive behaviour as they react to difficulties in their lives, such as mental health problems or undisciplined responses to things that go wrong in the family or relationships, such as child abuse or domestic violence.

Introducing MI

When working with people who are ambivalent about changing their lifestyle, you can introduce this method by acknowledging that external pressures aren't enough for them to make and maintain changes. For example, the risk of losing care of their children may push neglectful parents into changes. To keep going over the long term, though, they must build up confidence that they really want to make and maintain the changes. This practice model aims to help them with this. Because MI is about conversations, check that it's acceptable to make brief notes and use these as reminders of what people say that you can reflect back to them.

Action sequence

Engaging and focusing in the pre-contemplation phase

People are not usually *prêt-a-changer* that is, ready-to-go with personal and social change. Explore what clients think the helping process will be like. Demonstrate how you will behave as part of your alliance for change with them. Most important lifestyle changes are not about doing something, but about making choices. This involves setting an initial goal, then moving towards it with smaller choices. MI develops conversations about choices that help people make and stick to them. Change talk is about:

- **D**esires
- **A**bilities
- **R**easons
- **N**eeds

What is important to the client, what makes them feel good, what do they expect?

Focusing means extracting a clear direction of thinking, talking and eventually acting. If that doesn't emerge readily, try agenda mapping. Can we think about some topics that we might discuss? Offer a possible list. Perhaps this might be a page with bubbles covering physical health, relationships, social life, alcohol use, finances and some blanks to be filled in. When you have an agenda, you move on to orienting. Unlike task-centred practice, you don't prioritize because most issues depend on others. You zig-zag round the options to work out a direction that takes in the right possibilities in a sensible order.

Evoking, pre-contemplation moving to contemplation

Draw out and articulate clients' potential and future possibilities; this is called *evoking*. What would it be like? Are there alternative options? What would people, their children, parents, work colleagues, say if they achieve that change? Clients are ready for planning when the amount of 'change talk' increases in your conversations. People talk about considering, getting around to, hoping, thinking, trying.

To move to planning, flag up and recapitulate this change talk, using your notes. Then, use a key comment or question to stimulate planning; 'I wonder where we are going with this?' Then make a pregnant pause; a gap in the conversation for the client to move towards planning. If they don't do this, they're not ready and you need to return to evoking.

Develop discrepancy. This means helping clients to look for the things that will be better if they make the change. Imagine, envision how it will be different and so much better. Review things that the client has done that they can repeat and would be good steps towards the goal.

Use five key MI communication skills

The mnemonic is OARS:

- **O**pen questions open doors by opening multiple options for answering; they help the conversation move towards being more specific and clearer. Ask them one at a time, don't ask too many (one question to three reflections), ask how or what, not why.
- **A**ffirming prizes what is true and positive about clients or their actions. Take a 'glass-half-full' attitude to the client's behaviour and problems.
- **R**eflecting is your main form of communication. Most words and phrases can mean a variety of possibilities. The mnemonic is SAD.
  - **S**imple reflections (not too often) repeat the words to check you've understood. Emphasize the client's own experience, not complaints about others. Complex reflections make a guess about their meaning, offering options or openings for explanation; 'I wonder if feeling "depressed" means that your mood is generally low now, or that you have had a bad experience?'
  - **A**mplified reflections exaggerate the point the client made to help them realize that they may be going too far. Following the 'depressed' example, 'Of course, being depressed gets in the way of lot of things'. You can move on to '... but it perhaps doesn't need to be like that.'
  - **D**ouble-sided reflections present the ambiguity that lies behind the client's talk. Same example: 'Thinking about being depressed may stop you from doing things, but also makes it clear you are working on what stops you from moving forward.'
- **S**ummarizing collects several items of information together, links them and makes a transition to a new phase of the conversation.

Guiding and troubleshooting planning

MI aims to 'guide' rather than direct or enforce movement. Focus conversations on clients' needs and desires. Elicit a need or wish for advice or information. Ask permission: 'would it help to know more about ...?' Provide the advice or information, not too much – the main priorities; ask if clients disagree or can't use it. Leave it so they can respond. Elicit the response. For example, ask about how the client interprets the advice or information and what options it might open for them. Identify how important a change option is: the importance ruler is a one-to-ten scale of importance; after trying it, think what might improve the score.

Move clients on from 'sustain' talk, about things staying the same. Talk about sustaining changes is an expression of ambivalence: 'I'm not sure I can do this.' This may be particularly important if something has been tried and there has been a relapse. Emphasize clients' autonomy and choice to act, turn it into a challenge, listen carefully to the problems then remind clients, perhaps from your notes, what they said about motivations.

Discord may get in the way of making progress. Typical conversational signals of discord include: blaming others, minimizing problems, justifying inappropriate behaviour, interrupting, trying to argue or persuade you. Respond by apologizing and easing off until there are stronger signs of change, suggesting things to think about, being affirming and shifting the focus to positive things.

Evoke and strengthen confidence. Talk about how to start something, connect developments to clients' strengths, think through how to deal with obstacles. The confidence ruler is a one-to-ten scale (remember, the importance ruler was a feature of an earlier discussion). After trying it, think what might improve the score. Give more information and advice, identify and affirm strengths, review past successes and reframe things that went wrong, connecting both to present aims. As you hear confidence talk, ask clients to elaborate examples, using OARS. Work on solutions to challenges.

Moving to change

Mobilize the change talk towards action; evoke activation talk. Is there a clear goal or do options under discussion suggest a goal? Work on preparation for the change. Run through the options, and check what clients feel will be best. Choose neutrality as clients explore the options open to them. Ask for commitment: is this what you've decided? Develop specificity: what are you going to do to get ready? Set target dates. Prepare for the first step.

Troubleshoot the plan, or one or more options, together. What do we need to be prepared for? What or who might get in the way? What will you need to do this? If that happens, what will you do?

Explore reluctance; what ambiguities of feeling and attitude does it reveal? Evoke solutions from clients.

Listen for commitment talk: 'I plan, I'm going to, I promise I will ...' Evoke an 'implementation intention' (Miller & Rollnick, 2013: 286–7): this is a clear plan, that another person will see or check; recruit family or friends to do the checking. Develop clinical psychology MI towards social work MI by working on family and community supports.

Help clients to believe in their self-efficacy; they do have the resources to have an impact on achieving this change. Build on past achievements to show they have done it before. Model and rehearse what can be effective. Show how hopeful you are. Get others to express confidence in them, especially if in the past they have been doubtful but can now see the progress being made. Agree how you both will get others to be involved: the child's teacher, your client's supervisor at work, the doctor or health visitor.

Supporting change involves supporting persistence. Relapse is a chance to identify high-risk elements or stages of the change process. Revisit plans, and replan them where they have come adrift. Pay attention to what you have learned now through working together that may be problematic. Set up a system of reminders. Refocus if motivation seems to be getting diffuse. Test how motivation is fluctuating and reinforce the discrepancy gap again. Re-engage with clients who seem to have cut you off.

Rolling with resistance

Rolling with resistance involves accepting the ambivalence and difficulties that clients can see in what you're trying to do because this allows you to engage with them about it. There's another mnemonic, *scared*:

- **S**hift focus, at the same time acknowledging and going with the client's main area of resistance. 'I can see you're angry with me; how do find people respond to you being angry with them?' You can then go on to show how you and other people can handle anger.
- **C**oming alongside, accepting that the resistance prevents action now, but continuing change talk about how things could be better.
- **A**greement with a twist, accepting what clients say, but reframing it. 'I understand you are angry, and that is helpful because it makes clear that I have not found the best way of helping you yet.' Saying this sort of thing allows you to move on to a discussion of alternative options.
- **R**eframing accepts the resistance, looking at it in a different way. 'I accept you feel strongly about it; that's a good way of showing how important this area is for you.'

- **E**mphasize personal control. 'Only you can make the decision about this.'
- **D**isclose personal feelings or responses. 'I'm sorry to make you angry, but for me how you keep your children safe is very important, so I have to remind us all the time of that part of what we are trying to achieve.'

Things to think about

It can be disheartening, both for you and clients, to be constantly slipping off the path of progress that you jointly mapped out. MI stresses going through stages of change, based on a 'transtheoretical model' about changing health behaviours originally developed for smoking cessation (Prochaska, Redding & Evers, 2008). It assumes that it takes time for people to get to the point of wanting to make an important change, then making and establishing the change in their lives. The six stages are:

- Pre-contemplation. Not likely to act within six months, people are aware of a problem in their lives. You help raise their consciousness about it. They think over the gap between negative aspects of their current lifestyle and the attractiveness of realistic possibilities for the future.
- Contemplation. People are intending to take action within the next six months. They work out a path from the present damaging lifestyle towards future improved possibilities, and making those life upgrades more concrete.
- Preparation to change, within the next 30 days, and are making concrete plans to get their ducks in a row, external supports in place, setting targets and time limits, planning how to overcome difficulties that we know about and how to react to unexpected setbacks.
- Action to make the change, during a six-month timeframe, working through the difficulties that result.
- Learning from relapse, so that you can pick up the change process again.
- Maintaining the change – thinking in advance about what might go wrong or knock client off balance and planning how to react when this happens.

These timescales derive from the health education purposes of the original research. In most agencies, social work involvement is likely to be intermittent in the earlier stages, with people being part of a broader agency service rather than being actively engaged in MI.

This stage model stresses thinking and planning over a period before acting. This is unlike, for example, task-centred practice, which is more 'do-it-now' in emphasis (see Chapter 13). Difficult change is like decorating a room: a good outcome is all about preparation. Don't rush on until you've shared the thinking through. But don't concentrate on what's bad: the focus here is the gap between what's bad now and fruitful possibilities of the future. How are you going to thrash through that gap?

The model helps you hold on to the stage you're at. When things throw you off course, you can step back to the plan: was this something you hadn't contemplated? In that case, you revert to the past cycles and build in this new factor. Had you thought this might happen, but not built up a strong enough plan to counter it? Kick yourselves for the unjustified optimism and think how you might toughen up your reaction next time.

The stage model also helps you keep and make explicit between you the markers of progress through the stages; you both need to see how far you've come. If you miss the path, or everything seems uphill, you can check back on how far you've come and that helps you through the down times.

If you bear in mind the 'MI spirit', it pulls in social work's values, even while working with someone who is tough to work with. The mnemonic is PACE:

- **P**artnership, MI is done with and for people, dancing rather than wrestling. You don't pressurize people to change, you activate their motivation.
- **A**cceptance means that you emphasize clients' autonomy and worth, affirm them as people, acknowledging achievements, and try to maintain person-centred 'accurate empathy' (see Chapter 7).
- **C**ompassion, demonstrating your 'passion' for co-producing, actively promoting and giving priority to the changes they want to achieve. See Chapter 7 for more.
- **E**vocation, means not implying that clients have deficits, but drawing out and expressing their strengths and skills.

This may be obvious to social workers, particularly when they take a strengths or solution approach, remembering that MI is also connected to the currently popular positive psychologies (see Chapter 9). It is perhaps less part of clinical psychology, where this originates, hence the emphasis on MI spirit in the original texts. But it reminds us that it is tough to maintain these principles with people who are very resistant to change and prone to relapse. So bear them in mind.

Further resources

Corcoran, J. (2016). *Motivational interviewing: A workbook for social workers*. New York: Oxford University Press.

Hohman, M. (2012). *Motivational interviewing in social work practice*. New York: Guilford.

Both are good, brief practical guides, applied to social work with lots of examples and so better at representing the broader functions of social work than the original clinical psychology focus of the theory.

Miller, W.R. & Rollnick, S. (2013). *Motivational interviewing: Helping people change*. (3rd edn). New York: Guilford.

The latest edition of the original text, written for clinical psychologists.

Check the online resources at policy.bristoluniversitypress.co.uk/how-to-use-social-work-theory-in-practice/online-resources/chapter16 for a full list of references for this chapter.

17

Advocacy, human rights and welfare rights

Setting the scene

What are advocacy, human and welfare rights?

Advocacy includes representing the interests of clients within your agency and with other agencies, in some cases taking this on to action that seeks changes of policy relevant to your clients' interests. It is a long-recognized social work role; Wilks' (2012) text is a comprehensive introduction.

Human rights are privileges that people possess because they are human beings. They are defined by general codes agreed between nations, or by national codes or constitutions. Some rights are formulated to apply to specific groups, for example children, disabled people, prisoners. Rights also emerge from codes of practice, statements of policy and legislation-granted access to services; but these are not necessarily human rights because they come from political decisions to accord rights, not because of people's humanity. The latest edition of Ife's (2012) account of human rights in social work is an important statement.

Welfare rights are people's rights, deriving from their citizenship, to receive help and resources from or on behalf of the state to promote their wellbeing. Bateman's (2006) account of practice is well regarded.

Aims

You can distinguish different kinds of advocacy and their aims. In case advocacy you work to change the impact on clients of policy or practices in your own or other agencies. To do that, you work directly with the client and people around them to identify what you should advocate for and how you might do it in this case (this is called 'instructed' advocacy because you follow the client's instructions as a lawyer would). On other occasions you are in the position of arguing for your client in decision-making processes without their knowledge

PREPARATION

Consider the representation issue
Consider the level of advocacy
Establish people's points of view
Identify and refine arguments
Collect relevant information

LEVEL OF ADVOCACY

1 Giving information
2 Referring on
3 Rights casework
4 Representation
5 Mediation
6 Appeal

REPRESENTATION ISSUE

Take-up
Complex applications
Agency support
Professional support
Mediation
Appeal
Complaint, restitution

DIMENSIONS OF ADVOCACY

Decide on the type of advocacy
Decide your position on each dimension

£*!&?

Plan work in one or more forms of advocacy

- Speaking for clients ↔ Enabling clients to speak
- Persuasion ↔ Voicing clients' views
- Arguing for provision ↔ Expressing views
- Individual needs ↔ Collective concerns

REPRESENTING PEOPLE

Be assertive, not passive or aggressive
Work out ideal aims, with fall-backs
Test assumptions and judgements
Devise arguments
Provide information
Plan for likely disagreements and questions
Collect initial and back-up evidence

Representation
Picturing people
Forwarding their interests

RIGHTS WORK

Give advice and information on rights
Advocate for compliance with rights
Activate dormant rights
Explore organizational or policy development
Consider community and social development

POLICY ADVOCACY AND ACTIVISM

Agree on issues to work on and who is affected
Bring together people with shared interests
Review their readiness to act
Look at strength of motivation
Explore potential conflicting interests
Consider who benefits and loses
Plan aims and actions
Consider who to influence
Devise realistic timescales
Carry out actions
Monitor responses to your actions
Negotiate social activism with managers

Poverty and inequality
exclude and isolate people

VEHICLES FOR ACTION

Interpersonal
Information and advice
Case advocacy
Working groups
Community projects
Social action
Political action

or involvement ('uninstructed' advocacy). You might do this within your agency as an official, representing the interests of a member of the public you are charged with helping, using your professional judgement and discretion. This is often your role in case conferences or where decisions are being made by a panel to commission adult social care services. Social workers also often present their clients' needs on their behalf to decision makers outside their agencies, such as creditors.

Advocacy includes enabling, supporting or training clients to represent their own interests. They might do this on their own (self-advocacy) or with others who share the same interests (group advocacy) or with others in the community who volunteer to work on their behalf (citizen advocacy). The benefit of doing self-, group or citizen advocacy is that they build self-efficacy (belief by people that they can make a difference to life by their own efforts), independence and capacity among clients and people in their communities.

Policy, or cause, advocacy seeks changes in the aims and provision of policies and services to your clients and people like them. It often builds on advocacy, particularly citizen advocacy, on behalf of or alongside clients. Although it may contribute to social action to create important changes in society, as a social work practice it focuses on clients' interests. Activism on broader social objectives is a responsibility that you act on separately through professional and specialist organizations, stimulated and informed by your experience of clients' needs and their communities' interests.

Uses

Advocacy is one of the basic functions of social work, necessary in most practice. Practitioners use it in most cases. It is often useful at the outset, to get quick results that strengthen clients' positive attitudes about you, your agency and using social work services. Public officials and professionals such as social workers are required to comply with human and legal social rights in their work and to argue for the rights of clients with other agencies and in society generally. This extends to activating rights that lie dormant, unexpressed and unimplemented. Advocating as part of a system of provision may be restricted by the assumptions written into the system. Be aware and transparent about conflicts of interest that such issues may raise. Resist pressures to make it quick and easy to sort things out, if this is inappropriate.

Introducing advocacy and welfare rights

Representation has two aspects: how you picture a client in your own mind and to others, and how you press forward their interests in your agency or outside it. The picture in your mind comes partly from your attitudes to clients' characteristics and position, for example children or people with intellectual disabilities have a special position because they may not have the capacity to represent their own views. Others may have different views, expecting special groups to be more dependent on others speaking for them than they need to be. Considerable variation among such groups, for example between older and younger children, less or more competent people with disabilities, means that you need to negotiate what advocacy is appropriate between clients, the people around them, your agency and potential targets of advocacy.

The picture in your mind also partly comes from the fact that social workers hold a large amount of information and often provide this to others for their clients' benefit. This is expected of them for example by the courts, or decision-making agencies. The data comes from general processes like assessment. Explain to clients how you might be going to use the information they provide you with as you collect it, or early in your relationship. Remind them of this when using their information within your agency or elsewhere comes up again.

There are other positions where the advocacy role should be made clear:

- Applying for services, when you will be presenting their case. To promote transparent accountability, explain about how the process works. Enable clients to check and adapt the representation of them that you created in their application.
- Requests to take up a case with another agency. Where this is required or likely, take an 'instructed advocacy' position. Describe the agencies you will be approaching on their behalf. Say you will be acting as their 'voice' or, going further, to argue the case using professional judgements to support their voice, for example supporting a social housing application. Work out jointly the case that they want you to put on their behalf. Consider enabling them to do it, developing clients' skills or training them to do some or all of this, on their own or with you alongside them.
- Negotiations. Make clear that negotiations involve giving you discretion to get the best deal you can. Ask about their ideal outcome or target, and whether there are any 'red lines', outcomes that they will not accept.

Action sequence

Level of advocacy

Consider the complexity of service you need to offer, and whether you and your agency have the time and resources to help at each level:

1. Providing relevant information, referring and signposting to other services and explaining the system. All social work involves this level of advocacy.
2. Human and welfare rights casework: carrying out an assessment of what can be pursued, setting out options, encouraging people to act on their own behalf or with other groups and making applications or negotiating with service providers, including your own agency. Other aspects may include referring to other sources of help, such as specialist welfare rights organizations, citizens advice bureaux or law centres. You might also support them through the process while they act on their own behalf – this is a lengthier process than encouraging them to do so. Most social work involves these kinds of actions but practitioners need to be realistic about whether they have the expertise, resources (such as understanding of processes and reference books or websites) and time to do these things properly.
3. Representation and mediation with appeal systems, tribunals, courts and ombudsmen services. Most social workers refer people on to services providing this level of advocacy, unless they are part of a specialist agency.

In advocacy casework, assess the representation issue:

- take-up of services or benefits, where clients have been unaware of eligibility;
- help with making applications, especially where these are complex;
- providing agency support for applications, where this is part of broader provision you are responsible for;
- making applications, where access to services within your agency or a relevant charity may require the worker to make recommendations, using professional judgement and discretion;
- mediation with other agencies, where a stronger case or additional discretion is needed;
- appeal against a decision;
- complaint or requests for restitution for things that have gone wrong.

You can then act accordingly. Some actions require a non-instructed position because your professional decision or judgement is essential to your role.

Instructed or non-instructed

Decide with clients whether you are taking an instructed or non-instructed position or some combination of these. If you take an instructed position, they brief you to argue their views, as a lawyer would, for example a children's or family's advocate in a case conference or family meeting. Keep them informed about what you are doing and why. When you agree to do something, pursue it actively and quickly, letting the client know about any slow-downs or barriers and how you plan to overcome them. This transparency preserves their sense of control over the process, and boosts their knowledge and understanding of what to do on their own in future. Consequently, while you may be positive and optimistic, it heightens clients' control if you are impartial and frank in offering advice and assessments about what might be possible.

If you are taking a 'non-instructed' position, explain your professional judgements and decisions about what should be represented for example if you are contributing to a meeting allocating a care home place, or resources for home care. Explain both your decision and also how and where you will be making the case. If clients or carers disagree with your decision, how can they have a separate 'voice'? Inform them how to appeal. Alternatively, should you try to explain their view alongside your own? Share with clients any difficulties about that.

Share written reports and documents, in age- and ability-appropriate form, for example with children and people with intellectual disabilities. If necessary, explain any unclear implications.

Dimensions of advocacy

Discuss to clarify with clients and your managers a shared understanding of the balance of four dimensions of advocacy you are involved with, and where on the continuum of provision you will be operating.

- Purpose: to what extent are you speaking for clients or enabling them to speak?
- Perspective: to what extent is your aim persuasion on behalf of clients or giving voice to their views?

- Focus: to what extent are you aiming to gain specific benefits or services for them or to have the nature of their difficulties or position expressed?
- Scope: to what extent are you concerned only with a client's individual needs, or the implications of concerns felt by a collectivity of people (Wilks, 2012: 24)?

Gain support from managers and work with your team to arrive at agreed views about appropriate stances, to create a shared practice and get support in specific cases. Record clearly where you are instructed to act in your agency's interest or in accordance with its policies. Do this especially where the agency interest is contrary to your clients' interests or views. Seek agreement for ways to represent clients' voices. This is particularly important where they are not fully able to represent themselves, for example children, mentally ill people, people with intellectual disabilities.

Representing people

Representation work should be neither passive nor aggressive but assertive (Wilks, 2012: 137). Clarify with clients and express to decision makers a clear target outcome; consider fallback positions with your client. Test your own and the decision makers' assumptions and judgements. Devise arguments and provide information that meet decision makers' requirements. Envisage potential disagreements, issues and questions, and prepare initial and back-up evidence to contest potential alternative positions. Remain measured, cooperative and prepared to compromise. Identify a range of potential solutions, grading and presenting them in order of priority for your client at least to know about and ideally approve. Gain agreement on each issue, building further elements of your case on it.

Rights and human rights

Social work roles in rights work includes:

- advice and information to clients and the public about what rights exist (see Chapter 4 on advice and information);
- compliance with rights;
- activation of rights. Because human rights derive from our humanity, it may not be obvious when they are transgressed;
- advocacy;

- organizational and policy development to improve responses to injustice and failures to accord human rights;
- broader community and social development, allied with economic development, to provide a stable society in which rights may be fully activated.

Public and private rights

Rights work is not only a matter of organizational, public or state compliance with human and legal rights. Rights may be degraded in private, for example through oppressive child care, family violence and oppression, violence between intimate partners, abuse of older people. Be alert to situations in which individual and social rights are lost in private situations. Provide advice and information to people involved. Be respectful of alternative perceptions. People acting oppressively may not be aware that their actions transgress others' rights, for example where a parent or carer is trying to protect a child or adult at risk. Identify where rights and responsibilities are in conflict that needs to be resolved and where different family or community members have conflicting rights. Work with people to identify alternative ways of behaving. Advise people about ways in which their rights may be asserted. Consider calling the police or other agencies responsible for ensuring compliance with human, legal and social rights.

Policy advocacy and activism

Advocacy for changes to policy or in support of social causes sometimes emerges from experiencing various forms of case advocacy, or supporting people's voice in particular matters. You identify issues that require changes in policy, social attitudes or administrative and social practices. While you may be influential as an individual, such advocacy normally requires collective activity, which may involve professionals and client or community groups. Collect people of like mind through informal discussion and formal meetings. Identify client groups, partner agencies and specialist colleagues with shared interests, and engage their commitment. Think seriously about whether individually and collectively you are ready to spend energy, time and other resources to pursue the issue; think through your shared and possibly conflicting motivations for example anger at injustice, improving services. Agree on the issue and who is affected, positively and negatively by the present position. Review solutions and work out benefits and losses to relevant groups and interests. Identify aims, who you want to influence, timescales, potential ways of acting. Carry out the activities, keep track of attempts to influence and any successes. Monitor the issue as it develops. As with rights work, a community work or social development approach may be a helpful aspect of seeking policy change.

At every stage, think whether potential vehicles for action are helpful:

- informal, interpersonal influence to change opinion, including internet and social media;
- formal working groups within your agency or across agencies;
- involvement in evaluation or community research projects;
- organized case advocacy, to influence law, procedures and their implementation;
- information gathering and dissemination, for example surveys, reports;
- political action, for example lobbying, action through trades unions;
- social action, for example press campaigns, rallies, public demonstrations.

Some of these vehicles are ordinary processes for policy change within agencies, in which clients and staff can participate. In other cases, professional and trade union organizations may provide a vehicle for public engagement. Social activism, vigorous engagement in mechanisms for public influence, may be inconsistent with an employee role and carried out as a private individual. Negotiate with managers about the appropriate separation of roles. Accept that employees may not be allowed to engage in social activism directly relevant to their employment. On the other hand, you may be successful in arguing that active participation in relevant public matters enhances agencies' community credibility. Transparency of your actions and involvement provides a degree of protection.

Things to think about

Before using advocacy, rights interventions and social activism, start from clients' best interests. Check whether alternatives may be better. Enable clients, families and community activists to do as much as possible for themselves. Work out information and guidance to help them. Can you share tasks with them? Advocate in ways that enhance or don't damage relationships between you and colleagues and agencies whose help you rely on in other cases. Identify any approvals or support from managers or team colleagues that would benefit your advocacy or that they have the right to require.

After using advocacy techniques, consider whether there would have been better ways to help clients gain experience and skills in representing themselves. Assess barriers in your own or other agencies and think about ways of removing them or reducing their effects. Think through how to repair or reduce any damage to relationships between you, your agency and other agencies. Identify learning that might help colleagues or contribute to social action to achieve policy change. Explore how you and colleagues could collect and use information that might contribute to improving policy or procedures in the future.

Poverty always occurs in a family context, whether it is absent (for example among single, homeless or disabled people), expanding (for example where children are cared for) or contracting (for example in old age). The stage of the family cycle (Feldman, 1957) affects how individuals experience poverty and the use of money. It also adds emotional pressures of anxiety, fear and love to financial insecurity. Think about how to help mitigate these pressures and variations in living patterns when advocating.

We live in a money world (Feldman, 1957), where wealth and inequality affect political and social perceptions that may exclude or isolate people in poverty. Boost self-confidence by emphasizing clients' achievements, skills and competence.

Further resources

Dalrymple, J. & Boylan, J. (2013). *Effective advocacy in social work*. London: Sage.

Wilks, T. (2012). *Advocacy and social work practice*. Maidenhead: Open University Press.

Two good general books on the theory and practice of advocacy.

Check the online resources at policy.bristoluniversitypress.co.uk/how-to-use-social-work-theory-in-practice/online-resources/chapter17 for a full list of references for this chapter.

18

Empowerment, anti-oppressive practice and power

Setting the scene

What is empowerment and anti-oppressive practice?

Empowerment practice enables people to gain influence and control in their social relationships, and to claim their rights as participative citizens in social institutions. This develops their self-efficacy, the sense they have that they can make a difference to the direction and quality of their life experience. An important source is Solomon's (1976) classic statement about black empowerment in the US. A modern interpretation is Mullaly and West's (2017) practice text.

Anti-discriminatory practice combats social pressures to make judgements about a category of people that leads to unfair social or political treatment, because they are perceived as different from other people. Thompson's (2016) regularly updated text is widely valued.

Anti-oppressive practice, a development of anti-discriminatory practice, focuses on the misuse of social power. You help people understand and make use of their human and relationship resources to overcome social barriers to fulfilment of their wishes and feelings. It also contests burdensome, harsh and unfair treatment of them that comes from differences between their social identity and that of powerful social groups. The lack of social agency, the capacity to have an impact in social relations and to achieve change, and the oppressiveness of social barriers to fair treatment derive from inequalities in power in society. Dalrymple and Burke's (2006) text on social work using the law appropriately is an important statement.

Aims

These approaches have three connected aims:

- Through interpersonal practice interventions, to enable people to attain control and influence within social institutions and social relationships and to facilitate their human and social rights.

APPROACH

Develop social connection • Encourage diversity • Support solidarity
Collaborate to encourage dialogue and partnership • Be helpful and responsive to increase trust
Build people's expertise, strengths and relationships • Explore possibilities and solutions
Emphasize clients' explanations and evidence

PRAXIS

Explore narratives of clients' experiences
Understand experiences of discrimination...
...in economic, political and social relations
Identify experiences of oppression

NARRATIVES TO EXPLORE

Exploitation • Marginalization
Powerlessness • Cultural imperialism

CULTURAL COMPETENCE

Develop cultural competence...
Build diversity in social relations
Build ethnic-sensitive practice
Examine multiculturalism
Adapt practice to minorities' preferences
Develop regular training and staff development

ANTI-DISCRIMINATION AND ANTI-OPPRESSION

Help people find exit opportunities
Support expression in people's own voices
Use rights-based provision
Use authority, influence and power appropriately
Comply with administrative and legal constraints
Minimize interventions
Explain and promote clients' rights
Listen and respond to fears about agency oppression
Acknowledge political and social demands
Build critical awareness of social constraints
Explore impact of political issues

EXPLORING OPPRESSION

Aggression and hatred
Aversion and avoidance
Impacts on identity
Compliance with majority cultures
Threats to identity
Withdrawal

TYPES OF POWER

Enforcement • Authority
Management

EMPOWERMENT

Develop people's motivation and skills
Build their comfort and self-esteem
Explore action for social change
Contest tokenistic participation
Encourage mutual aid and peer support
Build partnerships
Use the law and discretion creatively
Develop prevention
Build social consciousness
Support multifocus views of issues
Provide practical help for collective activities

You cannot give power, only help people take it

TYPES OF PREVENTION

Diversion • Early prevention
Heavy-end • Restorative

MULTIFOCAL VIEW OF ISSUES

Explore meanings • Develop identity
Encourage resistance
Shift perceptions
Boost questioning attitudes

- Through social and structural interventions, to counteract and overcome economic and social barriers, arising particularly from inequalities, between social groups to beneficial social change. Removing barriers that people experience as oppressive aims to facilitate personal achievement and self-realization for individuals, social groups and communities disadvantaged by social inequalities.
- Through developing appropriate professional attitudes, competences, skills and values, to ensure that social work and all social provision avoid unfair discrimination and stigmatization on grounds of social divisions by age, class, disability, ethnicity, sexuality and spirituality.

Uses

These practices help put social work on the side of the people it serves. At least, it will be competent in dealing with social diversity and avoid discrimination in its practice, and will be a force for related agencies also to avoid discrimination. Better than that, it will reduce the distress caused by oppression, helping clients overcome barriers and limitations in their lives and improve their capacity to manage the direction and quality of their lives more successfully. Doing this provides some balance to failings and inequalities in social relationships and institutions. Empowerment and anti-oppressive practice also help agencies and society more generally, by ensuring competence in major social provision in dealing with diversity and inequality that might otherwise lead to social tension and disruption.

Introducing empowerment and anti-oppression

Implement these practices in all practice models. Aim to be explicit with clients about building an alliance to work towards goals that you are going to agree together. Explain that many people work with social workers to overcome barriers to a good quality of life, despite any difficulties they might have. A lot of these are created by our society and people's attitudes. You try not to let taken-for-granted assumptions prevent us from using positive and practical ways of tackling the causes of troubles as well as the troubles themselves.

Action sequence

Empowering, anti-oppressive approaches

Your approach should include:

- having a focus on connection, diversity and solidarity and rejecting difference as a way of categorizing people;
- emphasizing collaboration, consultation, dialogue, engagement, partnership, responsiveness, trust not distant professionalism, shared help not therapy;
- enabling clients to own their strengths, their expertise in their experiences and relationships;
- stressing possibilities and solutions (see Chapter 8);
- encouraging clients to elaborate and clarify their explanations, allowing evidence from their voices to have a strong influence on your practice together;
- encouraging powerful expression of black and oppressed peoples' perspectives on issues of concern to them.

Praxis – clients' narratives co-produce practitioners' strategic conceptions

Praxis is the process of allowing clients' experiences of oppression to inform and direct your practice decisions. Using some of the techniques explored in Chapter 10, listen and be responsive to the narratives of clients' or communities' lives to identify, clarify and discuss different forms of oppression of ethnic and other social groups:

- exploitation, others benefiting from using an oppressed person's financial and personal resources;
- marginalization, being treated as peripheral, of no concern, being excluded from consideration;
- powerlessness, clients seen as lacking the capacity to act;
- cultural imperialism, affected by adverse assumptions about the inferiority of the civilization and culture of some nations and ethnic groups.

Interrogate critically how social practices and services may discriminate against client groups and individuals you are working with. In advocacy, pursue rights-based approaches (see Chapter 17).

Explore with clients how these may emerge from economic, political and social relations in society, for example educational opportunities seem pointless, politics seems irrelevant, unemployment is alienating. How can these relations be transformed?

Extract from clients' narratives personal experiences of different kinds of interpersonal oppression and explore them and the personal reactions and social relations they lead to:

- acts of aggression and hatred;
- acts of aversion and avoidance;
- impacts on identity, causing people to shift aspects of their personal and social identities to fit in, perhaps to the extent of mimicking majority identities;
- forming their identity to comply with cultural and social expectations of influential majorities, rather than groups with which they identify;
- threats to identity, for example risks of loss if they maintain an important identity, assuming responsibility for others' criticisms of their identity;
- withdrawal in social situations to avoid oppression behaviour.

Cultural competence and ethnic sensitivity

Strategies include:

- 'Cultural' competence, or being 'culturally grounded' (Marsiglia & Kulis, 2009). Build awareness and understanding of important features of the identity of ethnic and other cultures you are involved with, and important cultural priorities within these.
- Diversity. Model and encourage acceptance of environments that engage people with many different cultural, social and spiritual identities. This offers a richer experience of humanity, enabling people to learn and grow from a stimulating and interesting variety of experiences. Develop support groups that include a variety of perspectives. Clients and practitioners need to confront the complexity and emotional content of living with difference, for example attitudes to lesbian, gay, bisexual, transsexual and queer/questioning (LGTBQ) or gender-fluid ways of living.
- Ethnic-sensitive practice. Ensure that all practice is sensitive to the special needs of minority ethnic groups. Ask about important ways in which your practice or your agency's service can respond to cultural and ethnic preferences. Avoid using generalized guides

to beliefs and faiths since families and communities will vary in how they interpret important beliefs and values in their lives. Do not expect clients to educate you in their cultural, ethnic or faith beliefs, but check how they interpret these values in their family or community.

- Multiculturalism affirms cultural and ethnic diversity, valuing minority groups' contributions to a holistic culture. It may devalue cultural, ethnic and spiritual complexity by promoting only incomplete understanding.

Adapt to the cultural preferences of the minority, for example some people expect more directive than non-directive involvement from an official, others avoid eye contact or a handshake. Other examples: discomfort in expressing feelings, avoiding acceptance of mental illness in the family, refusing discussion about the end of life. Most minority ethnicities have as wide a range of cultural and spiritual preferences as white Christians or Jews; some people are not strict adherents to religious requirements. Some cultures prefer family or community involvement in decision making, rather than a confidential relationship with a professional, so do not assume conventional values in helping. Ask people about their preferences; do not assume the impact of disadvantages or identities, for example poverty, faith or spiritual commitment.

Seek and support regular training, staff development and discussion opportunities on cultural and ethnic issues relevant to your populations, for example LGTBQ, older people, particular ethnic minorities.

Anti-discrimination and anti-oppression

Unfair discrimination arises from interactions of individual biologies and biographies in personal and interpersonal feelings and ideas, community and cultural, and wider social and institutional relations. Discrimination is usually oppressive because unfair treatment is distressing and restrictive to people's dreams and hopes. It is worse if this is because of people's social identity since this engages complex social interactions. Ensure that identifying, as part of assessment and care provision, people's personal characteristics and social identities does not lead to discrimination and oppression, for example in making service-commissioning decisions.

Anti-oppressive practice involves being aware, and making others aware, of the way unfair discrimination is part of many social institutions, social structures and social relations. Use that awareness to eradicate or reduce the impact of that unfairness. Explain your understanding of how social processes attack the dignity of and stigmatize oppressed groups in society. Avoid and draw attention to disrespectful language use. Discuss this regularly with colleagues to develop a shared approach in your agency and locality. Keep yourself and your team informed about developments in these issues.

Oppression is the use of power to treat people in burdensome and harsh ways, often over a prolonged period, leading to assumptions and expectations that unfair and insensitive treatment is normal. Contest discriminatory judgements and processes that lead powerful groups to become oppressive. Avoid and challenge oppressive uses of power, even if people are initially unaware of the oppression: 'it doesn't have to be like that.'

Three fundamental strategies for anti-oppressive practice are:

- Exit opportunities from standardized, agency-defined services in favour of client and community-defined alternatives, for example cash-for-care direct payment provision, personalized decision mechanisms.
- Voice, opportunities to express choice and personal preferences in practice approaches and service provision. Be transparent about your methods.
- Rights-based provision, rather than discretionary services. Use discretion to benefit clients.

Avoid oppressive behaviour in everyday practice. Routinely avoid using authority, influence and power that is available to you, unless it is necessary; and if it is necessary, explain why you must use it. Comply with administrative and legal constraints on your actions. Use minimal interventions. Explain rights to advocacy help, complain, participate in decision making. Make sure that leaflets and posters promoting rights are available in your office and community organizations in your locality. Listen to people about how authority, influence and power have been used against them in the past and their fears about how you and your agency might use them. Respond to these concerns by transparency about your actions. Acknowledge the political and social demands on you and your agency about issues that will engage the use of power.

Allow praxis to build a critical awareness of issues that ordinary people experience in the social and political world and that affect social work provision. Discuss current issues about service provision with team members.

Empowerment

Anti-discrimination and anti-oppression aim to combat negative social forces. It is difficult because it involves challenging existing and taken-for-granted patterns of social power. Empowerment tries to deal with these issues positively, by building people's own capacities and strengths to overcome unfair social barriers. This includes helping people find ways to cope and adapt to discrimination and oppression. This helps them build motivation towards change and develop skills to achieve it. As important is maintaining personal comfort and self-esteem in spite of oppression and finding ways to resolve problems that arise from the way they are treated. They can also move towards individual action and collective group engagement in social change.

Empowerment strategies contest tokenistic participation. Examples include routinized statements of rights for example codes of practice with no attempt at implementation. Also relevant are commodified or consumerist approaches, which are mainly about giving choice in a market which incorporates budgetary or service limitations. Interpersonal practice that treats personal development as the main way of empowering people, or structural practice that changes organizations without focusing on interpersonal practice, fail to be transformational because they only seek change at a personal or societal level, without connecting these holistically (Dominelli, 2012a).

Encourage mutual aid and peer support. Help people build and develop social capital, that is social networks of relationships that are or may become important to them. Review people they have been in contact with or people who have been informally supportive. Discuss with them the possibility of making a regular round of contacts, to the local shop, the local park, charity shops, local drop-ins, clubs, community organizations and churches. Help people think about arrangements that will improve their safety or quality of life, for example for older people preventing falls. Work with your team to ensure you have information about as many community opportunities as possible.

Find ways of building partnerships with clients, for example service user advisory groups, so that other people with similar problems can go to self-development courses alongside people with experience of overcoming some of the difficulties. Increase channels of communication with a wide range of organizations.

Use legal responsibilities to increase support for clients and communities. Avoid use of legal powers, except for their benefit. Use discretion creatively to improve provision and responsiveness of services.

Consider preventive approaches:

- Diversionary prevention. Help people to deal with important issues before problems occur for them. Shift them from a 'problem-saturated' narrative of their lives to a 'solution-oriented' view (see Chapters 9 and 10).
- Early prevention. Be responsive to people who are worried about developing problems.
- Heavy-end prevention. Focus on important and complex issues that have not yet led to risk or safeguarding issues, for example runaways from foster care or children's homes predicting placement breakdowns, disputes in families before they turn violent.
- Restorative prevention. Improve community or family environments, or services for people who have had difficulties to return to, for example drop-in centres or other support for people with mental illnesses.

Work to change people's consciousness of the issues that affect them towards empowering clients and the people around them and transforming their view of their concerns. Try to build a 'multifocal' view of the issues (Lee & Hudson, 2018: 146–7), so seeing them from different perspectives based in the variety of their life experiences:

- Meanings of the issue for clients and communities. Discuss how central an issue has become to their identity, whether they like it or not. Or is it peripheral, with other things in their life being more important? How do they understand their difference from others, and how much do they see themselves as the same? Talk through how this has varied at different stages of their life and in different relationships. For example, does poverty drain their capacity and energy to build family life, or is it a struggle that they manage with the help of family support?
- Identity in relation to the characteristic and differences between the client and others who share the characteristic. Help people work out how much they share with others and how much their experience is individual.
- Resistance. How much do they resist being associated with the category? What do they do to resist others' attitudes? How successful is that? What successes can they build on?
- Shifting perceptions. Discuss, with clients and groups, alternative conceptions of the major social institutions, for example rather than seeing their nuclear family as the cornerstone of living, should

we accept and value alternative patterns of different family life? And rather than see churches as mainly about being conventionally religious, see them as a community resource for finding people of goodwill who can get some useful things done in the community.

- Discomfort and questioning. Encourage individuals and groups to move from unquestioning acceptance and cooperation with oppressive perceptions. What makes them uncomfortable about how people look at this issue? What questions can be raised about views of the issue?

From these revisions to accepted views, individuals may be encouraged to move towards interest groups, and groups towards collective organization, to protest, to challenge the status quo and articulate alternatives.

Help clients and organizations who are attempting such activities with:

- practicalities – arrange access to resources, a creche, funding, meeting space, photocopying, printing; simply making people aware of these practicalities quickens their progress;
- education – facilitate access to knowledge about how to do things, the issues they are dealing with, for example get local adult education colleges to run courses of interest;
- access – links with decision makers, information about consultations;
- alliance – always be available to help, but not take over.

Building on community work techniques, encourage a focus on specific shared problems in the community.

Things to think about

You cannot give people power: if you have given it, you retain the power to take it away. You can be relaxed about people taking on power, though, and help them do it.

There are different forms of power and ways of understanding it. One dimension of power is the capacity to enforce your will on someone who prefers otherwise. Look at how someone could do that, for example physical violence or the threat of it, disinformation, distraction or dishonesty. We see this in interpersonal relationships, for example in some marriages that are going wrong. Help clients to see that power is not only applied by others, but may be available for them to take up.

Another dimension is the ability to get your way through having authority, a right recognized by the law or social assumptions, for example in the rights accorded to employers to manage their workforce, schools to discipline children or the criminal justice system. Help clients to see that the law also limits authority and offers protections.

Being able to get your way by setting the agenda or managing the environment so that others are not aware of alternatives is another form of power, for example not publicizing the availability of social benefits, making applications for benefits complex and restrictive, the restrictive impact of surveillance through closed circuit television (CCTV). These uses of power interact. For example, a disabled man, already aware of a restrictive and judgemental regime for evaluating applications for benefit, may find that extensive CCTV surveillance is used not only for the helpful purposes of preventing crime and controlling traffic, but for the personally oppressive recording of evidence of an active life contributing to disability benefit assessments.

Further resources

Dalrymple, J. & Burke, B. (2006). *Anti-oppressive practice: Social care and the law* (2nd edn). Maidenhead: Open University Press.

Devore, W. & Schlesinger, E.G. (1999). *Ethnic-sensitive social work practice* (3rd edn). Boston, MA: Allyn & Bacon.

Mullaly, B.(R.P.) & West, J. (2017). *Challenging oppression and confronting privilege: A critical approach to anti-oppressive and anti-privilege theory and practice* (3rd edn). Don Mills: Oxford University Press.

Important books from different perspectives.

Check the online resources at policy.bristoluniversitypress.co.uk/how-to-use-social-work-theory-in-practice/online-resources/chapter18 for a full list of references for this chapter.

19

Groupwork

Setting the scene

What is groupwork?

Groupwork is social work with clients and others meeting together, a practice concept implementing a range of theoretical perspectives. Most groupwork in social work is in 'primary groups', small enough for face-to-face interaction among all members so that all are aware of each other's contributions. This usually means between three and 12 people plus one or two practitioners. Larger numbers are used for educational or informational aims.

Groupwork stems from the historical roots of social work in the settlement movement and Christian youth work (Reid, 1981; Andrews, 2001). During the 1950s it became more therapeutic, with the psychoanalyst Wilfred Bion (1961) influential in the UK. Mullender, Ward and Fleming's (2013) account of practice using a democratic and empowerment model to achieve both individual and social change has been influential.

Aims

Three common aims of groupwork (Papell & Rothman, 1966) are:

- Social goals, developing mutual action and support in a community or social group with shared interests and concerns. The practitioner enables influence through shared activity. Example: working with a group of migrants to develop conversation opportunities with English-speaking adults.
- Remedial goals, restoring or rehabilitating people's capacities to respond to problems in their lives. The practitioner is a change agent. Example: a group of young offenders sharing experiences to build non-criminal interests and opportunities.
- Reciprocal goals, building groups members' capabilities to interact with social institutions to meet their needs better. The practitioner

PREPARATION

In planning, consider:

Community and agency aims and needs
Political and management demands and constraints
Leadership in the group, its membership and size
Should it be open-ended or time-limited?
How frequent and how long should meetings be?
Focus: on internal relationships or external issues?
The aims of the programme
Resources needed
Dealing with difficulties
Connections with other colleagues and other work
Reporting back to agency and colleagues
Recording and confidentiality records
With ongoing groups: provide for new members

GROUP PROCESS ISSUES

relationships
leadership
power
boundaries
roles
tasks
what is brought and taken?

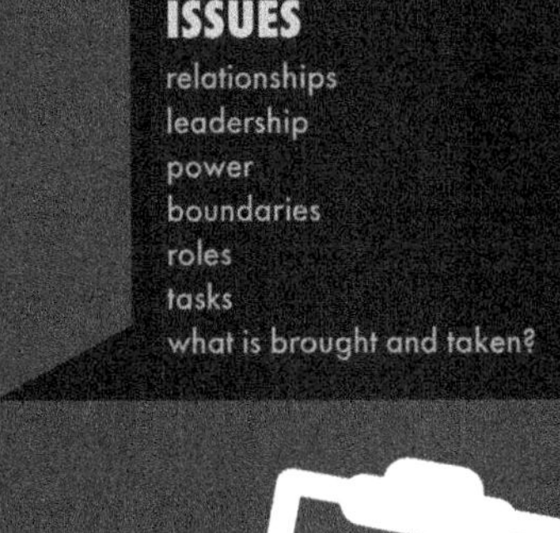

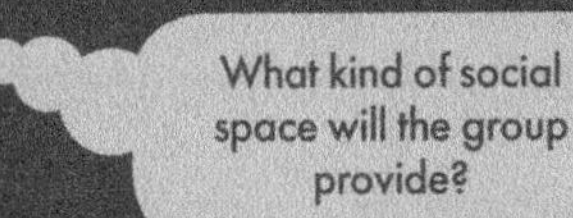

INTERVENTIONS

When making interventions, consider:

Your aims: education, information-giving or therapy
Maintaining a safe climate in the group
The group's structure and ground rules
The issues that the group needs or wants to tackle
How you can guide discussion helpfully
How you can manage behaviour appropriately
How you can stimulate the start of group activity
Model reactions

INTERVENTION TARGETS

Individual members
Whole group
Parts of group
Leaders within the group

INTERVENTION AIMS

Facilitating interaction
Enabling relationships
Developing structure
Working on members' aims
Developing norms of behaviour

ENDING AND LEAVING

Remind members in advance of the group ending
Encourage expression of feelings about ending
Encourage planning for a future without the group
During the final meeting work on planning and review
Ongoing groups: make provision for people leaving

mediates between organizations and group members. Example: a group of women who have experienced domestic violence developing education programmes for schools and community groups.

Uses

Groupwork creates an additional temporary social space in clients' lives, enabling them to achieve valued aims. Building on a sense of belonging and commonality of feeling and experience, groups offer friendship, mutual support and relationships that break down isolation and loneliness. They also offer chances to recognize shared experiences and feelings. Members have opportunities to help as well as to be helped. Groups may also provide education, information and different perspectives on issues. Practice in residential care usually contains significant elements of groupwork. Here, the milieu or life space in which people live can provide boundaries and directions for working on personal development.

Regular meetings may boost hope and motivation to deal with difficulties. During a difficult period, they form a safety net, increasing members' sense of security in managing their affairs. Members may experience how to exercise control and power within personal relationships and develop capacities to achieve change. Groups provide opportunities to learn and test interpersonal and other social skills, and gain feedback on behaviour and efforts to cope with problems. Members may model themselves on other members or practitioners in the group.

Introducing groupwork

Groups may already exist, for example a school or work group. They may also arise spontaneously, for example members of a youth group recognizing shared interests. Others are formed by practitioners from among clients or a specific population, for example spouses of people experiencing domestic violence. They may also arise from a larger meeting, which wants to work on an issue, for example a community group concerned about housing repairs. Help people with anxieties about whether they have the skills or confidence to set up and run a group.

Where groups arise or already exist, facilitate a discussion about aims and structure. If necessary, see each potential member individually to help them decide to commit to the group. Where you are forming a group, identify potential members and encourage them. Help them to make the choice by explaining potential benefits and downsides, so that consent to participation is informed. Agencies may require a consent form, especially for children whose parents need to consent.

Action sequence

Preparation and beginnings

Groups are effective where members or potential members can help each other to achieve shared outcomes and where your agency is hospitable to forming and supporting both groupwork and this group. Tune in to potential group members' needs: why is a group best for these clients or this situation? Use this knowledge about the members to plan and prepare for the group. Turn constraints into positives around its structure:

- Community, agency or political issues, for example is social change among your aims? Do you need to get management support?
- Leadership, by members or practitioners; gender and numbers of leaders; style.
- Membership, how to recruit, similarity vs. diversity in experience and needs, selection process.
- Size.
- Open-ended or time-limited.
- Open or closed to new members joining.
- Session timing: days, duration, frequency, times of meeting.
- Internal or external focus: on the group and its relationships or on external issues for example developing a community project.
- Aims for activities, programme, speakers or subjects. Programmes may aim at enabling or increasing human contact among members, enabling education and information gathering, rehearsal with others of behaviours, for example to increase confidence and skill in communication or relationships, which may enable people to raise and share difficult issues.
- Resources. Staff, supervision, location, rooms, equipment, transport, refreshments.
- Dealing with difficulties, for example members' distress. Explain the arrangements to members if a colleague is available to see them about distress during or after the group. Having two practitioners in the group, so that one can take time with a distressed member, also needs to be explained.

Practitioners responsible for individual clients, which may be you and colleagues, may do work arising from the group in other settings. Make plans for this explicit before the group starts. Clear space for group-related discussion within other interactions so that it does not interfere with other work. Identify if you need to report back on the group or individuals within it and plan how this will be done, for example to colleagues who refer clients to the group, to parents or teachers of children, the courts or spouses in domestic violence cases. Clarify this before seeking consent to involvement. Remind people of this commitment where they seem to need reminding, but don't use this as a threat, for example don't imply you will report bad behaviour.

Consider and gain consent for recording sessions, and confidentiality of records. Agree rules about members making records or keeping information for example photographs, mobile phone use. Give people the chance to feed back to you or the agency about individual sessions and the whole group. Take suggestions for improvements seriously.

Interventions

In groupwork, you make interventions with people within the group and so you need to consider the target of each intervention you make and whether this has consequences for what you say and do:

- one or more group members
- the whole group
- parts of the group, for example children or parents, younger or older
- other group leaders

You can make useful interventions in four areas to help members to:

- facilitate and understand interactions between all members;
- enable groups to develop consistent patterns of relationships and a social structure, including sub-groups;
- identify and work towards the agency's and members' objectives through activities and tasks;
- develop norms of behaviour, cohesion, influence and a supportive social climate.

Potential interventions:

- giving information or educating members;
- creating, or recreating, a safe climate;

- setting and maintaining structure and ground rules. This is important to reduce the impact on group relations of social inequalities and oppressive behaviour carried over from everyday life, for example stopping bullying in the group;
- raising or renewing issues;
- guiding discussion so that you cover the issues for example about bereavement;
- interpreting or managing behaviour;
- starting an action for example an activity;
- modelling appropriate reactions, for example when a member cries, is angry, walks out.

Is your intervention appropriate and timely? Consider waiting to see how others in the group react. Give them the chance to make the same response you would have made. Managing the use of limited time in the group, by moving discussion on, contributes to its climate and structure.

Human behaviour is always ambiguous. Achieving change through social influence in remedial groups involves helping members make social comparisons with other members of the group, practitioners or people outside the group. How another behaves is a model for them to accept, modify or reject. Within the group process, members may move from rejecting change, towards compliance with behaviours, identification with a role model and eventually internalization of a change. Discuss behaviour or experiences that members may want to eliminate, reduce, maintain, enhance or modify. Try to build support within the group for such movements. Does group process settle down into being tolerant, not rocking the boat by trying out difficult skills or picking up controversial aims? You may need to confront it if the group always takes the easy way out. For example, you could offer practice in new ways of behaving, such as responding to bullying.

Ending and transition out of the group

When time-limited groups are to end, allocate time in the previous week to reminding members of this. Encourage them to express their response to the approach of the end, and draw attention to planning for a future without the group. The final meeting will include elements of celebration, planning and review.

Ongoing groups need rules that make provision for people leaving, for example giving notice to other group members, and for saying goodbye.

Things to think about

Explore the kind of social space for interaction that the group provides, what enables members to feel that they belong, the structure of relationships within and outside the group. Reflect on and openly mediate between group members' objectives, agency aims and the interests of others, for example parents, spouses, teachers, the courts. See conflicts as ways to identify and work on group issues, modelling how to deal with conflict creatively. Consider the balance between achieving tasks and participating in process in the overall purpose of the group and the interactions that take place.

Groups often develop a life of their own, moving away from formal objectives. Guide people to keep to their aims, while recognizing where new directions are relevant.

As you work in a group, you are alert to and constantly evaluating 'group process'. Group process is a contribution to the group by a member, leading to reactions or lack of reaction by other members; both the contribution and the reactions to it are an item of process. Interactions provide evidence about overt and inexplicit reasons for making the contribution and the reactions. Also relevant are the contributions of this element of group process to the aims of the group. A sequence of connected contributions and reactions may offer stronger evidence of process. In understanding the reactions, look at how the contribution and reactions reflect:

- relationships between the members;
- the use of leadership and power within those relationships;
- the boundaries of the group, for example what behaviour, contribution and reaction is permitted by its culture and what is less acceptable;
- interpersonal roles in relationships with other members;
- tasks undertaken to achieve or obstruct the group's activities and aims;
- what is brought into and taken away from the group;
- the balance between group processes and task performance, role of the leader in holding the group to the task within the group process;
- the balance between democratic, authoritarian and laissez-faire leadership.

Look at whether behaviour in your group appears inappropriate to the set aims of the group. People may be unaware of tendencies:

- to prefer groups that have strong leadership (this avoids taking responsibility for their own relationships);
- to feel best-supported where they can form a relationship with another member (this may limit engagement with other members and lead to jealousy);
- to deal with feeling insecure in the group by getting into or avoiding conflicts with others (which may disrupt interactions aimed at getting the job done).

When you see patterns of behaviour emerging that obstruct the group's aims, challenge it, either in the group or by private discussion. Collect evidence of consistent patterns of behaviour and draw attention to it, giving evidence from previous interactions in the group.

Further resources

Lindsay, T. & Orton, S. (2014). *Groupwork practice in social work* (3rd edn). London: Sage.

A good practical general text.

Mullender, A., Ward, D. & Fleming, J. (2013). *Empowerment in action: Self-directed groupwork*. Basingstoke: Palgrave.

A practical groupwork text, focused on critical social objectives.

Check the online resources at policy.bristoluniversitypress.co.uk/how-to-use-social-work-theory-in-practice/online-resources/chapter19 for a full list of references for this chapter.

20

Community work and macro practice

Setting the scene

What is community work and macro practice?

Community work is enabling people with shared interests to come together, identify and examine important needs and act to meet those needs, by developing projects to meet them or by campaigning to ensure they are met by others. It is a practice concept implementing a range of theories, and like groupwork goes back to the beginnings of social work in the settlements of the 19th century (Gilchrist & Jeffs, 2001). It is sometimes called macro practice because it focuses on broad interests shared by groups associated with localities or social concerns raised by and for significant populations, for example disabled people.

Professions other than social work, including housing, planning and youth work, play significant roles in community work. Also, community members often build on their practical experience to attain paid community work roles.

Because this book is about social work practice, I do not look at community work as a form of social activism; it may have this purpose for some participants. My focus is on community work from the perspective of a social work agency or team that wants to engage people with shared interests in collaborative efforts to work on their concerns.

Aims

The main aim of community work within social work is to move practice beyond caring and helping roles to develop the resilience, skills and social capital of clients to facilitate them in working collectively to meet shared concerns and interests.

COMMUNITY AND MACRO PRACTICE 20.1

PREPARATION

Negotiate agency support
Build knowledge of the locality or field of concern
Communicate your commitment to community members

ENTERING, EXPLORING THE COMMUNITY

Build team support and participation
Develop partnerships with coordinating organizations
Cultivate relationships with key people
Carry out a social audit or information project
Work on a shared action plan or...
...engage with a host organization on a project
Develop education on and exploration of concerns

STRATEGIC FOCUSES

Community resources
Cultural projects • Documentation
Environment • Ethnicity
Evaluation, assessment
Excluded communities
Health, housing • Information
Intergenerational issues
Reaching out • Training, skills

UNDERSTANDING TYPES OF COMMUNITY WORK

Be clear about the main emphasis of your aims

- *Community action* is network-based, aiming to increase solidarity and support
- *Community planning* is participation-based, aiming to share in identifying and meeting needs
- *Community action* is issues-based, aiming to help powerless people achieve social change

COMMUNITY WORK INTERVENTIONS

Blend forms of intervention...
...but maintain your focus on community aims
Build collaborative projects on issues of concern
Link people with relevant organizations
De-emphasize difficulties but...
...encourage community expression
Develop leadership and representational skills
Foster skills in applying for resources

DEALING WITH CONFLICT

Community work raises political struggles...
...but involves social work in social change
Be assertive about the evidence on needs but...
...also emphasize community need and wishes
Engage and reconfirm agency support
Justify relevance to agency roles
Build professional support and defences
Avoid making your personal views public

Uses

For most social workers, community work is not a major activity but the American idea of 'generalist' practice favours a practice that incorporates community work alongside groupwork into work with individuals and families where it usefully meets some of the needs of clients through collective action. Partnership working in the community stimulates social engagement by involving a range of individuals, groups and organizations. Timescales are different so practitioners need to plan how it will fit with their individual work where that must take precedence. For teams, collectively building work in the local community can improve practice with individuals and families. It benefits information collection that supports individual practice, improves understanding of the community context, identifies supportive community strengths and builds knowledge of other organizations that might be helpful to clients. It allows teams to extend existing resource systems and set up new ones. Community involvement also supports self-help, through engaging community members' commitments in improving services, but, worryingly, it may compensate for cuts in public services. Use community innovations to make the case for improvements in provision and development models of practice such as social entrepreneurship that finance community endeavour.

Community action, by encouraging community education and political and social awareness, shifts the balance of power in communities. Groupwork in community contexts builds relationships and confidence (see Chapter 19). This empowers relatively powerless people to influence social change. They gain confidence and skills for doing so in other aspects of their lives. Community work can also support strategies to combat poverty, oppression and stigmatization affecting, for example, families in poverty or people recovering from mental illness. Experience of engagement in developing new services can also give people an interpersonal and organizational basis for negotiating with government and private agencies where conflict arises.

Needs assessment through developing area and community profiles improves information for wider social work and contributes to community confidence and resources. Participatory action research, in which community members set research priorities and methods and learn skills, is a useful approach (Chevalier & Buckles, 2013).

Introducing community work

Community work is used in two different contexts:

- with people who have shared interests for example a medical diagnosis, disabilities, being carers;
- with people who live in and have an affinity with a locality, whose social concerns derive from issues affecting that locality.

In a disaster, for example a major accident or climate damage, most people understand that mutual aid and support is valuable. Otherwise, people mostly expect social work to be for an individual or family. Introducing community work, therefore, needs to be explained. Say to your client that other people share the same concerns and it sometimes helps for them to work together to plan, organize and campaign for services to meet their shared needs.

Action sequence

Preparation

Taking a community work approach requires agency acceptance. Negotiate with managers to achieve at least their acquiescence or ideally support. Nurture your own grasp of possibilities and resources in the area that you work in. Feeding this into the team builds acceptance of the need to act on issues within the community. This helps to find issues and opportunities that engage your professional curiosity, colleagues' support and local concern. It also improves what you bring to individual and family work.

Build knowledge and understanding of the locality or field of concern. Visit localities in the way that community members do, by public transport and walking around. Drink and eat in local bars and cafes, go to local community and leisure events, experience local ethnic diversity, and participate in local religious and faith-based activities. Visit relevant agencies, such as hospitals or schools, as a member of the public. Attend public meetings of relevant charitable and official organizations. Talk to local people during such visits. Look at and subscribe to relevant websites and print media, both local and those covering your fields of concern. Gather and document as much information as you can about issues of concern. Consider establishing blogs, vlogs and other social media to demonstrate commitment and contribute on these topics. All of this improves your picture of the community, its needs and its dreams, and your colleagues' acknowledgement of the importance of local issues. It also demonstrates your commitment in the eyes of people in that community.

Entering and exploring the community

Share out interests and responsibilities among team members and report back to each other. A small number can do this informally, even if all do not participate and the team avoids official commitment. Identify coordinating organizations, both those based in the locality and those with wider links and responsibilities. Establish partnerships with organizations and individuals concerned about the same issues. Collaborate to call conferences and meetings to explore topics of concern and identify needs and issues.

Meet the key people and others involved in relevant organizations, build up relationships and information banks on topics of concern. Engage with a local general organization, for example a coordinating body like a community council, to promote a formal social audit of a community, or an information project on a topic of concern.

Develop a shared action plan and find or create an organization to host the planning process. Develop education about and exploration of the topic, including building skills and knowledge among community members.

With a base in a social care agency, balance work aimed at service development with work responding to clients' and residents' priorities. This is because people in most localities do not give priority to social care issues: education, employment, health, housing and poverty are generally more important to them and have a longer-term impact on needs for and responses to social care.

Community work interventions

Develop projects to involve community members in activities to meet their needs, develop their skills, increase participation and increase their power.

There are three main forms of community work intervention:

- Community development is network based.
  It aims to increase solidarity and mutual support among people living in a defined, usually small, locality.
  The aim is to increase social capital, the resources that social networks in the locality can bring to action on shared concerns.

Look for groups of people with shared interests and bring them together. It's easier if you include some people who already have organizational skills. Start with mutual support groups, or obviously practical local projects. Service coordination and development of projects between agencies may be an important vehicle for community engagement.

- Community planning is participation based.
  The aim is to identify and meet service needs and to facilitate citizen participation in developing and managing service provision to meet social needs. Connected with this, an important British practice, 'community social work', going back to the period after the formation of local authority social services departments in the 1970s (Hadley & McGrath, 1984), involves locating teams of social workers, alongside social care provision, in identifiable localities, to improve knowledge of and links with those communities.

  Develop knowledge of local opportunities for participation in consultations, decision making or service development. Build inter-professional collaboration to support community engagement. Facilitate other agencies to build liaison and make links with communities you know. Encourage and accompany clients to first meetings. Advise people on how they can maintain contact and build their roles. Motivate them: it may seem extra effort, but helpers gain psychological benefits.

- Community action is issues based.
  It aims to assist social groups excluded from influence and power to campaign collectively to achieve social change, so that society responds better in meeting their needs.

  Look for issues that clients, families or community members feel strongly about. Facilitate links with other people with similar concerns. Help them get in touch with organizations covering these interests. If these interests are not widely shared, make links with organizations in related areas and try to connect these new interests with similar ones. Approach general organizations, such as colleges, churches, faith groups, health consultation groups, local community groups, including schools and youth groups. Many of these may benefit from becoming involved with a local community issue, for example setting up a bereavement service may help hospitals, faith groups and private sector interests such as funeral directors.

Any community activity may include more than one of these focuses, but control the range you take on with any initiative to avoid stretching people's commitment and focus.

Strategic focuses include the following:

- Develop community resources, working with clients and local people together. Examples that often command support are counselling projects, early years child care facilities with preventive aims in children's social care, holiday playschemes, day or drop-in centres for adult social care client groups, support for carers or support for people in deprived communities, visiting and befriending schemes for housebound people.
- Cultural projects involving expressive skills enable excluded voices to reach self-expression. Examples are community arts generally, bands, community choirs, large arts projects such as mosaics, murals, sculptures. Historical projects enable people to explore their roots and they build information about the client group, community or special interest. Oral history allows older people and people with excluded voices to contribute information, using audio and video recording that is now cheap and easily available. Old postcards, photographs and objects can lead to exhibitions and increased local commitment. Sports and physical exercise projects, running tracks, physical exercise and walking routes can boost health awareness and interest.
- Discovering and documenting a community's life contributes to social capital and solidarity.
- Environmental improvement, development of ponds, lakes and rivers, open areas, rubbish clearance raises and responds to environmental policy concerns (see Chapter 24) and improves local amenities. It may also improve fitness and help with other public health objectives.
- Ethnicity may be a useful focus for solidarity. Multicultural approaches focus on increasing understanding and links between different ethnic groups, for example using cultural experiences. Service development focused on faith groups may help provide for otherwise under-provided groups.
- Evaluation and assessment of community facilities and opportunities provides information about the community and useful resources for campaigning. It may also boost education and skills, including communication, interactional and social skills for participants.
- Excluded communities may enable you to work with client groups that have few resources, for example drug abusers, unemployed people, young offenders, women.

- Health and housing projects produce similar benefits. They may be focused around particular excluded groups, for example disabled people, homeless people, older people, young people, or around general environmental improvement.
- Information projects, providing information around the community's amenities and facilities or around service needs, can improve the level of knowledge and understanding of health and social care needs.
- Intergenerational projects seek to build links between older and younger population groups.
- Reaching out, through having stalls or other contributions at local events, raises visibility for social care services and helps make links. Subject matter should be of general health and social interest, rather than simply advertising or promoting services. Include activities to engage people more strongly.
- Training and skills development opportunities associated with community activities increase human resources available to the community. They may also assist people involved with future work opportunities.

As you make your interventions, shift away from difficulties, so that people can work on the positives, but also do not neglect expression of important issues. Therefore, balance needs against strengths, oppression against opportunities, and your expertise against the voice of excluded people.

Develop leadership skills among people involved. Enable people to take leadership and representative roles in formal and informal organizations and in meetings. Foster skills in making applications for financial resources and resources in kind from charitable and business sources. Nurture support from local businesses, for example pubs for catering, meetings. They are often motivated to promote sales and public approval in this way; it is not a gift, so feel free to ask.

Build skills in understanding and working with business and official organizations, for example how to approach, influence and interact with them.

Things to think about

Community work often becomes involved in political and social conflict. It has the capacity to draw attention to inequalities in service provision and power which lie behind severe deprivation or public concern about an issue, and working in this field includes you in struggles between people in powerless positions and the powerful.

Once you get involved, you may be criticized in public and in the print and social media. Pressure in your job from managers and politicians may lead to sanctions. As you become involved, gain and regularly confirm support from colleagues, your family and people in the community, particularly those with influence or high status. Be ready with careful justification of the positions that you take and also your activities' relevance to your job role. Build relationships with people with administrative competence and legal expertise who can defend you in threats to your employment or professional standing. Never do anything in secret, never say anything that can be misinterpreted or misrepresented, never do or say anything that you would feel unhappy about being reported on the evening television news bulletin. Keep your managers and supervisors informed of your actions and obey their instructions. Engage them in ambiguities or uncertainties.

Consider broader political contexts that form a background to community concerns and conflicts among groups you deal with, for example economic and political responses to employment and industrial change, such as globalization, migration, neoliberal economics. These may add to pressures for action or inaction, and managerial pressures on your position. As a social worker, you are also positioned between the state and its role in managing social order and that element of community work that generates social dissent.

An important element of community work practice is your own assertiveness in pushing clients' and community engagement forward. Balance your own commitment against clients' or other local interests.

Further resources

Burghardt, S. (2014). *Macro practice in social work for the 21st century: Bridging the macro-micro divide* (2nd edn). Thousand Oaks, CA: Sage.

Gilchrist, A. & Taylor, M. (2016). *A short guide to community development* (2nd edn). Bristol: Policy Press.

Two good introductory texts.

Check the online resources at policy.bristoluniversitypress.co.uk/how-to-use-social-work-theory-in-practice/online-resources/chapter20 for a full list of references for this chapter.

21

Systems practice

Setting the scene

What is systems practice?

Systems practice focuses on links within the social relations around clients so that they may adapt to and manage, with others, change and complexity in their social environment. Our work integrates individuals within their social environments. There are two overlapping practices, based on general and ecological systems theory. Recent developments in chaos and complexity theory based on research in 'complex adaptive systems' inspire us to seek patterns; Hudson (2010) provides a comprehensive introduction and Hood (2018) a guide to more recent research on complexity theory.

Aims

The main aim of systems intervention is to input energy, for example information, resources, into a target system, for example an individual client, family, group, community. Systems have identifiable boundaries. We then influence throughput, how the energy is used within the system. As we observe the output from the use of energy within the system, we can promote feedback loops to influence further input into the system.

Systems ideas help us add options and targets for indirect intervention to direct work with clients. Also, systems analysis helps us identify a clear focus within a complex system.

All parts of our service system connect with other practitioners and agencies (Munro, 2011).

Multisystemic therapy is a practice which aims to help young people in the context of relationships within their families.

Uses

Systems theory helps us understand the networks of relationships that affect people, the transactions between them and the boundaries

IDENTIFY LEVELS AND ROLES OF SYSTEMS

Explore the 'person-in-environment'
How do changes in the system have impacts on people in it?
Understand biopsychosocial and spiritual issues in the system
Reflect on patterns of transaction and relationship
Look at interaction of systems and subsystem
Consider the reciprocal influence of individuals
Think about circular causality

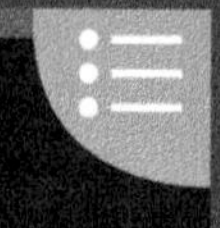

TARGET SYSTEMS

Client • Change agent
Target • Action

IDENTIFY RELEVANT SYSTEMS TO WORK WITH

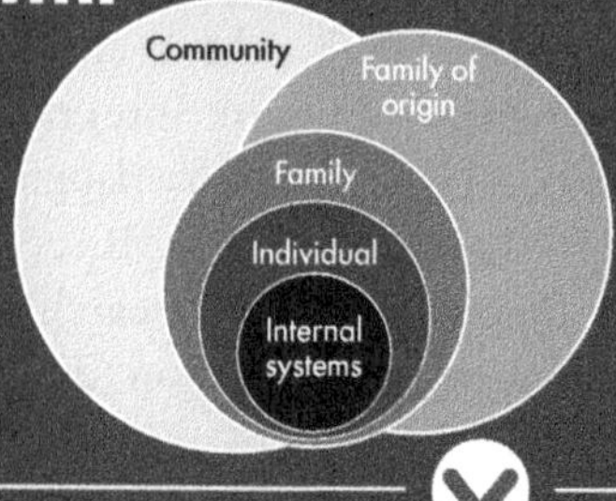

HELPING SYSTEMS

Informal and natural systems
Formal systems • Societal systems

SERVICE APPROACH

Make connections
Integration • Adaptation
System maintenance

PLAN INTERVENTIONS AND SERVICES

Decide your approach
Decide on types of service
Design your intervention
Ensure plans are feasible, viable, sustainable and adaptable

SERVICE TYPE

Direct intervention
Coordination • Governance
Control • Support • Surveillance
Intelligence • Policy-making

WORKING ON ISSUES

Engage with people involved
'Respectful curiosity'
Rehearse new ideas
Use strategic and structural approaches
Examine environments
Explore person-environment interventions
Work to develop networks
Think about multisystemic practice

DEALING WITH PROBLEMS

Change the number or range of systems involved
Upset equilibrium in the system
Work to overcome slow progress
Instil confidence and hope
Establish trial periods and...
...if they fail, devise a new plan
Set short-term interim goals...
...building towards longer-term aims

STRATEGIC APPROACHES

Reframing
Directives
Communication

STRUCTURAL APPROACHES

Belief systems
Organization
Communication and problem-solving

TARGET NETWORKS

Family group decisions
Support networks
Mentoring relationships
Mutual aid
Group activities

PERSON-ENVIRONMENT NETWORKS

Belief systems
Organization
Communication and problem-solving

around those systems. Boundaries may be realities, for example distance between family members or walls, doors and floors in buildings. They may also be perceptions, for example a gang territory in a housing estate. Exploring how people see the systems in their lives helps them make judgements and decisions about changing the pattern of their relationships.

Systems ideas also empower people by acknowledging and enabling work on the complexity in links and relationships among groups and organizations that affect them. What uncertainties and volatilities make interactions difficult? How may they be managed? Complexity and chaos theory point to the reality that stability and order are not always present, and so we must find ways of managing instability and rapid change. Aspects of situations may create islands of stability or redirect change in helpful or emotionally acceptable directions.

Introducing systems interventions

Explain systems views early on; you are looking at individuals, and also at things, outside clients themselves, that affect them. Explain why you are seeking information about family members, friends or neighbours; you want to see who is already involved and who might be able to help. Also, information about agencies involved with clients or their families, or present in their community, gives us and them ideas about who might offer something.

Before starting an intervention, say that it is good to identify in an organized way, target and encourage people and agencies to help. By running through a list of who is involved, it becomes easier to see where we might make more links, building on existing contacts. By trawling through possible collaborators, we model what to do if clients face future difficulties. The language of systems may be useful: talk about making links or building cooperation is less stigmatising than talking about help or support.

Help clients to think about these issues. Because systems practice is indirect, not always involving the client, they may not realize the importance of contacting other agencies or getting other people involved. Working on systems broadens perceptions, so people can see that their own issues involve other people or agencies. Sometimes it is obvious, for example parents caring for children. Other times, less so, for example people may not be aware that police community liaison staff work with domestic violence, rather than their stereotype of uniformed officers. People may resist wider interventions, for example a mother who thinks her husband is useless with a teenage daughter's difficulties, whereas she and you may be able to build an alliance that calls on his abilities.

Action sequence

Explore systems to identify levels and potential roles of systems

Systems theory proposes that human systems develop patterns of relating over time. These patterns place them within a context or environment of other systems. You understand the person in relation to that environment, and how that environment gives meaning and reacts to the person. You collaborate with clients and people in the system to understand unique features of that 'person-in-environment' (PIE; see Chapter 11 on psychodynamic relational theory to see the source of this idea). You explore sometimes long chains of causality and ripple effects of events at a distance and what they mean now for people in the system. You can look at the whole network of links that a system represents or at personal social networks, the various links associated with an individual or social group, such as a family or community.

Rather than aiming to change interpersonal relationships, think through how changes within a system might have an impact on those involved. Identify a range of systems and networks involved and their patterns of behaviour and relationships. For example, are groups involved in a community hostile to or supportive of each other? Perhaps their reactions to other groups are conditional on how the external groups behave. Perhaps views vary depending on which group members are involved in an activity.

Examine biopsychosocial and spiritual issues for relevant individuals, families, groups, communities and explore the social environments with which they have links. Do not try to label and create a typology of systems, for example families are often more than parents plus children, or less than this. Instead, view networks (points and the links between them) and systems (groups or spaces with a lot of interaction) as patterns of transactions and relationships. For example, a family system in which brothers interact together much more than parents with their children contains two subsystems with differing characteristics; you work with the systems as they are, not assuming a focus on parent–children relationships.

Systems, therefore, have an interactional quality. Look at how each system and each part of each system are interacting with the others. Part of human systems is, similarly, relatedness. Interaction and relatedness creates a culture within the system. This is also true of internal interventions for individuals, for example helping people understand conflicts, perceptions, emotional and physical reactions. Look for reciprocal influence between system members, circular causality, a pattern in which a particular behaviour often stimulates the same reaction, and for events and parts of the system that are often unpredictable. For example, patterns of relationship in a family may be affected by a volatile member; some members accept the volatility, others might try to manage the conflicts that result or avoid them by keeping out of the way.

Identify and explore different system levels to see how individual clients or groups are positioned and what influences their position. These include:

- community
- family of origin
- family
- individual
- internal systems

For example, a disabled person may be mainly concerned with the impact of their disability on self-care (internal systems), or with how their child has reacted to their disability (family), how, despite their living independently, their parents are over-concerned to supervise and control their lifestyle (family of origin) or local people are bullying and hostile (community). Other relevant systems may cross the boundaries of these levels or be only part of them for example work groups.

From the first contact and assessment materials, identify:

- The client system. If it is an individual, look for the subsystems you will work with, for example attitudes, perceptions, relationships. If the system is wider than the individual, will it be identified as part of another system, for example siblings, immediate or nuclear family, extended family?
- The change agent system. The practitioner may be the sole person involved but there are likely to be supervision, management, other team members, care workers, informal caregivers.
- The target system. Will you work mainly with the client, or with others such as family members, school or work colleagues (for example to prevent bullying), other community members? You might also work with other agencies, for example housing or healthcare providers.

- The action system, the people you work with to have an impact on the situation. With an older person recently diagnosed with dementia, this might include specialist and general practice healthcare teams, domiciliary care agencies, day centres, care homes. List and set aims for your work with them. Agree how you or clients will engage them and get their agreement to participate.

Different types of system offer resources to clients, groups and communities; you approach them differently:

- Informal and natural systems, for example community, family or volunteer caregivers. You often approach these informally and interpersonally.
- Formal systems, for example charities, community organizations, member organizations, trade unions. Identify whether and how you or the client should make applications. Think about other members of the client system, for example a relative whose work role gives access to a specific charity, or a local pub that will fund-raise.
- Societal systems, for example education, healthcare, housing, local authorities, social security agencies, commercial and private sector service providers. Consider formal liaison systems and rights to service.

Plan and generate interventions and services

Systems ideas generate three basic approaches to intervention:

- Building connectedness and integration among individuals and systems (mainly from general systems ideas).
- Facilitating adaptation of individuals and systems to each other (mainly from ecosystems ideas). In this practice, you see individuals, families, groups and communities as becoming something new in relation to others.
- System maintenance, keeping systems going that are beneficial to clients and improving their capacity to respond to clients' and community needs. Examples include increasing the diversity of services and responses to clients and social issues; increasing organizations' capacity to deal with diversity among clients and communities. For example, traditional mobile meals services may need additional organizations to provide ethnically appropriate menus.

What kinds of service are you going to undertake?

- Intervention or direct service provision by a practitioner or team. After agreement with clients, gain support from colleagues or supervisors.
- Coordination of services provided by other practitioners and services. How will you or other members of the action system contact them, plan with them, deal with problems? Timescales need to be worked out; work according to agencies' approaches, for example adolescent mental health services may have waiting lists, while general practitioners and primary care teams react more rapidly.
- Governance or support and control. For example, in a child safeguarding situation, who is responsible for investigation, how are regular visits and support to be organized, when will reviews take place?
- Surveillance and intelligence. Regular visiting or checking with care workers or family members about adults at risk; setting up systems and agreements with others to make sure you've covered the situation. Picking up and collating information about local care homes and their offerings.
- Policy making for the long term, for example contributing your experience of supported housing for older people to planning by housing providers.

Working on individual, family and environmental issues

Design your intervention; think about:

- Feasibility; can you and target and actions systems achieve potential plans?
- Viability; can you, the agency and clients sustain the effort and costs?
- Environmental sustainability.
- Adaptability; to what extent can you adapt interventions that do not quite work out?

Engage people in the system to work together. Take a stance of 'respectful curiosity'. Work with people to appreciate issues in their relationships and try out new ways of relating through reviewing experiences in a focused way. Try rehearsing new ideas.

Strategic approaches (from family therapy) look at how relationships have led people to get stuck in unhelpful patterns. Practices include:

- Reframing, adding positive connotations to see things in a new light.
- Directives, encouraging systems to practise behavioural tasks between sessions.
- Communication patterns. What are members' working hypotheses about relationships? Get people to describe common patterns; what triggers them and stops them? Circular questioning, going round each person in the system in turn, elicits members' perspectives on communication and system changes.

Also from family therapy, explore the system structure. How might patterns of relationships be restructured or strengthened? Perhaps healthier alliances can be built. For example, a less-involved parent might plan to spend time with a child, or a brother agree to visit a disabled family member regularly. Plan to block unhelpful coalitions. Rehearse techniques, for example sculpting, that allow people in the system to play with changing roles and relationships. Work on:

- Family or group belief systems: what is the meaning that family or group members ascribe to the adversities or opportunities they face or have faced? Help them to develop a positive outlook. Facilitate transcendence, the capacity to rise above adverse experiences, and spirituality, the capacity to value learning from adversity.
- Organizational factors: how can the system be made more flexible and connected?
- Communication and problem solving: how can information be communicated more clearly, comprehensively and flexibly, perhaps using new media? Get people to try writing instead of speaking, making signs rather than talking, making short films on their phone for people to see. Encourage people to express emotions more openly in social situations. Facilitate collaboration in reviewing people's reactions to events.

Also explore the environment in which a human system lives. Useful environments to examine are:

- the perceived environment as constructed by individual and collective beliefs, for example families that perceive schools as hostile, leading to poor relationships with teachers;

- the physical environment, natural and built, for example does an older person have appropriate transport, and are they able to reach the nearest bus stop or train station?
- social and interactional environments in the system: patterns of human relationships and levels and types of intimacy;
- institutional and organizational environments, organizations that affect how people live, for example doctors' surgeries, closeness to hospitals, police stations, churches;
- cultural, social and political environments, for example clubs, pubs, social media, social care policies of local councils, immigration policies.

Problems in living are often the result of stress because of a poor fit between people and these environments. Life stress is affected by people's individual and system coping ability and their resilience (see Chapter 6). Another relevant factor is the degree of power they have over events, or the extent to which and way in which they see others as being powerful in influencing their lives. Person-environment interventions focus on adapting the individual or family aspects of this:

- Improve clients' sense of mastery, so they feel they can manage stressful life situations, using resources, for example finance, family members, to do so.
- Get active engagement from multiple professions and agencies.
- Promote collective action to link individual concerns with social empowerment.

Ways of working on networks include:

- facilitating family group decision making in conferences where several members of families need to agree on a course of action, for example in hospital discharge;
- building volunteer and informal supportive networks; build on existing organizations and relationships and community members who are perceived as effective in supporting others;
- building mentoring relationships for people who recognize the need for support in making changes in their lives; allow them to choose their own mentor and the type of relationship.
- initiating and supporting mutual aid among people with similar problems.
- enabling people to participate in group activities that build their knowledge and skills in carrying out domestic, personal and social tasks.

Dealing with unexpected change in a system raises the possibility of self-organization. This is the characteristic of complex systems to organize themselves spontaneously into unpredictable structures and behaviours. This change appears to be triggered by minor inputs, but what is happening is that stresses build up in a system until a period of instability and uncertainty pushes it into a fundamental change. Increasing diversity in a system helps to reduce this, for example get more and different people and activities involved in a community centre where there are problems with young people's behaviour.

Multisystemic practice involves planning for a range of professions and practitioners with a variety of skills to agree on issues and interventions where they would all contribute.

Dealing with problems

Strategies for dealing with difficulties that arise in systems practice include:

- involving wider numbers or ranges of systems, to strengthen or reduce pressures on those involved;
- upsetting the equilibrium in some way: change the pace, input more information, work in different settings, use a crisis to change what you're working on;
- acknowledge slow progress, problems, obstructions; plan to overcome them;
- remaining confident, providing hope, reinforcing objectives, for example 'there is a good chance that this will work if we keep at it';
- starting with a trial period, then agree plans;
- setting short-term interim goals.

Things to think about

One crucial difference between general systems theory is its focus on working on connectedness, while ecological systems theory is concerned with adaptation. Consequently, general systems lead us to a concern with networks, while ecological systems lead us towards a focus on patterns and groups of links and their adaptation to one another.

Systems ideas connect individuals with the widest aspects of our world through interlinked identifiable structures. Because they are interlinked, you can see how everyone is part of a continual interplay between individuals and social structures. Representing these graphically through specialist and general ecomaps, genograms and network diagrams illustrates and helps us understand the complexity of people's situations and the pressures on them. They can also help you think through whether you have appropriate contacts.

Further resources

Gitterman, A. & Germain, C.B. (2008). *The life model of social work practice: Advances in theory and practice* (3rd edn). New York: Columbia University Press.

The most recent edition of a comprehensive account of systems practice influenced by ecological ideas about adaptation and fit.

Hood, R. (2018). *Complexity in social work*. London: Sage.

A good account, using up-to-date systems ideas, of how to understand complexity in relationships and interactions.

Check the online resources at policy.bristoluniversitypress.co.uk/how-to-use-social-work-theory-in-practice/online-resources/chapter21 for a full list of references for this chapter.

22

Critical and structural practice

Setting the scene

What are critical and structural practices?

Critical practice works with clients to identify and explore the impact of social structures on the issues that face them in their lives. It then builds, together with others sharing similar social interests, creative ways of transforming those social impacts. The aim is to generate collective progress towards personal and social liberation from oppressive and restrictive social structures. At the same time, engagement with this process also empowers and helps individuals in taking their place successfully in society.

Elements of what is now called critical practice go back to radical social work, particularly in the US, in the 1930s (Reisch & Andrews, 2002) and more widely in the 1960s (Lavalette, 2011). Important current formulations include Fook's (2016) and Mullaly's work on structural practice (Mullaly & Dupré, 2019).

Aims

Critical and structural practice aims to be emancipatory, liberating or transformational. This means it seeks to overcome social limitations on people's freedoms to achieve their own self-fulfilment. It also seeks to achieve significant change in the social environment, so that those limitations do not recur, and so that the increased freedom is available to both clients and others in oppressed positions. Social work is important as a mechanism for helping people take action on their own behalf, and is a profession able to use its understanding to create social change.

Uses

Critical and structural practice demands that 'the social' contributes to explanation of issues presented to social workers and that social change is part of their intervention. Its postmodern element requires

RITICAL AND STRUCTURAL PRACTICE 22.1

PPROACH

phasize human rights, social justice and equalities
e social models of health and disability
ild participative citizenship
actise cooperatively in equal, dialogic relationships
lp clients use their autonomy
assessment start with urgent needs
parate material needs from people's personal functioning
ise people's self-esteem, their capacity to act and their skills
lidate cultural, religious and spiritual diversity
and strengths

TERVENTIONS

ree forms of critical and structural intervention
ange how the current social order...
affects people's development and survival
srupt the current social order's impacts on social identities
ild practice on critical political and social analysis

EVELOPING AND SURVIVING

e consciousness-raising
ild family and community cooperation
anage the effects of being units of
consumption
sure social work care is not controlling
hance people's problem-solving
able people's voices to be heard
elp people link with others
pport strengths in families and communities
e co-production to share planning and
action
e techniques to engage alienated people

SOCIAL IDENTITIES

Focus on damaging effects of oppression
Work on language use to combat oppression
Reach out to indigenous and minority groups

SOCIAL AND CRITICAL ANALYSIS

Help agencies to plan with oppressed groups
Evaluate and learn from failed provision
Use feedback to redesign services

AINTAIN BALANCES BETWEEN...

dividual helping and group empowerment
gency demands and good social work practice
ocial justice and service economy
ients' voices and judgemental social attitudes

EVELOP CRITICAL SOCIAL WORK PRACTICE

ngage with working class and indigenous organizations
ecentralize and democratize teams and practice
void individualizing explanations of social issues
ioritize relational units valued by clients

every explanation to be open to question and subject to a reframing of reality. Its structural element entails a structural analysis as part of that questioning of reality. This enables us to understand how social formations and movements create the individual and interpersonal that is the main inclination of social work thinking. Its feminist element (see also Chapter 23) sanctions a recognition of and response to disquiets and inequalities in the dialogues between human beings and dialectics about our work and our clients' personhood, the internal reasoning that we use in making decisions and judgements.

We use these ideas to inject the social in our practice, to reject the tyranny in our thinking of discourses that accept uncritically the existing social order and to identify ways of creating social change that benefit clients individually and collectively.

Introducing critical and structural practice

Many clients expect you to work on the individual and specific problems they bring to you. Community groups, similarly, assume you will focus on the issues you identify in partnership with them. One of the aims of critical and structural practice is to help you expand the consciousness of people you are partnering with. You aim to develop longer-term perceptions and more complex understanding of the sources of the issues they are facing. Before doing this, explain your approach, so that the people involved can give informed consent to work with you in this way. The points to cover are as follows:

- You will work from their own aims and priorities, and you encourage them to let you know if they think you are not focusing on their main concerns.
- You will pick up and work on immediate and practical concerns as they arise.
- You will also look at the wider consequences of what's happening for their own personal feelings and emotions and things that affect their family and community.
- You will look not only at the obvious factors that have led to the barriers or problems they are facing, but also to longer-term and hidden factors, and policies or systems that are unfair or not working properly. This is so that you can make sure that solutions you come up with to put things right for them endure for the long term, and also may help other people in the same position.
- If you make official or professional decisions, you will try to take a fair course of action that respects their wishes and feelings and

sustains their opportunities and rights following the same principles that we examined in Chapters 17 and 18 on advocacy and rights practice, and empowerment and anti-oppressive practice.

Action sequence

Your approach

Critical practice takes the conventional social work action sequence and shifts our approach to it. It contains three important elements at every stage:

- Emphasize human rights and achieving social justice for clients, their families and communities and between social groups, seeking to reduce inequalities that are part of the structure of societies.
- Focus on social models of health and disability, and people's participative citizenship.
- Practise in equal, dialogic relationships with clients and colleagues so that they may experience cooperation in building social improvements.

Emphasize your efforts to learn but don't expect them to teach you about their community, culture or religion. Appreciate clients' feelings, honour their culture and individuality, empathize about social issues they are concerned about. Get feedback on what they find helpful. Keep them informed about agency processes, for example decisions affecting them. Ally with clients who are contesting abuses of power and participating in social movements that support their rights. Explain and suggest opportunities to do this.

Try to retain and offer to clients as much autonomy of decision making and action as you can. Give them a chance to practise using their autonomy in worthwhile actions.

In assessment and initial intervention, start with urgent survival needs. Assist in dealing with material problems; avoid entwining these with personal difficulties. Identify power issues that can be resolved, for example oppressive creditors, housing providers.

Raise people's self-esteem and capacity to take action themselves. Validate culture, religious and spiritual diversity, and strengths. Reframe clients' skills, reducing self-blame and finding new skills that they can build on. Practise open listening, model power sharing, point to narratives that help clients appreciate their successes and opportunities.

Intervention ...

Three forms of critical and structural intervention are:

- practice changing the impact of the current social order on people's capacity to develop and survive, for example advocacy, dialogical practice, family support, self-help, peer support;
- practice disrupting adverse impacts of the current social order on people's social identities;
- practice building on critical political and social analysis and understanding;

... on developing and surviving

Consciousness raising develops self-confidence to become more assertive about clients' own needs and about getting others' support and involvement when existing social structures disadvantage and oppress them. Start with how their needs have arisen and ways of gaining control of at least some of them.

Build up cooperative and consciousness-raising elements of community and family life. Resist forces that limit opportunities. Enable communities and families to provide settings for good personal experiences to combat the alienation of adverse social policies and living conditions.

Identify and support ways to cope with being units of consumption. Promote effective management of demands on children and family members to be consumers, for example unhealthy, poor-quality food choices, excessive passive media use. Enable families to find ways to develop their personal capacities and participate through education and shared activity in collective action. Avoid supporting oppressive family structures, in which men's work dominates their families' economic resources. Facilitate women to achieve financial and emotional equality. Extend opportunities for children to develop opportunities for longer-term life satisfaction. Do all this as part of working on agency responsibilities.

Where appropriate, look for ways of helping people understand and respond to family and interpersonal conflicts as conflicts between social expectation and their own preferences. Support them to find ways of implementing (at least some of) their own priorities. Help people understand and avoid strengthening social conflicts in their lives and communities.

While social control that social work imposes differs from oppressive social control by political regimes or by police and security forces, caring and helping can also be experienced as controlling. Avoid practice actions that reinforce social control by others. Avoid actions that control people's freedoms unnecessarily and that reinforce powerful groups' definitions of social issues that view negatively your clients and social groups in which clients live. Avoid secret surveillance; instead engage clients in recording adverse events and planning how to overcome them.

Work with people on their own problem solving; enabling their voices to be heard can empower them to go further, either with your help or on their own. Normalization aims to grow understanding that what seemed like an individual's problems are widely shared. Build links with others who are similarly affected.

Identify and support strengths in individuals and families, especially where they are affected by discrimination and oppression. Help potentially excluded people tell their stories in their own words in the early stages. Work with them to appraise how external forces have influenced what happened to them. Identify ways they can avoid this in future.

Use co-production in planning and delivering services, sharing the planning and tasks of service provision. Identify individuals and groups who can contribute to consultations and initiatives by private sector enterprises and government initiatives. Engage people in thinking through their own conceptions of services appropriate to their own interpretations of their needs.

Strengths, narratives and solutions approaches and MI techniques allow practitioners and agencies to engage with disengaged and hostile individuals, families and groups.

... on social identities

Focus on oppression and its damaging effects in work with individuals and families, using counselling on how existing social arrangements affect them and how they can minimize detrimental effects, for example stigma. Critical reflection (see Chapter 25) helps clients see how they can achieve some social change in their lives. Encourage clients to set up or join groups of people in similar situations to develop confidence in projecting a new identity, for example people in a run-down area of public housing. Stimulate collective engagement, forming groups of people with similar experiences. Redefine people's assumptions that there is no action they can take. Show how a few small steps may lead on to further achievements.

Attend to use of language and interpret how it marks negative influences of hostile and oppressive uses of culture and power. This is especially important with people from minority ethnic groups and those affected by sensory disabilities that affect how they understand the world and how they are treated.

Reach out to indigenous and minority groups, rather than expecting them to present themselves to agencies in ways that the agency can cope with. Help professionals and services in other agencies with less engagement in minority communities engage appropriately. Assist them to participate actively in multi-professional decision making. Raise the representation of minority groups' interests.

... on critical political and social analysis

Facilitate local agencies and government to engage with social groups in planning services and social provision. Mediate with organizations representing clients' and communities' interests to help them engage with civic and other local decision making.

Evaluate failed provision. Where services have failed, or your service doesn't seem to help, evaluate those failures carefully for lessons to be learned and make clear changes to respond to issues identified.

Seek out, listen and do something about feedback on help and services provided to individuals, on broader service changes and complaints. Try to redesign the pattern, style or timing of services that are unsatisfactory; the team can say among themselves: 'how can we do that better?'.

Critical approaches to social work responsibilities

Seek information and understanding from working class and indigenous organizations, such as local community organizations, human rights and activist groups, trade unions and workers' organizations. Support community, macro and collective practice that involves such groups. Be aware of and if possible respond to their critiques of practice. Avoid transgressing their boundaries, enabling them to pursue their legitimate objectives rather than trying to limit their freedom of action.

Decentralize and democratize teamwork, so that even busy practitioners can be aware of and involved in responding to at least some local community issues.

Avoid using individualizing explanations of social problems which blame clients for the impacts on their lives of social oppressions.

Work as much as possible with relational units valued by clients, for example a child's family unit, an older person's family or community carers. This avoids separating clients out into special categories such as children in need or people at risk. Be wary of the use of agency or coordinating documentation, such as the English common assessment frameworks for adults or children, to label clients similarly, rather than identifying their unique characteristics.

Things to think about

Critical practice also involves critical reflection (see Chapter 25). An important difficulty in critical and structural practice is balancing the value of interpersonal relationships, at both the individual and macro level, with a focus on structural and political issues. Developments of the social model of disability faced this issue. Initially, the model focused on how social and economic structures in society excluded disabled people from full participation. More recently, listening to the voices of disabled people, the social experiences created by the impairments that lead to disability in an excluding society were important in creating disabled people's personal and social identities. This had consequences for their lives and relationships.

As with community work (see Chapter 20), be prepared for conflicts with powerful forces that oppose opening out clients' and communities' opportunities, and with agency and management systems that try to limit your range of action.

Constantly examine the balance of concern for:

- clients' voices seeking good listening, respectful treatment, concern for emotional and material support and awareness of family and community context against external demands for moral and social judgement;
- creative social work that seeks justice and equality of treatment both individually and among different social groups against economies in service provision;
- overcoming administrative and procedural demands for efficiency and compliance with legal and policy requirements against the barriers this creates to achieving an appropriate role for social work practice that meet clients' needs and wishes.

Be aware of and avoid potential conflicts between being a personal and a political change agent. Seeking prompt and extensive systemic change may be incompatible with working on personal change. Maintaining social order and the social fabric of society also supports a secure life for clients and others in oppressed communities. Despite this, structural interventions can be developed within micro practice, by taking small steps. Bring together specific groups to identify and plan work on their own issues. You, your agency or your profession don't have to do everything – give clients space to act for themselves, and their group or community.

Maintain a balance between individual helping and group empowerment. Both interventions are valuable and they achieve different things. Individual help and support develops mutual trust among people who may never have experienced it before. It frees up people's capacity and openness to help themselves and others through group and community activity. Group empowerment amplifies individual and family efforts by sharing ideas, providing empathetic mutual support and enabling people to experience the value of helping others.

Be aware of costs, emotional, financial and organizational, for agency partners, clients and colleagues of decisions about intervention. Draw attention to the full range of personal costs of social work practices and social care policies to avoid interventions whose saving private or public sector money imposes costs that are damaging to clients.

Further resources

Kennedy-Kish, B., Sinclair, R., Carniol, B. & Baines, D. (2017). *Case critical* (7th edn). Toronto: Between the Lines.

A long-standing (under Carniol's authorship) account of critical practice in a Canadian context.

Williams, C. & Graham, M.J. (eds) (2016a). *Social work in a diverse society: Transformative practice with black and minority ethnic individuals and communities*. Bristol: Policy Press.

Excellent general account of critical social work, focused on issues of ethnic diversity, but broadly applicable.

Check the online resources at policy.bristoluniversitypress.co.uk/how-to-use-social-work-theory-in-practice/online-resources/chapter22 for a full list of references for this chapter.

23

Feminist practice

Setting the scene

What is feminist practice?

To develop feminist practice, you need to be open to the value of women's experience, knowledge and perspective. If you centre your understanding and intervention on women's experience, you are taking into your thinking an essential aspect of political and social understanding. Without the benefit of women's perspectives, you exclude vital elements of human life and relationships.

Feminist practice emerged explicitly alongside radical social work (see Chapter 22), with Dominelli and McLeod (1989) making an important early contribution. It is a key element of both anti-oppressive and critical social work (see Chapters 18 and 22). Current concerns are well illustrated in Butler-Mokoro and Grant's (2018) edited collection.

Aims

Feminist practice is two things. It is, first, part of a movement that engages women and men in understanding how gender in conventional patriarchal societies oppresses everyone and especially women. It aims to shift practice in which the state reinforces women's gendered positions towards empowering and liberating them.

Second, feminist practice aims to raise consciousness and increase women's control over their lives, particularly in areas of social relations where gender divisions oppress them.

Uses

Feminist practice addresses how gendered social conditions in society and in social work give rise to oppression. It has a strong role in providing physical and emotional care for people with social needs, in domestic and partner violence, in prostitution and sexual abuse, and in women's management of inequality and poverty in social provision.

APPROACH

Dialogic interaction
Equalized relationships
Open about alternatives and opportunities
Liberate social relationships
Raise consciousness of gendered assumptions
Raise women's oppression in practice

Women's roles, positions, contribution, experience, relationships

Gender-sensitive, not gender-blind

STRENGTHS-BASED PRACTICE

Envision transformation
Live through challenges
Live out moves
Act with intent

Explore alternatives, not binary options

FEMINIST WORK WITH MEN

Gendered society is two-way
Do masculinity differently
Cooperation
Mutual support
Make contributions

WORK ON RELATIONSHIPS

Everyday gender issues • Shift towards non-oppressive • Assertiveness for both partners
Family feelings about mothering • Mothering in childhood & now
Carer and cared for person • Respect for dignity

ISSUES ABOUT caring

Conflict, unequal power
Mothering, maternity
Emotional support
Relationship support
Caring relationships
Contexts of caring
Receptivity, responsiveness
Equal sharing in caring
Options in education

ISSUES ABOUT relationships

Life experience
Relationship equity
Equal, open parenting
Good intimate relations
Positive shared feelings
Multiple roles
Maintain family ties
Support systems
Power-sharing
Role flexibility
Self-esteem
Assertiveness
Self-expression
Problem-solving
Conflict resolution
Violence

ISSUES ABOUT identity

Valuing gender
Valuing sexuality
Empathy
Open to new experiences
Dialogue about identities
Socialization
Gender and other identities
Microaggressions

Intersections
Other inequalities, poverty, oppression

Addressing gender oppression requires listening to and responding to women's experience of oppression.

Some feminist practice is women centred, aimed at helping women who are directly affected by gender oppression. Helping women to voice their concerns, expectations and experiences develops their wider understanding of how gender inequality affects society, allowing them to make a contribution to combating that. This may also benefit the resources and relations within families and within the care of children, disabled, ill and older people, because women play a primary role in organizing and providing care.

Work with men is also important. This is because repositioning the social behaviour and role of men who are oppressive, unthinking or violent in exercising gendered power moves society towards more equal and satisfying gender relationships. Focusing only on individual practice with women and family-based social work may not address such issues.

Introducing feminist practice

Start feminist practice by explaining and modelling self-disclosure of identity and social position. In doing so, demonstrate the right to control and restraint in revealing personal information. Later, you may wish to show how identity may be fluid by disclosing important changes during the lifecourse that have affected you. Point out how issues that emerge in assessment may be connected to the roles that women are expected to take up in families and wider society. You are not saying that woman are necessarily oppressed or disempowered, but that society is organized in ways that do not value women's contributions. Everyone benefits from exploring and understanding the strengths of women's participation in relationships and social institutions.

Action sequence

Approach

Use a dialogic style of interaction, making your relationship as equal as possible; that's why being self-revealing at the beginning is important. Aim to enable open conversation about alternatives and opportunities that will liberate women's positions and women and men's social relationships. Raise both women's and men's consciousness of gendered assumptions and satisfying alternatives, for example through discussion groups, exploration of issues presented to the agency. A strengths-based approach developed with Latina women in the US may be generalized, the mnemonic is ELLA (Gloria & Castellanos, 2016):

- **E**nvision the transformation sought. Help people think about the kind of gender relationships they would like to have in their lives.
- **L**ive through the challenge this change will require alongside clients. Review what changes would be needed to arrive at these improved relationships, both personal and interpersonal and in people's expectations of their relationships.
- **L**ive out the process of moving away from accepted cultural gendered norms. Look at the priority in the situation you are working on to take steps in this direction. Plan and rehearse ways of implementing them, discussing potential difficulties and how to overcome them.
- **A**ct with intent to make the change. Test out the changes in real life; review the changes achieved and how these alter clients' visions of what is needed, and take up further priorities.

Attend to issues of women's oppression raised in the three following important areas of practice.

Caring

Direct attention to how caring is undertaken in families. Explore conflict, unequal power and abuse of power, in which carers experience different treatment, for example men may be given services while women care without help. Explore everyday life and the ordinary in the relationships. How can this relationship be shifted in trusting and non-oppressive directions? How can each partner in the caregiving develop assertiveness about their potential and actual contributions and needs?

Working on child care issues, focus on mothering. How did women clients experience this in childhood? How are demands for mothering different now? Explore differing feelings in the family and power dynamics within the nuclear and extended family to help clients understand the nature of pressures to comply with social norms in accepting maternity and in mothering responsibilities. Are emotional, financial, practical and relationship support present to enable mothering in the way clients desire? How might they be put in place?

Explore both sides of caring relationships. How are thoughts and needs shared between carer and cared-for person? Do institutional and social contexts support care relationships? For example, do wider family and community members and formal care services support interpersonal relationships of carer and cared-for person and needs and personal autonomy of the carer? Ethics of care views focus on receptivity, relatedness and responsiveness rather than moral or social rules, for example how partners respect dignity, rather than a wife or daughter's duty to care. Enable couples involved in caring responsibilities to consider how these may be equally shared.

Examine options for women carers to continue or take up education, employment and leisure opportunities. Advocate for and enable women to take up carers' rights to separate assessments for their own needs from the assessments of the cared-for person.

Identity

Enable clients to gain a secure valuation of their gender identity and sexuality. How do we or clients benefit or suffer from exclusion or privilege? Reflect on your own and clients' positions with empathy for their experiences, cultural humility in accepting their experience of the impact of inequalities. Help people be open to exploring unfamiliar experiences. Encourage dialogue between groups with varying identities.

Explore how current issues derive from socialization into inappropriate roles and behaviours, for example in family and school in childhood, in leisure interactions, in workplaces as an adult. Look at how important social identities emerged in interactions in various social locations, particularly where these intersect with identities connected with body shape, class, ethnicity, sexual orientation, spirituality. Also relevant are care, health, housing and social security or other financial experiences. Explore how oppression and male privilege may feed into experiences around gender identity. Look at examples of emotional reactions generated by intentional and unintended micro-aggression in interpersonal relationships. Uncover similar experiences with institutions, for example education settings, housing providers. Examine how these relate to structural inequalities, for example the wage gap between women and men's pay, attitudes to sexuality that affect transgender people.

Examine the intersection of women's experiences and other conditions, for example ageing, disability, sexuality.

Intimate and family relationships

Help clients sift through how their life experience prepares them for or hinders them from successful intimate relationships. These include experience of attachments (see Chapter 12), the need for proximity, emotional, physical and social, and the need to belong in long-term caring relationships. Explore with couples and individuals building self-esteem as an important basis for experiencing attraction and acceptance in relationships. Encourage couples and individuals to review equity in the balance between costs and rewards derived from the relationship, reciprocity in interpersonal and social exchange and styles of verbal and non-verbal communication. Encourage people dissatisfied with relationships to rehearse and practise alternatives together.

Work on improving problem solving, resolving conflicts and sharing power in relationships to reduce negative and increase positive emotions and interactions. Help people practise balancing positive and negative emotional reactions to each other, to understand and appreciate the other's feelings, learn to express approval for the other's efforts and positive reactions in general. Develop a shared positive view of women, value women's coping strengths, encourage flexibility in roles between men and women and work on strengthening personal identity in both partners. Explore the effect of cultural assumptions on attitudes to gendered behaviour.

Develop women's capacity for assertiveness and self-expression. When working with children and parents, point to controlling or limiting arrangements and relationships in the home and in child care, in the past or now. With financial problems, identify if economic relationships are inappropriately gendered. Explore alternatives, for example separate control of finances, explicit discussion of financial responsibilities. Encourage equal and open relationships for both parents; point to ways of avoiding children feeling powerless in family arrangements. Support equality in family activities, for example confront and find alternatives to mothers managing family arrangements, with fathers prioritizing work or male social relations. If parents separate, for example, facilitate both parents' relationships with children's schools. Work one step at a time, not all at once.

Probe the extent to which violence is an issue. Women are strongly affected by violence in war, for example migrants from war zones, sexual health, sex trafficking, prostitution and also in women's health, especially mental health and substance abuse issues. Help women affected by child sexual abuse, intimate partner violence and sexual violence understand that gendered cultural and ethnic assumptions shape these life experiences. Build appreciation and understanding of the important multiple roles women take on. Explore actual and potential support systems, and contributions to stability and achievement in faith and spirituality. Argue for accepting official and state responsibility in responding and providing support.

Because of these difficulties, women are in jeopardy of entering the criminal justice, homelessness, immigration control and mental health systems. Assist them to maintain ties to family and children. Look for ways of maintaining good-quality healthcare. Aid the maintenance and re-establishing of supportive relationships and re-entry to normal life. Establish protection against exploitation, suicide and violence in institutions or by people in their lives. Promote opportunities for psychological and supportive treatments, rather than monitoring and surveillance and medication.

Men

Feminist practice does not neglect working with men because gendered thinking in men as well as women has a negative impact on relationships and changing this benefits everyone. Help men recognize how they create gender inequalities and restrictions for women, and get them to think about alternative ways of doing masculinity. Explore how cooperation and mutual support rather than dominance is appropriately masculine. Discuss how men contribute to caring and household responsibilities. Look at the two-way impact of gendered thinking: does it influence both how men think, feel and interact and also women's satisfaction with relationships and treatment? Men should reflect on gendered socialization and interaction with significant male others and how this shapes their identity and behaviour.

Boys may be perceived as troublesome or troubled in family relationships (Thomas, 2016), particularly in black minority families. Help parents examine whether these interpretations value cultural views about the nature of strength, the strong man and potential alternatives.

Things to think about

Feminist practice requires constant collective engagement in developing awareness and evaluating women's role and position in social relations and in organizations. This is because it builds on personal experience of women's lives where oppression and subordination lead to women's social contribution, experience and relationships being devalued, for example where there is sexual exploitation and violence towards women, where important inputs in social life as carers are devalued.

Avoid focusing on gender to the exclusion of other issues. Poverty is important because women are often poorer than men and are responsible for earning a significant contribution to income and for financial management in many poor families. This often intersects with other sources of oppression, for example age, disability, ethnicity and sexuality, and inequality and institutional disempowerment of women. To develop a secure position for women in social care organizations and more widely, and especially for women involved in situations where social work help is required, constant attention to gender inequalities and exploitation is required.

Develop arrangements for your work that facilitate participation and co-production. Model equality in your helping relationship. Make yourself accessible, offering contact numbers and being clear about availability. Institutionalize regular feedback about you, the relationship, the arrangements and the agency. Provide for collective representation so that clients can meet as and respond as a group.

Avoid trying to be gender blind. Instead, practise gender-sensitive practice. Highlight ways gender-based roles, identities and behaviours connect to wider structures of power and inequality and seek alternative ways of thinking.

It is respectful and represents equality in your work with clients to make sure that your arrangements are efficient, well coordinated and take account of clients' life pressures.

Avoid binaries, explanations of something as having only two options. Prefer seeking a wider range of alternatives.

Further resources

Butler-Mokoro, S. & Grant, L. (eds) (2018). *Feminist perspectives on social work practice: The intersecting lives of women in the 21st century*. New York: Oxford University Press.

A useful collection of articles.

White, V. (2006). *The state of feminist social work*. Abingdon: Routledge.

A good research-based account of practitioners' struggles to implement feminist practice.

Check the online resources at policy.bristoluniversitypress.co.uk/how-to-use-social-work-theory-in-practice/online-resources/chapter23 for a full list of references for this chapter.

24

Ecological and green practice

Setting the scene

What is ecological and green practice?

Ecological and green practice improves sustainable interconnections among human beings in transactions with their social environment and with the natural environment. This aims to help people be aware of and respond to how interpersonal, natural and social environments interact and how this affects them. Also, it seeks to stimulate supportive reciprocity in interpersonal, group and community relations. As public policy begins to enforce personal and social responses to climate change, many social work individual clients and communities will have their way of life disrupted, and will need help with this and policy-change interventions.

Ecological systems theory (Gitterman & Germain, 2008, of which elements were included in Chapter 21) is a largely American practice connected with other systems theories of practice. Coates (2003) developed an important early attempt to create a practice concerned with environmental and ecological concerns, and recent contributions by Dominelli (2012b), Gray, Coates and Hetherington (2013) and McKinnon and Alston (2016) focus on practice aimed at environmental justice.

Aims

Ecological systems theory aims to help clients and the people around them see how being part of a holistic system of interrelationships not only generates some of the problems in their lives, but also offers opportunities and resources to help overcome these challenges. Thus, young people, people with disabilities and mental illness, and older people all benefit from support from family and community networks, and in making contributions in exchange.

Ecocritical or ecocentric theory enables clients, families and communities to understand how the natural and built environment has an impact on their wellbeing. This creates opportunities to cooperate

ECOLOGICAL AND GREEN PRACTICE 24.1

APPROACH

Focus on interlocking relationships and social links
Interdependence between social structures and organizations
Look at behaviours in social or physical spaces
Assess natural behaviour and interactions
Look at support in interlocking systems
Examine long-term social impacts of events and experiences
Take a holistic view of people's lifecourses

ASSESS INTERLOCKING

Physical spaces
Micro and meso systems
Macro systems
Exosystems

INTERVENTION AIMS

Sustainability – to endure, develop, grow
Long-term harmony – to resolve conflict

Links between people and groups create wholes
Achieving a better environment and reversing damage
Use animal, human, natural resources well
Build positive experiences through adventure pedagogy
Develop people's citizenship and reduce de-citizening
Respond to economic issues through local social enterprise
Work on effective energy use
Oppose environmental degradation and conflict

INTERVENTIONS

Practical support and resources to build links
Facilitate links to increase social capital
Broaden support networks beyond dyads and triads
Increase people's experience of offering social support
Build on satisfying experiences and interests
Promote participation in social activity and social action
Encourage partnerships with others with mutual concerns
Extend interests for those with limited options

with others to secure improvements in those environments. These can be motivating because they fulfil personal and social aspirations. Increasingly, concern for green issues engages people's commitment to social justice and to meeting global challenges. Promoting equality involves commitment to equity in making resources available to diverse individuals and communities.

Uses

Early social work saw environmental interventions as practical, rather than concerned with a client's inner experience. It was also indirect, tackling social and agency barriers to personal and interpersonal progress (more on this in Chapter 21). This approach to ecological concerns work is now only a starting point.

Ecological and green practice focuses on change in natural and human environments and social networks. This lifts intervention away from the individual's problems and actions to help people share better in families and communities. Examples are projects for unemployed young people, age-friendly neighbourhoods and building dementia-friendly organizations. The networking or systems elements of this are most relevant to helping clients gain control of how they can participate in families and communities and in important social institutions, such as neighbourhoods, schools or workplaces. Attachment to place, such as a drop-in centre or a neighbourhood, is an important instrument for achieving this.

The sustainability and social justice elements may usefully motivate and stimulate people to participate in group or community activity concerned with these issues. They may also be personally motivating for individuals.

Introducing ecological and green practice

Elements of this practice inform other approaches, or might be picked up where you have long-term care responsibility. If first contact and assessment processes identify someone with a concern with the environment, raise the possibility of helping them through working on these issues. With others, you pick up on the aspects of their goals or problems that are about making whole their connections with the wider world, rather than those that focus on troubled interpersonal relationships. Examples might be isolated disabled or older people, migrants trying to establish themselves, young offenders alienated from social relations. Suggest that you should work together on making their lives more relevant and social relations more responsive to people in their position.

Action sequence

Approach

Assessment in ecological theory sees people's environments as interlocking relationships and social links. Look at their interdependence with others and with social structures and organizations. While you analyse and work with this complex, if the concern is behaviour, this is site-specific and takes place in identifiable social spaces or physical places, for example, poor facilities on an estate of social housing properties, violent or bullying neighbours of people with intellectual disabilities. You focus behavioural concerns in those spaces. Assessment prioritizes observation of natural behaviour and interactions. Ecological assessment of individuals and families engages with supports and limitations for clients in various interlocking systems:

- physical places, for example home, residential care setting, hospital, locality;
- micro and meso systems, for example family, neighbours, school–home and home–work links;
- macro systems, for example economic, industrial and government structures;
- exosystems, for example age, culture norms, power, privilege, social class.

You assess the development of links that affect clients, how each system links with and alters others. Genograms of relationships and ecomaps of important links and factors may be useful. Social impact assessment evaluates the long-term impacts of events in your focus and actions you might propose.

Think holistically about clients' lifecourses, what these bring to them and the barriers created by them. Work on understanding how present issues and future aspirations emerge from that life experience. In the future, change might involve redirection or rebalancing of that lifecourse, but help the client see its importance to their identity and the social systems it has created, or changing attitudes among people around them. An example is where neighbours will not help an older person because of local stigma around their past life choices, such as a criminal record, debt, drug use or mental ill-health.

Focuses for intervention

In general, ecological practice focuses on building links within and across communities, exploiting a sense that a community, family or individual lifecourse needs working on holistically. Positive focuses include promoting a better local environment, housing or urban or rural setting, reversing environmental damage and its social consequences, and using an increased range of animal, human and natural resources more effectively. Adventure pedagogy is a strategy of using activities and experiences in challenging and wild environments to develop young people's self-esteem and confidence, and can be applied to other populations.

Citizenship development can offer a focus for personal and relationship development. Work with people who see themselves as excluded from local communities or from service provision to explore their rights to participation. Evaluate with clients their experiences of becoming de-citizened, losing aspects of their citizenship, for example through being made dependent on carers, on services or on others' help, through not being informed about their rights or services available, through losing self-confidence in providing for their own needs. Re-citizen them through groupwork, mutual aid and rehearsing and building experience that will renew their participative rights. Encourage and facilitate them to take part in creative and arts opportunities, especially where this involves social relationships, for example amateur acting, community choirs.

Economic issues are often political, societal or global issues. Economic growth may be damaging to natural and social environments. The economic system may limit people in pursuing ecologically sustainable environments. But developing local enterprises, particularly social entrepreneurship and microfinance for small-scale social development, are all possible strategies for community groups (Schmitz, Matyók, James & Sloan, 2013; Dominelli, 2012b).

Energy use is an important focus. Families under economic pressure and older people may be helped with insulation, using renewable energy and more economical use of cooking or heating. Often financial help is available.

Helping people to look at issues of environmental degradation, pollution and scarce natural resources may lead to local and inter-country conflict, for example between travellers and settled people, between migrant and local populations. Parents might work on protecting children from traffic fumes, or rubbish dumping on derelict land locally. More positively, families might be encouraged to work to improve local spaces for play. Working on green spaces or community gardens may be useful strategies for people with intellectual disabilities. Look for ways in which patterns of relationships and mutual support may be developed.

Personal and social identities may be bound up with experiences of place, for example in youth gang memberships, family social mores. Social policies and practices, such as urban planning and policing, may produce opportunities and reinforce successes, or encourage people to resist the patterns of privilege and oppression seen in wider landscapes of power (Zukin, 1991). Place may be 'stretched' (Kemp, 2010), helping people make links between their local, interpersonal options and wider dimensions of place. For example, inner city oppression of black and minority ethnic groups and individuals may link with outer suburbs' need for the economic resources of the city and region. And black and minority ethnic groups' links with former countries show how stretchy space enables people to move into and out of environments and make use of distant as well as local resources. Individuals, families, groups and communities may be helped to rethink how their location affects their identities and how stretching towards alternative locations, or remaking their present environment, can change the barriers affecting their life and their opportunities.

Human and natural disasters, for example famine, flooding, fires, transport accidents, may encourage people to come together to use natural resources in their locality more effectively, or to encourage greater equality in sharing. Examples might be food distribution schemes, attempts to redistribute resources.

Spirituality and political concerns about the meaning and value of clients' lives in the community may be strongly relevant to older people or other isolated clients, for example a parent living alone with a client with intellectual disabilities. Contacts with resources such as local churches, faith groups and community groups, links with sympathetic local helpers, education and leisure opportunities, work with animals, companion or assistance animals, riding for disabled people may all be relevant.

Raise awareness of work, the workplace and employment as a potential location for building social relationships. Engage clients in understanding whether work locations generate personal and social reactions, for example alienation or satisfaction, being valued or devalued by labour. Might work relationships also create opportunities for helpful social change? It also raises important issues of social organization, such as industrialization, loss of rural lives and traditions, and urbanization, which affect people's mental and physical health. As people come to understand this, examine strategies to improve social relations and health, for example part-time work, leisure and social connections at work, changing work conditions. Help people move to positive community activities and work, away from drug-using lifestyles. Find strategies to help people move on from working in the black or gig economy.

Intervention

Deliver practical support to clients, families, groups and communities through:

- goods and services as resources to provide practical help;
- information about how to get things done;
- emotional support, using yourself, volunteers or help identify people in the community – companionship, compassion, empathy, exploring experiences, considering options and discussing feelings are all relevant;
- affiliation, organizing links with others promoting identity and belonging.

Add people and links to increase clients' social capital. Broaden support networks beyond the dyads and triads in clients' lives. For example, with young people and people with intellectual disabilities, develop wider contacts, extending links with parents or siblings. With people with disabilities, build community networks as well as strengthening marital relations. Older people might develop adult education, church or community group relations, as well as links with children and grandchildren.

Increase experiences that offer social support, shifting engagement from unhelpful towards supportive people. Increase the number of supportive contacts people have, helping people to change or experiment with the style of their relationships.

Explore what experiences and interests clients have found satisfying and build on them. Encourage participation in social activities or social action. If clients do not have financial resources, they may be able to offer time. Encourage clients to build partnerships with others with similar concerns and interests. For young parents, this may be around children or provision for family support. For disabled, mentally ill and older people these can be built around local community concerns or personal interests. Where people's options are limited, extend the range of interests they have contact with, helping them evaluate new options and build on those that engage them.

Things to think about

An important objective of ecological and green practice is sustainability, the capacity at least to endure and ideally to develop and grow. Sustaining interventions contribute to supporting and stabilizing a person or group so that they can continue or improve their chances of survival and development. In ecology, sustainability in natural systems derives from their diversity and long-term productivity. The idea of sustainable social development aims to meet the needs of the present 'without compromising the ability of future generations to meet their own needs' (Brundtland Commission, 1987). It combines ecological, economic and social development achieved in concert. For social workers, this involves considering ecological and economic wellbeing alongside their work on the social.

The nature of the community's resources is an important issue. Think about the environment, natural or human; for example, the lakeside, seaside or ocean environment, the urban environment, the market town, the rural environment. Is industry in an urban environment a heavy or a service industry? Does it involve old and possibly declining industry or new technology? How can you help people respond to these changes as individuals, families or communities?

Another important ideal is to seek long-term harmony and conflict resolution. Can a new story for this community, family or individual be created?

Further resources

Gitterman, A. & Germain, C.B. (2008). *The life model of social work practice: Advances in theory and practice* (3rd edn). New York: Columbia University Press.

The most significant text using ecological systems theory in a practice model.

Mary, N.L. (2008). *Social work in a sustainable world*. Chicago, IL: Lyceum.

Dominelli, L. (2012b). *Green social work: From environmental crises to environmental justice*. Cambridge: Polity.

Two texts focusing on sustainability as a social justice issue in social work.

Gray, M., Coates, J. & Hetherington, T. (eds) (2013). *Environmental social work*. London: Routledge.

McKinnon, J. & Alston, M. (eds) (2016). *Ecological social work: Towards sustainability*. London: Palgrave.

Two edited collections that engage extensively with theoretical and practice debate in these areas.

Check the online resources at policy.bristoluniversitypress.co.uk/how-to-use-social-work-theory-in-practice/online-resources/chapter24 for a full list of references for this chapter.

25

Ending and critical reflection

Setting the scene

What is ending and critical reflection?

Ending or, in jargon, 'termination', completes a social work process. Not all models of social work practice are explicit about this process; some chapters earlier in the book include how to end practice where theories provide for it. This chapter explores more general aspects of human and interpersonal aspects of ending, include preparing the people involved for ending or transferring contact. On transfer, you help people involved to accept and begin to value a new relationship. With ending, you help clients to plan and accept responsibility again for their own further progress on the issues you have worked with.

Both interpersonal and administrative processes at this stage may include review and evaluation, as part of agency and professional accountability. Review involves looking back over the contact, summing up achievements, challenges that arose and how they were dealt with. Look at progress towards aims set at the beginning and during the process. Try to send people out on a high, but, for your own professional development and your agency's improvement, identify things that went less well and try to understand why. If they are still appropriate aims, think about how to help clients to take them on in the future. Evaluation is a formal process of seeing what was of value in the process, whether what has been achieved meets the aims set, was worthwhile in the context of clients' lives and met agency aims. Agencies often have formal processes for doing this.

Reflection, sometimes called 'critical reflection', structures your standing back, considering the process and outcomes of your work in a case, in a group of cases and in general. You follow consistent procedures for considering knowledge and understandings that emerge from the work, avoiding the taken-for-granted organizational, professional and social assumptions that sometimes inform our actions. Doing so may enable you to develop and contribute new knowledge and understanding in your practice to your team, agency and profession. For some writers, for example White, Fook and

ENDING AND TRANSFER

Look back • Achievements • Challenges
Progress on aims • Understand what went wrong
Go out on a high • Aims in the future • Evaluation

EMOTIONAL REACTIONS

Acting out, clinging on
Defensiveness, denial
Old problems return
New problems emerge
Anxiety about change

EASING ENDINGS

Prepare for ending • Feelings about transfer
Prepare for new worker • Prepare new worker
Re-do missing endings • Ceremony

FACTORS AFFECTING REACTIONS TO ENDING

Involvement, satisfaction, success
Fulfilling relationships • Previous losses • Your leaving

(CRITICAL) REFLECTION

Cognitive thinking
Affective thinking
Values thinking
Reflection-*in*-action
Reflection-*on*-action
Reflection-*for*-action

Criticality: Scepticism
Social barriers in clients' lives

IDENTIFY A CRITICAL EVENT

Focus on a critical event • Review a period of work
Evaluate outcomes • Be reflexive • Co-production with clients

CHOOSING THE EVENT

It went well
It included mistakes
You were unconfident
You enjoyed it
You felt pressurized
Clients were hard-to-value
You didn't know enough
You felt unsupported

DESCRIBE THE CRITICAL EVENT

Account of events • Roles, actions, consequences
Your role, interventions, actions • Others' reactions
Value issues • Meanings, understandings

ANALYSIS

Synthesis and integration
Appropriation and validation
New effective state
New direction or connection
Move outside present 'frames'
Bring ideas to the surface
Use journals, supervision, group

EXPLORE ALTERNATIVES

Critique, interpret, explain
Problematization
Genealogy of issues
Archaeology of discourses
Deconstruction

CHANGE OR REAFFIRMATION

Examine earlier reflection
Alternative areas to work on
New skills, ideas, understandings
Experimentation, research • Overcome barriers

USE ALTERNATIVE DISCOURSES

Health or social care
Law, economics or management
Psychology or sociology
Rights, spirituality or environment

Gardner (2006), 'critical' reflection requires you to incorporate analysis that does not take for granted the existing social order or economic, political and social policies or which identifies contradictions in rational explanations of evidence. 'Critical thinking' means using disciplined ways of thinking about ideas and practice objectives, often using reasoned thinking and empirical research.

Reflection in professional education, developing from the ideas of John Dewey (1933) and the work of Donald Schön (1983), is an important mechanism for education and theory development. Three dimensions, cognitive, affective and values thinking, allow you to explore a range of practice issues which may have been obscured in daily practice (Thompson & Thompson, 2018: 27–47). It has become a commonplace procedure in many professions for continuing professional development and organizational review. Agency reflective processes may involve groupwork with carers, clients and colleagues and professional supervision arrangements. Reflection helps to develop humanity, an ethos of learning and responsiveness in agencies.

Reflexivity involves two-sided or 360° observation and analysis, putting yourself in others' shoes and seeing how your actions influence them. You explore others' understandings of your work, seeing how others perceive your responses and the effects of your actions on the people and environment you were involved with. Thus, you can understand better how differing conceptions of events may be valid and need to be understood and responded to.

Aims

Four important aims in ending are:

- reviewing, looking back on, and perhaps summarizing, what has happened during the intervention;
- evaluating the success of the interventions from relevant points of view, especially the clients';
- disengaging from relationships;
- stabilizing intervention, so that there is no relapse and clients can use skills learned and make further progress.

A further aim in critical reflection is:

- using review and evaluation of your work to examine the process and outcomes of your work and identify changes and improvements in your practice and understanding that you can adopt in the future.

Uses

Ending processes help you and clients feel a sense of closure, and perhaps achievement, in using social work services. Critical reflection as part of ending enables you to develop your skill and understanding. You can then contribute that improved understanding and skill to agency and professional policy and practice.

Introducing ending and critical reflection

The main approach to ending is to give advance notice of it. You also help people gain a realistic future expectation of help being renewed if problems recur or different problems arise. If further help may not be available, help to clarify how to deal with changing problems or future goals. Engaging people in reflection about your work together can help with this. Try to demonstrate that until the actual ending, you remain the practitioner within this relationship. Carry on being empathetic, forward looking and helpful until the last moment.

Particularly in a brief intervention with a clear time limit, ending starts at the beginning. If there are open-ended tasks, try to hold clients to complete at least part of the task. This can help you both towards a perception of successful mastery.

Where you expect long-term contact, talk this over with people as part of starting out, for example will you go on until a child reaches the age of 18 years, or for the length of time that a disabled person needs your services? Build in the assumption that in long-term cases there will be regular reviews involving a resetting of your work, and transfers of responsibility, for example when clients or foster carers move house; when practitioners move to new jobs.

Action sequence for ending

Be accepting of a range of behavioural and emotional responses when ending or transfer becomes likely. These may affect clients and others involved, and yourself and colleagues. Reactions vary according to the degree of involvement, satisfaction and success; whether the relationship has been fulfilling; whether people have mastered losses around previous endings and complications if you are leaving, for example administrative issues, a feeling of leaving before finishing.

Be ready, therefore, to respond to:

- emotional reactions such as anger, fear, irritation, pleasure in achievement, or relief;
- acting out behaviour, that is, aggression, annoying behaviour, unrestrained expression of emotions, which previously clients have been able to control;
- clinging on, for example constantly ringing for advice or reassurance;
- defensive reactions, for example not letting new workers make contact;
- denial reinforcing a sense of worthlessness, for example not needing help, not being worth helping;
- recurrence or repetition of old issues;
- introducing new problems;
- anxiety about substitutes and replacements, for example fears when foster care arrangements end.

If you are transferring responsibility to another agency or practitioner, expect apprehension or hope about a new relationship, possibly both. Renewing the helping relationship or renewed negotiation of aims may be stressful. Explore possible feelings and help people find a route through worries.

While you may be preparing clients for a new worker, you are also preparing the new practitioner for these clients. Try to provide clear and realistic information without prejudicing their own engagement, and share records and information, checking what people involved need to pass on.

If you pick up a case where there has been no ending with previous practitioners, do the ending before you start: 'I think we should look at how your previous contact with our agency came to an end.'

If closure can be planned for, at the next-to-last contacts with people involved, prepare clearly for ending. Try to make the experience of a successful ending an important self-actualizing growth opportunity, a positive learning experience about how to move on, for you and clients.

If you are a long-serving practitioner, beginning and ending may happen several times between you and a client or their family. Prepare for the possibility of future contact for you or the agency, acknowledge and review previous involvements.

People may be ambivalent about ending: it may be a difficult or propitious moment. Make leaving a ceremony, even if it's just a handshake or hug. Celebrate as well as mourn.

Action sequence for (critical) reflection

Reflection can be reflection-*in*-action, taking place as you work alongside your client, or reflection-*on*-action, done at the end of a piece of work or as a case is closed. In both, you aim to make sense to yourself and your client of what has happened. It may also be a reflection-*for*-action, where you know that you are going to take an important step, and reflect on the progress towards it and what you will do.

Reflection is a circular process of:

1. identifying and describing an event or experience;
2. developing your understanding of it and the action you took;
3. exploring possible alternatives to that understanding and action;
4. forming plans for changing how you change or reaffirm your response to this event or experience in the future.

A successful reflection leads to improved clarity in how you change or reaffirm your future practice actions. Many formal review and evaluation processes within agencies, however, focus on your accountability to policy or procedures and do not seek to build on knowledge in this way. You can often, however, include professional development into these procedures, for example by doing a bit extra, and in supervision.

Using reflection-*on*-action in review or evaluation processes, look back at how well you carried out each of these four stages when you were *in*-action: reflexivity about clients' self-identity, changes in your understanding of their position, responsiveness to their narratives, enabling voice and choice. Focus on your relationships in each case, including within your own organization.

One important area of reflection is to incorporate or lead you to inquiry and research (Gardner, 2006). At each stage, you may identify areas where you did not have enough knowledge or the right understanding. One option may be to explore existing research more fully or form your ideas into possibilities for further research. Do this by looking at each of the issues raised in this case, how they were constructed and by whom, into issues that you intervened with, how the people involved thought about these issues and whether other voices or narratives need to be explored. How can each of these issues be better understood?

1. Identifying the event or experience

You cannot reflect on everything, so select an event or experience to focus on. One approach is to identify a 'critical event' or 'critical incident', an event which you plan to be, or which in retrospect turns out to be, a revelation in your understanding or turning point in your action. You could focus on a missing or new perspective in your thinking or a misunderstanding, for example where you are newly encountering people from a minority ethnic group. An alternative is to explore a period of your work on a case: this is a common process in agency periodic reviews or evaluations. At the ending of your involvement, you would reflect either on the whole period of involvement or simply on the outputs achieved.

Davies and Kinloch (2000: 140, slightly adapted) give examples of critical incidents to select for analysis, which you could apply to any form of review. These are where you felt:

- it had gone well, or better than expected;
- you made the wrong decision or other mistake;
- you lacked confidence;
- you enjoyed working with the client, group or community;
- under pressure;
- it was difficult to accept, understand or value a client;
- you did not know enough;
- unsupported.

Using reflection-*in*-action, be reflexive, putting yourself in the position of your clients and others you are working with. How might they see you? Examine their behaviour towards you or responses to your interventions. Agency evaluations and reviews involving satisfaction questionnaires or other measures may help. This can transform your understanding of people in minority or oppressed positions. Interrogate how they form their self-identity from their family and community experience, citizenship, culture and historical and geographical position. Be responsive to how they express their life experience, be curious about their narratives of what is important to them, but do not expect them to educate you about their life history, unless you need this to carry out your aims. Through co-production, enable them to have a voice and as much choice as possible.

Part of identifying the event or experience is describing it adequately, to enable you to reflect fully on all its implications. Ordinary agency records, or your memory, are not enough to achieve this. Many systems for reflection involve creating a detailed record of events, drawing diagrams or artwork, or maintaining a reflective journal covering your work, in which you both describe and work on your understanding events or experiences.

The description involves:

- an account of events;
- the roles of people involved;
- the actions they took, and how these related to their roles;
- the consequences of their actions;
- your own role;
- planned interventions and other actions you took;
- the consequences of and others' reactions to your role, interventions and actions;
- the consequences of others' actions;
- value issues that arose and how you dealt with them;
- how events and people's reactions illuminate, illustrate or suggest their meanings and understandings of what took place.

2. Analysis and understanding

Ways of thinking that help the analysis can include:

- synthesis, mixing different ideas to form a new conception;
- integration, weaving different ideas to look at things in alternative ways;
- appropriation, picking up an idea to use in the future;
- validation, confirming or becoming more confident that an idea is useful;
- new affective or emotional state, a new way of feeling, for example more optimistic; more confident that you can carry out a procedure;
- deciding on an engagement, taking a new direction or connection with people.

Try to move outside your present 'frame' of thinking, or to disrupt or unsettle it. For example, imagine yourself working with this client in a different agency: how would they present themselves differently? Would your different function in a school setting help you see a family differently? Or would a disability or mental health team approach your elderly client differently?

An important area of analysis is feelings, the immediate neurological, physical and psychological reactions to what happens in your life, and emotions, the longer-term state of mind that guides our behaviour and human relationships. Emotional states form a context in which immediate feelings affect us, but feelings contribute to how our emotional state develops. Therefore, explore clients' emotions and feelings and your own. It can be difficult to bring emotions to the surface. Ways of doing so are:

- writing in a journal or notebook – to free yourself from anxiety about self-disclosure, you could start separately from agency records, transferring a curated summary later;
- talking freely to a mirror, then making notes;
- talking into a recording, then writing the agency record;
- talking to a trusted colleague, who can help you be critical about your thinking and reactions;
- using supervision;
- finding a safe group where you are confident in people being supportive.

Often, particular environments, such as a families, social groups and workplaces, have 'feeling rules' (Butler, 2019) which set the pattern for how people are expected to express or repress their emotions: what are the rules for this client in this situation, and for you in your workplace? To explore this, look at how feelings and emotions are developed and regulated, and how they interact with rational thinking. Explore what systems people are part of that affect how they think about things, for example church or social group membership, or expectations in school or a care home. Think also about how people in this setting have constructed opposition to ways of thinking, or how they might do so.

Another useful approach is to explore people's own ways of managing their feelings and emotions or regulating how they express their emotions, for example can they delay a response until a more suitable moment, do they have social skills to avoid getting angry? You could also explore your emotional reactions to the situations you are working in, for example are you having to hold yourself in? What makes you like your client or how do they irritate you?

3. Exploring alternatives

Hodgson and Watts (2017: 238–9) identify several ways of looking at ideas critically:

- critique: compare present reality with ideal outcomes;
- interpretation: use theory or models to understand confusing or opaque actions or circumstances;
- explanation: account for phenomena and relationships between them;
- problematization 1: interrogate anything that appears natural for hidden assumptions;
- problematization 2: question conceptualizations of issues to understand the conditions that created them;
- genealogy: trace how issues are analysed, classified and regulated;
- archaeology: understand how discourses and other practices have generated perceptions of phenomena, but exclude human consciousness and interpretations;
- deconstruction: analysis of relations between signs in language and symbols and what they signify.

Critical reflection requires engaging with alternative theoretical discourses within your services and alternative practice perspectives (Healy, 2014):

- health and medicine
- welfare or social services
- legal
- economics
- management and effectiveness
- psychological ideas
- sociological ideas
- citizens' rights
- religion and spirituality
- environment

Planning to change or reaffirm your practice

The first three elements of the reflective processes lead you to plan alternative action in the future. You examine the early stages of social work to understand anew: identify alternative areas where you should re-engage and reassess the situation, negotiating new approaches with clients and others involved. Your reflection will identify where changed or improved skills work more effectively, and if necessary work with others to improve your skills or seek training, support or supervision.

Skills improvement focuses on how you could have been:

- differently creative;
- more or differently analytical;
- more successful in managing and relating to staff in commissioned services, colleagues and other practitioners involved;
- focused more or differently in the interpersonal relationships involved in the case;
- communicating in different ways (Thompson, 2018; Thompson & Thompson, 2018: 132–3).

The third stage of analysis may identify alternative ideas and perspectives that alter your understanding of the situation.

Planning will involve clients and the people around them, supervisors and managers and working with colleagues in formal and informal discussion groups. Reflection leads to experimentation to test out new options for practice, but ethically should be done as a form of inquiry into the success and value of these options both to a particular case, to your wider practice and to the wider practice of your team, agency and profession. A strategy to test new interventions, report back and discuss with colleagues is essential for accountability. Using formal evaluation and research can help to confirm innovations for yourself, in the agency and more widely.

Planning may also need to identify how to overcome barriers to reflection in the agency, such as:

- time pressures, for example build thinking time into your work, manage workload;
- minimizing the value of reflection and skill development, for example cooperate with like-minded people, use reflective diaries and thinking;
- 'managerialism', a focus on top-down objectives enforced by compliance with quantitative output measures, rather than human qualitative evaluation, for example find support for more enlightened views, through professional organizations, present alternative views in employee feedback, form groups to do your own reflection, find an informal mentor.

Things to think about

Particularly with brief interventions, endings and critical reflection may leave us and clients with feelings about work left undone. Have we been thorough enough? What should we have done to be more or differently thorough? Have you kept a case open for too long – why? What do you or the client get out of that? Are you or the client feeling guilty because you didn't achieve what you'd hoped and planned? Do you feel your relationship is so good that nobody else can do it as well? You may have these feelings; so may clients. To deal with these sorts of issues, in your review or evaluation, try to be clear what you did achieve, and think about things that another practitioner might succeed with.

Feelings and emotions are generated in endings. People may feel good about achievements and progress, hopeful for the future. Or they may experience loss, a break in progress or a fear or risk of deterioration. Is it, musically, a climax or *rallentando*, a trumpets and drumroll ending, or a slowing and falling away. There are many OK possibilities, and people may have varying views about what's OK; similarly, so-so judgements and downright bad evaluations.

Reflection develops your self-awareness of how you acted and your aspirations for improvements in how you are going to be in the future; see also Chapter 3. Focus on evidence and thinking about the relationship between you and the people involved and how this expresses their thinking and emotions. Formulate objectives to increase your knowledge, theoretical understanding and skills, either through formal staff development or training, or setting out on a self-development programme of your own, or with a few colleagues who share aims.

Critical reflection and reflexivity involves two processes. One is building and maintaining a general scepticism about standardized processes within both the agency and social work practice. If you responded to the event or experience you are looking at using conventional ideas or practices, ask yourself if there were less commonplace alternatives you could have tried. The second process is to use critical theory to identify clients' social environment, life experiences or social relationships and structures that created barriers to achieving the outcomes that you aimed for, and see how these might be overcome.

Further resources

Johns, C. (ed) (2017). *Becoming a reflective practitioner* (5th edn). Chichester: Wiley.

A wide-ranging, multi-professional collection of information and practice guidance.

Bruce, L. (2013). *Reflective practice for social workers: A handbook for developing professional confidence*. Maidenhead: Open University Press.

A useful practical guide for social workers.

White, S., Fook, J. & Gardner, F. (2006). *Critical reflection in health and social care*. Maidenhead: Open University Press.

An important, thoughtful and practical collection of papers.

Check the online resources at policy.bristoluniversitypress.co.uk/how-to-use-social-work-theory-in-practice/online-resources/chapter25 for a full list of references for this chapter.

Bibliography

Note: Page citations following some books listed here indicate the chapter in this book where use has been made of a particular point in the cited text.

Adame, A.L. & Leitner, L.M. (2008). Breaking out of the mainstream: The evolution of peer support alternatives to the mental health system. *Ethical Human Psychology and Psychiatry. 10*, 146–62.

Adams, J. (1995). *Risk.* London: Routledge.

Adams. R. (2009). Advocacy and empowerment. In R. Adams, L. Dominelli & M. Payne (eds) *Critical practice in social work* (2nd edn) (pp 178–88). Basingstoke: Palgrave Macmillan.

Alameda-Lawson, T. & Lawson, M.A. (2002). Building community collaboratives. In M. O'Melia & K.K. Miley (eds) *Pathways to power: Readings in contextual social work practice* (pp 108–27). Boston, MA: Allyn & Bacon.

Aldgate, J. & Gibson, N. (2015). The place of attachment theory in social work with children and families. In J. Lishman (ed) *Handbook for practice learning in social work and social care: Knowledge and theory* (pp 80–98). London: Jessica Kingsley.

Allen, G. & Langford, D. (2008). *Effective interviewing in social work and social care: A practical guide.* Basingstoke: Palgrave Macmillan.

Allen-Meares, P. & Lane, B.A. (1987). Grounding social work practice in theory: Ecosystems. *Social Casework. 68*(9), 515–21.

Anderson, J. (1996). Yes, but IS it empowerment? Initiation, implementation and outcomes of community action. In B. Humphries (ed) *Critical perspectives on empowerment* (pp 69–83). Birmingham: Venture.

Andrews, J. (2001). Group work's place in social welfare: A historical analysis. *Journal of Sociology and Social Welfare. 28*(4), 45–64.

Aspinwall-Roberts, E. (2012). *Assessments in social work with adults.* Maidenhead: Open University Press.

Backwith, D. (2015). *Social work, poverty and social exclusion.* Maidenhead: Open University Press.

Bailey, R. & Brake, M. (eds) (1975). *Radical social work.* London: Arnold.

Baines, D., Tseris, E. & Waugh, F. (2018). Activism and advocacy. In N. Thompson & P. Stepney (eds) *Social work theory and methods: The essentials* (pp 215–26). New York: Routledge.

Baldwin, C. (2013). *Narrative social work: Theory and application*. Bristol: Policy Press.

Baldwin, N. and Walker, L. (2009). Assessment. In R. Adams, L. Dominelli & M. Payne (eds) *Social work: Themes, issues and critical debates* (3rd edn) (pp 209–28). Basingstoke: Palgrave Macmillan.

Bassot, B. (2016a). *The reflective practice guide: An interdisciplinary approach to critical reflection*. Abingdon: Routledge.

Bassot, B. (2016b). Engaging with emotions. In B. Bassot, *The reflective practice guide: An interdisciplinary approach to critical reflection* (pp 65–78). Abingdon: Routledge.

Bassot, B. (2016c). The role of writing in reflection. In B. Bassot, *The reflective practice guide: An interdisciplinary approach to critical reflection* (pp 31–41). Abingdon: Routledge.

Bateman, N. (2006). *Practising welfare rights*. London: Routledge.

Baulkwill, J., Dechamps, A., Manning, J., van der Croft, N. & Payne, M. (2012). Young carers in palliative care: A groupwork project. *European Journal of Palliative Care. 19*(6), 296–9.

Bechelet, L., Heal, R., Leam, C. & Payne, M. (2008). Empowering carers to reconstruct their finances. *Practice. 20*(4), 223–34.

Beck, A. (1976). *Cognitive therapy and the emotional disorders*. Harmondsworth: Penguin.

Beck, N. (2017). Beginning with the body: The neurobiology of mindfulness. In T.B. Northcut (ed) *Cultivating mindfulness in clinical social work: Narratives from practice* (pp 43–62). Cham: Springer.

Beck, U. (1992). *Risk society: Towards a new modernity*. London: Sage.

Beckett, C. & Horner, N. (2016). *Essential theory for social work practice* (2nd edn). London: Sage (69–85, Chapter 17; 109–13, Chapter 24; 122–4, Chapter 11; 124–32, Chapter 12; 174–8, Chapter 13; 189–200, Chapter 21; 201–6, Chapter 19; 238–54, Chapter 25).

Beesley, P., Watts, M. & Harrison, M. (2018). *Developing your communication skills in social work*. London: Sage.

Bellinger, A. & Fleet, F. (2012). Counselling and contemporary social work. In P. Stepney and D. Ford (eds) *Social work models, methods and theories* (pp 152–65). Lyme Regis: Russell House.

Béres, L.G. (2009). Mindfulness and reflexivity: The no-self as reflexive practitioner. In S.F. Hick (ed) *Mindfulness and social work* (pp 57–75). Chicago, IL: Lyceum.

Bion, W.R. (1961). *Experiences in groups and other papers*. London: Tavistock.

Birdseil, K. & Kitchen, K. (2018). Mindfulness and social work. In F.J. Turner (ed) *Social work treatment: Interlocking theoretical approaches* (6th edn) (pp 325–37). New York: Oxford University Press.

Bolton, G. (ed) (2008). *Dying, bereavement and the healing arts*. London: Jessica Kingsley.

Borden, W. (2009). *Contemporary psychodynamic theory and practice*. Chicago, IL: Lyceum.

Boushel, M. & Farmer, E. (1996). Work with families where children are at risk: Control and/or empowerment? In P. Parsloe (ed) *Pathways to empowerment* (pp 93–107). Birmingham: Venture.

Bower, M. (2005). Psychoanalytic theories for social work practice. In M. Bower (ed) *Psychoanalytic theory of social work practice: Thinking under fire* (pp 3–14). London: Routledge.

Bowers, N.R. & Bowers A. (2018). General systems theory. In F.J. Turner (ed) *Social work treatment: Interlocking theoretical approaches* (6th edn) (pp 240–7). New York: Oxford University Press.

Bowlby, J. ([1988] 2005). *A secure base* (republished with a Preface to the Routledge Classics edition). Abingdon: Routledge.

Boylan, J. & Dalrymple, J. (2009). *Understanding advocacy for children and young people*. Maidenhead: Open University Press.

Brandell, J.R. (2004). *Psychodynamic social work*. New York: Columbia University Press.

Brandell, J.R. (2011). *Theory and practice in clinical social work* (2nd edn). Thousand Oaks, CA: Sage.

Brandon, D. (1976). *Zen in the art of helping*. London: Routledge and Kegan Paul.

Braye, S. & Preston-Shoot, M. (1995). *Empowering practice in social care*. Buckingham: Open University Press.

Brearley, C.P. (1982). *Risk and social work*. London: Routledge and Kegan Paul.

Brearley, J. (1995). *Counselling and social work*. Buckingham: Open University Press (54, Chapter 4).

Bricker-Jenkins, M., Hooyman, N.R. & Gottlieb, N. (eds) (1991). *Feminist social work practice in clinical settings*. Newbury Park, CA: Sage.

Bricker-Jenkins, S. (1991). Introduction. In M. Bricker-Jenkins, N.R. Hooyman & N. Gottlieb (eds) *Feminist social work practice in clinical settings* (pp 1–13). Newbury Park, CA: Sage.

Briscoe, C. (1976). Community work in a social services department. In P. Henderson & D.N. Thomas (eds) *Readings in community work* (pp 171–5). London: Allen & Unwin.

Brown, H. & Barrett, S. (2008). Practice with service users, carers and their communities. In S. Fraser & S. Matthews (eds) *The critical practitioner in social work and health care* (pp 43–59). London: Sage.

Bruce, L. (2013). *Reflective practice for social workers: A handbook for developing professional confidence*. Maidenhead: Open University Press.

Brundtland Commission (1987). *Our common future, from one Earth to one world.*

Buckle, J. (1981). *Intake teams.* London: Tavistock.

Bugental, J.F.T. & Sapienza, B.G. (1994). The three R's for humanistic psychology: Remembering, reconciling, reuniting. In F. Wertz (ed) *The humanistic movement: Recovering the person in psychology* (pp 157–69). Lake Worth, FL: Gardner.

Burack-Weiss, A., Lawrence, L.S. & Mijangos, L.B. (eds) *Narrative in social work practice: The power and possibility of story.* New York: Columbia University Press.

Burford, G., Pennell, J. & MacLeod, S. (2005). Family group decision making. In B.R. Compton, B. Galaway & B.R. Cournoyer (eds) *Social work processes* (7th edn) (pp 416–21). Belmont, CA: Brooks/Cole.

Burghardt, S. (2014). *Macro practice in social work for the 21st century: Bridging the macro-micro divide* (2nd edn). Thousand Oaks, CA: Sage.

Butler, G. (2019). Reflecting on emotion in social work. In A. Mantell & T. Scragg (eds) *Reflective practice in social work* (5th edn) (pp 39–61). London: Sage.

Butler-Mokoro, S. & Grant, L. (eds) (2018). *Feminist perspectives on social work practice: The intersecting lives of women in the 21st century.* New York: Oxford University Press.

Butrym, Z.T. (1976). *The nature of social work.* London: Macmillan (26–9, Chapter 5).

Campbell, C.L. (2018). Chaos theory and social work treatment. In F.J. Turner (ed) *Social work treatment: Interlocking theoretical approaches* (6th edn) (pp 23–33). New York: Oxford University Press.

Caplan, G. (1965). *Principles of preventive psychiatry.* London: Tavistock.

Carabine, J. (1996). Empowering sexualities. In B. Humphries (ed) *Critical perspectives on empowerment* (pp 17–34). Birmingham: Venture.

Carnes, R. & Northcut, T.B. (2017). Beginning with the clients: Mindfully reconciling opposites with survivors of trauma/complex traumatic stress disorders. In T.B. Northcut (ed) *Cultivating mindfulness in clinical social work: Narratives from practice* (pp 103–28). Cham: Springer.

Carniol, B. (1992). Structural social work: Maurice Moreau's challenge to social work practice. *Journal of Progressive Human Services. 3*(1), 1–20.

Cassidy, J. & Shaver, J.R. (eds) (2016). *Handbook of attachment: Theory, research, and clinical applications* (3rd edn). New York: Guilford.

Cavaiola, A.A. & Colford, J.E. (2018). *Crisis intervention: A practical guide.* Thousand Oaks, CA: Sage.

Chambon, A.S. (2007). Between social critique and active reenchantment. In S.L. Witkin & D. Saleebey (eds) *Social work dialogues: Transforming the canon in inquiry, practice and education* (pp 203–26). Alexandria, VA: Council on Social Work Education.

Chevalier, J. & Buckles, D.J. (2013). *Participatory action research: Theory and methods for engaged enquiry*. Abingdon: Routledge.

Children in Wales (2008). *All Wales child protection procedures*. Cardiff: Local Safeguarding Children Boards in Wales. Retrieved from: http://www.childreninwales.org.uk/policy-document/wales-child-protection-procedures-2008.

Chisnell, C. & Kelly, C. (2016). *Safeguarding in social work practice: A lifespan approach*. London: Sage.

Chui, W.H. & Ford, D. (2012). Crisis intervention as common practice. In P. Stepney and D. Ford (eds) *Social work models, methods and theories* (2nd edn) (pp 80–101). Lyme Regis: Russell House.

Cigno, K. & Bourn, D. (eds) (1998). *Cognitive behavioural social work in practice*. Aldershot: Ashgate.

Coates, J. (2003). *Ecology and social work: Toward a new paradigm*. Halifax: Fernwood.

Compton, B.R. & Galaway, B. (1989). *Social work processes* (4th edn). Belmont, CA: Wadsworth.

Compton, B.R., Galaway, B. & Cournoyer, B.R. (eds) (2005). *Social work processes* (7th edn). Belmont, CA: Brooks/Cole (23–65, Chapters 21 and 24; 207, Chapter 3; 319–25, Chapter 25).

Cooper, A. & White, E. (eds) (2017). *Safeguarding adults under the Care Act 2014: Understanding good practice*. London: Jessica Kingsley.

Corcoran, J. (2016). *Motivational interviewing: A workbook for social workers*. New York: Oxford University Press.

Corrigan, P. & Leonard, P. (1978). *Social work practice under capitalism: A Marxist approach*. London: Macmillan.

Cosis Brown, H. (2009). Counselling. In R. Adams, L. Dominelli & M. Payne (eds) *Critical practice in social work* (2nd edn) (pp 105–14). Basingstoke: Palgrave Macmillan.

Crawford, F. (2006). Research for and as practice: Educating practitioners in inquiry skills for changing cultural contexts. In S. White, J. Fook & F. Gardner (eds) *Critical reflection in health and social care* (pp 172–84). Maidenhead: Open University Press.

Cree, V. & Davis, A. (2007). *Social work: Voices from the inside*. London: Routledge.

Currer, C. (2007). *Loss and social work*. Exeter: Learning Matters.

Currie, R. & Parrott, B. (1986). *A unitary approach to social work: Application in practice*. Birmingham: BASW Publications.

Dalrymple, J. & Boylan, J. (2013). *Effective advocacy in social work*. London: Sage.

Dalrymple, J. & Burke, B. (2006). *Anti-oppressive practice: Social care and the law* (2nd edn). Maidenhead: Open University Press.

Dalzell, R. & Sawyer, E. (2016). *Putting analysis into child and family assessment: Undertaking assessments of need* (3rd edn). London: Jessica Kingsley (151–87, Chapter 3).

Daniel, P. (1970). Group processes and task performance: Their relevance for training groups for social workers. In Family Welfare Association London (ed) *The voice of the social worker* (pp 74–82). London: Bookstall Services.

Das, C. & Carter A.J. (2016). 'Pushing theory': Applying cultural competence in practice – a case study of community conflict in Northern Ireland. In C. Williams & M.J. Graham (eds) *Social work in a diverse society: Transformative practice with black and minority ethnic individuals and communities* (pp 21–37). Bristol: Policy Press.

Dattilio, F.M. & Freeman, A. (2007). Introduction. In F.M. Dattilio & A. Freeman (eds) *Cognitive-behavioural strategies in crisis intervention* (3rd edn) (pp 1–22). New York: Guilford.

Davies, H. & Kinloch, H. (2000). Critical incident analysis. In C. Macauley & V. Cree (eds) *Transfer of learning in professional and vocational education* (pp 137–50). London: Routledge.

Davies, L. & Duckett, N. (2016). *Proactive child protection and social work* (2nd edn). London: Learning Matters.

Davies, M. (1994). *The essential social worker: A guide to positive practice* (3rd edn). Aldershot: Arena.

Deacon, L. & Macdonald, S.J. (eds) (2017). *Social work theory and practice*. London: Sage (81–92, Chapter 24).

Department of Health (2014). *Care and support statutory guidance*. London: Department of Health.

Derezotes, D.S. (2000). *Advanced generalist social work practice*. Thousand Oaks, CA: Sage (9, 77–81, 126–8, Chapter 5).

Desai, S. (2018). Solution-focused practice. In N. Thompson & P. Stepney (eds) *Social work theory and methods: The essentials* (pp 141–52). New York: Routledge.

Devore, W. & Schlesinger, E.G. (1999). *Ethnic-sensitive social work practice* (3rd edn). Boston, MA: Allyn & Bacon.

Dewey, J. (1933). *How will we think?* Boston, MA: Heath.

Dhooper, S.S. & Moore, S.E. (2001). *Social work practice with culturally diverse people*. Thousand Oaks, CA: Sage (33–9, Chapter 2).

Dobson, D. & Dobson, K.S. (2017). *Evidence-based practice of cognitive-behavioral therapy* (2nd edn). New York: Guilford.

Doel, M. (2006). *Using groupwork.* London: Routledge.

Doel, M. (2009). Task-centred work. In R. Adams, L. Dominelli & M. Payne (eds) *Critical practice in social work* (2nd edn) (pp 169–77). Basingstoke: Palgrave Macmillan.

Doel, M. (2015). Groupwork. In J. Lishman (ed) *Handbook for practice learning in social work and social care: Knowledge and theory* (pp 275–86). London: Jessica Kingsley.

Doel, M. & Shardlow, S.M. (2005). *Modern social work practice: Teaching and learning in practice settings.* Farnham: Ashgate (23–46, Chapter 5).

Dolinsky, B., Jerin, R. & Johnson, B. (2018). Healthy and otherwise: Women in intimate relationships. In S. Butler-Mokoro & L. Grant (eds) *Feminist perspectives on social work practice: The intersecting lives of women in the 21st century* (pp 84–106). New York: Oxford University Press.

Dominelli, L. (2002). *Feminist social work theory and practice.* Basingstoke: Palgrave.

Dominelli, L. (2006). *Women and community action* (2nd edn). Bristol: Policy Press.

Dominelli, L. (2012a). Empowerment: Help or hindrance in professional relationships? In P. Stepney and D. Ford (eds) *Social work models, methods and theories* (pp 214–35). Lyme Regis: Russell House.

Dominelli, L. (2012b). *Green social work: From environmental crises to environmental justice.* Cambridge: Polity.

Dominelli, L. & McLeod, E. (1989). *Feminist social work.* Basingstoke: Macmillan.

Donovan, C. (2017). Feminism and social work. In L. Deacon & S.J. Macdonald (eds) *Social work theory and practice* (pp 93–102). London: Sage.

Doran, G.T. (1981). There's a S.M.A.R.T. way to write management's goals and objectives. *Management Review.* *70*(11), 35–6.

Douglas, T. (1979). *Group processes in social work: A theoretical synthesis.* Chichester: Wiley.

Dunlap, K.M. (2018). Functional theory and social work practice. In F.J. Turner (ed) *Social work treatment: Interlocking theoretical approaches* (6th edn) (pp 223–39). New York: Oxford University Press.

Dyke, C. (2016). *Writing critical assessments in social work.* St Albans: Critical Publishing.

Eamon, M.K. (2008). *Empowering vulnerable populations: Cognitive-behavioral interventions.* Chicago, IL: Lyceum.

Eby, M. (2000). Understanding professional development. In A. Brechin, H. Brown & M.A. Eby (eds) *Critical practice in health and social care* (pp 49–69). London: Sage.

Eby, M. & Gallagher, A. (2008). Values and ethics in practice. In S. Fraser & S. Matthews (eds) *The critical practitioner in social work and health care* (pp 114–32). London: Sage.

Edwards, K., Hallett, C. & Sawbridge, P. (2008). Working with complexity: Managing workload and surviving in a changing environment. In S. Fraser & S. Matthews (eds) *The critical practitioner in social work and health care* (pp 60–77). London: Sage.

Egan, G. (2010). The communication skills of therapeutic dialogue. In V.E. Cree (ed) *Social work: A reader* (pp 153–8). London: Routledge.

Egan, G. (2014). *The skilled helper: A problem-management and opportunity-development approach to helping* (10th edn). Belmont, CA: Brooks/Cole.

Emory, E.V. (1936). First interviews as an experiment in human relations. In F. Lowry (ed) (1939). *Readings in social case work 1920–1938: Selected reprints for the case work practitioner* (pp 187–206). New York: Columbia University Press.

Epstein, L. & Brown, L.B. (2002). *Brief treatment and a new look at the task-centered approach* (4th edn). Boston, MA: Allyn & Bacon.

Fawcett, B., Featherstone, B., Fook, J. & Rossiter, A. (eds) (2000). *Practice and research in social work: Postmodern feminist perspectives.* London: Routledge.

Feilberg, F. (2018). Counselling in social work. In J. Lishman, C. Yuill, J. Brannen & A. Gibson (eds) *Social work: An introduction* (2nd edn) (pp 395–408). London: Sage.

Feldman, F.L. (1957). *The family in a money world.* New York: Family Service Association of America.

Fenton, R. (1970). Long term clients and change of caseworkers. In Family Welfare Association London (ed) *The voice of the social worker* (pp 58–62). London: Bookstall Services.

Ferguson, H. (2011). *Child protection practice.* London: Palgrave Macmillan.

Ferguson, I. (2008). *Reclaiming social work: Challenging neo-liberalism and promoting social justice.* London: Sage.

Finley, R. & Payne, M. (2010). A retrospective records audit of bereaved carers' groupwork. *Groupwork. 20*(3), 65–84.

Fook, J. (2015). Reflective practice and critical reflection. In J. Lishman (ed) *Handbook for practice learning in social work and social care: Knowledge and theory* (pp 440–54). London: Jessica Kingsley.

Fook, J. (2016). *Social work: A critical approach to practice* (3rd edn). London: Sage.

Fook, J. & Askeland, G.A. (2006). The 'critical' in critical reflection. In S. White, J. Fook & F. Gardner (eds) (2006). *Critical reflection in health and social care* (pp 40–53). Maidenhead: Open University Press.

Ford, P. & Postle, K. (2012). Task-centred practice in challenging times. In P. Stepney and D. Ford (eds) *Social work models, methods and theories* (pp 102–22). Lyme Regis: Russell House.

Fortune, A.E. & Reid, W.J. (2011). Task-centered social work. In F.J. Turner (ed) *Social work treatment: Interlocking theoretical approaches* (6th edn) (pp 532–52). New York: Oxford University Press.

Foster, J. (2018). Women and criminalization at the intersections. In S. Butler-Mokoro & L. Grant (eds) *Feminist perspectives on social work practice: The intersecting lives of women in the 21st century* (pp 131–52). New York: Oxford University Press.

Freire, P. (1972). *Pedagogy of the oppressed.* Harmondsworth: Penguin.

Freud, S. (1974). *Introductory lectures in psychoanalysis.* Harmondsworth: Penguin.

Friedman, B.D. & Allen, K.N. (2011). Systems theory. In J.R. Brandell (ed) *Theory and practice in clinical social work* (2nd edn) (pp 3–20). Thousand Oaks, CA: Sage.

Galper, J. (1975). *The politics of social service.* Englewood Cliffs, NJ: Prentice-Hall.

Galper, J. (1980). *Social work practice: A radical approach.* Englewood Cliffs, NJ: Prentice-Hall.

Gardner, A. & Brindis, C. (2017). *Advocacy and policy change evaluation: Theory and practice.* Stanford, CA: Stanford Business Books.

Gardner, F. (2006). Using critical reflection in research and evaluation. In S. White, J. Fook & F. Gardner (eds) *Critical reflection in health and social care* (pp 144–55). Maidenhead: Open University Press.

Garrett, P.M. (2013). *Social work and social theory: Making connections.* Bristol: Policy Press.

Ghaye, T. (2011). *Teaching and learning through reflective practice: A practical guide for positive action.* Abingdon: Routledge.

Gibson, N. & Heyman, I. (2018). Narrative therapy. In J. Lishman, C. Yuill, J. Brannen & A. Gibson (eds) *Social work: An introduction* (2nd edn) (pp 353–64). London: Sage.

Giertz, A. (2004). *Making the poor work: Social assistance and activation programs in Sweden.* Lund: Lund University School of Social Work. Retrieved from http://lup.lub.lu.se/search/ws/files/4715275/1693304.pdf.

Gilchrist, A. & Jeffs, T. (eds) (2001). *Settlements, social change and community action.* London: Jessica Kingsley.

Gilchrist, A. & Taylor, M. (2016). *A short guide to community development* (2nd edn). Bristol: Policy Press.

Gilgun, J.F. (2005). An ecosystemic approach to assessment. In B.R. Compton, B. Galaway & B.R. Cournoyer (eds) *Social work processes* (7th edn) (pp 349–60). Belmont, CA: Brooks/Cole.

Gitterman, A. (2011). Advances in the life model of social work practice. In F.J. Turner (ed) *Social work treatment: Interlocking theoretical approaches*. (5th edn) (pp 279–92). New York: Oxford University Press.

Gitterman, A. (2018). Life model of social work practice. In F.J. Turner (ed) *Social work treatment: Interlocking theoretical approaches*. (6th edn) (pp 287–301). New York: Oxford University Press.

Gitterman, A. & Germain, C.B. (2008). *The life model of social work practice: Advances in theory and practice* (3rd edn). New York: Columbia University Press.

Gloria, A.M. & Castellanos, J. (2016). Latinas *ponderosas*: Shaping *mujerismo* to meniafest. In T. Bryant-Davis & L. Comas-Diaz (eds) *Womanist and* mujerista *psychologies* (pp 93–120). Washington, DC: American Psychological Association.

Golan, N. (1978). *Treatment in crisis situations*. New York: Free Press.

Goldstein, E.G. & Noonan, M. (1999). *Short-term treatment and social work practice: An integrative perspective*. New York: Free Press.

Goldstein, E., Miehls, D. & Ringel, S. (2009). *Advanced clinical social work practice: Relational principles and techniques*. New York: Columbia University Press.

Goroff, N. (1974). Social welfare as coercive social control. *Journal of Sociology and Social Welfare*. *2*(1), 19–26.

Gosling, J. & Martin, J. (2012). *Making partnerships with service users and advocacy groups work: How to grow genuine and respectful relationships in health and social care*. London: Jessica Kingsley.

Gould, N. & Taylor, I. (eds) (1996). *Reflective learning for social work*. Aldershot: Arena.

Graham, M. (2007). *Black issues in social work and social care*. Bristol: Policy Press.

Gray, M., Coates, J. & Yellow Bird, M. (eds) (2010). *Indigenous social work around the world: Towards culturally relevant education and practice*. London: Routledge.

Gray, M., Coates, J. & Hetherington, T. (eds) (2013). *Environmental social work*. London: Routledge.

Green Lister, P. (2012). *Integrating social work theory and practice: A practical skills guide*. Abingdon: Routledge.

Green Lister, P. & Crisp, B.R. (2007). Critical incident analysis: A practice learning tool for students and practitioners. *Practice*. *19*(1), 47–60.

Greene, G.J. & Lee, M.Y. (2011). *Solution-oriented social work practice: An integrative approach to working with client strengths*. New York: Oxford University Press.

Greene, R.R. (ed) (2012a). *Resiliency: An integrated approach to practice, policy, and research* (2nd edn). Washington, DC: NASW Press.

Greene, R.R. (2012b). Human behaviour theory: A resilience orientation. In R.R. Greene (ed) *Resiliency: An integrated approach to practice, policy, and research* (2nd edn) (pp 1–27). Washington, DC: NASW Press.

Guest, C. & Scarff, P. (2008). Counting the costs. In S. Fraser & S. Matthews (eds) *The critical practitioner in social work and health care* (pp 78–96). London: Sage.

Gutiérrez, L.M., Parsons, R.J. & Cox, E.O. (1998). *Empowerment in social work practice: A sourcebook*. Pacific Grove, CA: Brooks/Cole.

Hadley, R. & McGrath, M. (1984). *When social services are local: The Normanton experience*. London: Allen & Unwin.

Hall, C., Parton, N., Juhila, K. & Pösö, T. (2003). Conclusion: Yes, but is this of any use? In C. Hall, K. Juhila, N. Parton & T. Pösö (eds) *Constructing clienthood in social work and human services: Interaction, identities and practices* (pp 223–33). London: Jessica Kingsley.

Halmos, P. (1965). *The faith of the counsellors*. London: Constable.

Halmos, P. (1978). *The personal and the political: Social work and social action*. London: Hutchinson.

Hamblin, A. (1970). The world of the fair: Casework with a schizophrenic client and his wife. In Family Welfare Association London (ed) *The voice of the social worker* (pp 7–13). London: Bookstall Services.

Hardcastle, D. (2011). *Community practice: Theories and skills for social workers* (3rd edn). New York: Oxford University Press.

Hargie, O. (2016). *Skilled interpersonal communication: Research theory and practice* (6th edn). Abingdon: Routledge.

Harms, L. (2018). Narrative approaches. In N. Thompson & P. Stepney (eds) *Social work theory and methods: The essentials* (pp 117–28). New York: Routledge.

Hart, A. (2018a). Crisis intervention. In J. Lishman, C. Yuill, J. Brannen & A. Gibson (eds) *Social work: An introduction* (2nd edn) (pp 280–95). London: Sage.

Hart, A. (2018b). Reflective practice. In J. Lishman, C. Yuill, J. Brannen & A. Gibson (eds) *Social work: An introduction* (2nd edn) (pp 153–69). London: Sage.

Hart, M.A., Burton, A.D., Hart, K., Halonen, D. & Pompana, Y. (eds) (2016). *International indigenous voices in social work*. Newcastle upon Tyne: Cambridge Scholars.

Healy, K. (2014). *Social work theories in context: Creating frameworks for practice* (2nd edn). Basingstoke: Palgrave Macmillan (33–110, Chapter 25; 121–7, Chapter 24).

Henriques, P. & Tuckley, G. (2012). Ecological systems theory and direct work with children. In P. Stepney and D. Ford (eds) *Social work models, methods and theories* (pp 166–80). Lyme Regis: Russell House.

Heymann, D. (1971). A function for the social worker in the anti-poverty program. In W. Schwartz & S.R. Zalba (eds) *The practice of groupwork* (pp 157–76). New York: Columbia University Press.

Hick, S.F. (ed) (2009a). *Mindfulness and social work*. Chicago, IL: Lyceum.

Hick, S.F. (2009b). Mindfulness and social work: Paying attention to ourselves, our clients, and society. In S.F. Hick (ed) *Mindfulness and social work* (pp 1–30). Chicago, IL: Lyceum.

Hill, R. (1965). Generic features of families under stress. In H.J. Parad (ed) *Crisis intervention: Selected readings* (pp 32–52). New York: Family Service Association of America.

HM Government (2018). *Working together to safeguard children: A guide to inter-agency working to safeguard and promote the welfare of children*. London: HM Government.

Hodgson, D. & Watts, L. (2017). *Key concepts and theory in social work*. London: Palgrave (100–160, 192–206, Chapter 22; 228–42, Chapter 25).

Hoefer, R. (2012). *Advocacy practice for social justice* (2nd edn). Chicago, IL: Lyceum.

Hohman, M. (2012). *Motivational interviewing in social work practice*. New York: Guilford.

Holland, S. (2010). *Child and family assessment in social work practice* (2nd edn). London: Sage.

Hollis, F. (1970). The psychosocial approach to the practice of casework. In R.W. Roberts & R.H. Nee (eds) *Theories of social casework* (pp 33–76). Chicago, IL: University of Chicago Press (52, Chapter 10).

Hood, R. (2018). *Complexity in social work*. London: Sage.

Hothersall, S.J. & Maas-Lowit, M. (eds) (2010). *Need, risk and protection in social work practice*. London: Sage.

Howe, D. (2005). *Child abuse and neglect: Attachment, development and intervention*. Basingstoke: Palgrave Macmillan.

Howe, D. (2009a). *A brief introduction to social work theory*. Basingstoke: Palgrave Macmillan (29–41, Chapter 11; 42–8, Chapter 12; 75–82, Chapter 13; 96–7, Chapter 10; 108–20, Chapter 24; 145–51, Chapter 18; 162, Chapter 7; 170–4, Chapter 25).

Howe, D. (2009b). Psychosocial work: An attachment perspective. In R. Adams, L. Dominelli & M. Payne (eds) *Critical practice in social work* (2nd edn) (pp 137–46). Basingstoke: Palgrave Macmillan.

Howe, D. (2011). *Attachment across the lifecourse: A brief introduction*. Basingstoke: Palgrave Macmillan.

Hudson, C.G. (2010). *Complex systems and human behavior*. Chicago, IL: Lyceum.

Humphrey, D. (2018). Task-centred intervention. In J. Lishman, C. Yuill, J. Brannan & A. Gibson (eds) *Social work: An introduction* (pp 311–24). London: Sage.

Hunter, S. & Ritchie, P. (eds) (2007). *Co-production and personalisation in social care: Changing relationships in the provision of social care*. London: Jessica Kingsley.

Ife, J. (2012). *Human rights and social work: Towards rights-based practice* (3rd edn). Port Melbourne: Cambridge University Press.

Ingram, R. (2015). *Understanding emotions in social work: Theory, practice and reflection*. Maidenhead: Open University Press (20–2, Chapter 11).

Irvine, E.E. (1978). Professional claims and the professional task. In Open University Course Team (eds) *Professional and non-professional roles 1* (pp 85–113). Milton Keynes: Open University.

James, R.K. & Gilliland, B.E. (2017). *Crisis intervention strategies* (8th edn). Belmont, CA: Brooks/Cole.

Johns, C. (ed) (2017). *Becoming a reflective practitioner* (5th edn). Chichester: Wiley.

Johnson, L. & Yudilevich Espinoza, S. (2018). Mothering and child welfare. In S. Butler-Mokoro & L. Grant (eds) *Feminist perspectives on social work practice: The intersecting lives of women in the 21st century* (pp 107–30). New York: Oxford University Press.

Jordan, B. (1979). Memoirs of a long-distance tightrope-walker. In D. Brandon & B. Jordan (eds) *Creative social work* (pp 85–96). Oxford: Blackwell.

Kadushin, A. & Kadushin, G. (2013). *The social work interview* (5th edn). New York: Columbia University Press.

Kanel, K. (2017). *A guide to crisis intervention* (6th edn). Belmont, CA: Brooks/Cole.

Karls, J.M. & Wandrei, K.E. (eds) (1994). *Person-in-environment system: The PIE classification system for social functioning problems*. Washington, DC: NASW Press.

Keeler, A. (2013). Counselling. In A. Worsley, T. Mann, A. Olsen, E. Mason-Whitehead (eds) *Key concepts in social work practice* (pp 48–53). London: Sage.

Kelley, P. & Smith, M. (2018). Narrative theory and social work treatment. In F.J. Turner (ed) *Social work treatment: Interlocking theoretical approaches* (6th edn) (pp 338–50). New York: Oxford University Press.

Kemp, S.P. (2010). Place matters: Toward a rejuvenated theory of environment or direct social work practice. In W. Borden (ed) *Reshaping theory in contemporary social work: Toward a critical pluralism in clinical practice* (pp 114–45). New York: Columbia University Press.

Kemshall, H. (2015). Risk assessment and management: An overview. In J. Lishman (ed) *Handbook for practice learning in social work and social care: Knowledge and theory* (pp 174–88). London: Jessica Kingsley.

Kemshall, H., Wilkinson, B. & Baker, K. (2013). *Working with risk: Skills for contemporary social work.* Cambridge: Polity.

Kennedy-Kish, B., Sinclair, R., Carniol, B. & Baines, D. (2017). *Case critical* (7th edn). Toronto: Between the Lines.

Kennerley, H., Kirk, J. & Westbrook, D. (2017). *An introduction to cognitive behaviour therapy: Skills and applications* (3rd edn). London: Sage.

Kessen, C. (2009). Living fully: Mindfulness practices for everyday life. In S.F. Hick (ed) *Mindfulness and social work* (pp 31–44). Chicago, IL: Lyceum.

Keval, N. (2005). Racist states of mind: An attack on thinking and curiosity. In M. Bower (ed) *Psychoanalytic theory of social work practice: Thinking under fire* (pp 31–43). London: Routledge.

Kimberley, D. & Parsons, R. (2018). Trauma-informed social work treatment and complex trauma. In F.J. Turner (ed) *Social work treatment: Interlocking theoretical approaches* (6th edn) (pp 553–73). New York: Oxford University Press.

Kirkman, E. & Melrose, K. (2014). *Clinical judgement and decision-making in children's social work: An analysis of the 'front door' system: Research report.* London: Department for Education.

Kisthardt, W.E. (2009). The opportunities and challenges of strengths-based person-centred practice: Purpose, principles, and applications in a climate of systems integration. In D. Saleebey (ed) *The strengths perspective in social work practice* (5th edn) (pp 47–71). Boston, MA: Allyn & Bacon.

Knight, J. (1970). Casework with one partner in marriage problems. In Family Welfare Association London (ed) *The voice of the social worker* (pp 14–20). London: Bookstall Services.

Knijn, T., Martin, C. & Millar, J. (2007). Activation as a framework for social policies towards lone parents: Is there a continental specificity? *Social Policy and Administration. 41*(6), 638–52.

Koggel, C. & Orme, J. (eds) (2010, 2011). Care ethics: New theories and applications: 2 parts. *Ethics and Social Welfare* (Special issue) *4*(2), 109–216; *5*(2), 107–227.

Kondrat, D.C. (2014). Solution-focused practice. In B. Teater (ed) *An introduction to applying social work theories and methods* (2nd edn) (pp 170–86). Maidenhead: Open University Press.

Koprowska, J. (2014). *Communication and interpersonal skills in social work* (4th edn). London: Sage.

Kroll, B. (2010). Only connect … building relationships with hard-to-reach people: Establishing rapport with drug-misusing parents and their children. In G. Ruch, D. Turney & A. Ward (eds) *Relationship-based social work: Getting to the heart of practice* (pp 69–84). London Jessica Kingsley.

Langan, M. & Lee, P. (eds) (1989). *Radical social work today.* London: Unwin Hyman.

Langer, C. & Lietz, C.A. (2015). *Applying theory to generalist social work practice: A case study approach.* Hoboken, NJ: Wiley.

Lavalette, M. (ed) (2011). *Radical social work today: Social work at the crossroads.* Bristol: Policy Press.

Lavalette, M. & Ioakimidis, V. (eds) (2011). *Social work* in extremis*: Lessons for social work internationally.* Bristol: Policy Press.

Lawson, J. (2018). The 'making safeguarding personal' approach to practice. In A. Cooper & E. White (eds) *Safeguarding adults under the Care Act 2014: Understanding good practice* (pp 20–39). London: Jessica Kingsley.

Ledwith, M. (2011). *Community development: A critical approach* (2nd edn). Bristol: Policy Press.

Lee, J.A.B. (2001). *The empowerment approach to social work practice: Building the beloved community.* New York: Columbia University Press (66–7, 189–92, Chapter 2).

Lee, J.A.B. & Hudson, R. (2018). Empowerment approach to social work treatment. In F.J. Turner (ed) *Social work treatment: Interlocking theoretical approaches* (6th edn) (pp 142–65). New York: Oxford University Press.

Lee, M.Y. (2018). Solution-focused theory. In F.J. Turner (ed) *Social work treatment: Interlocking theoretical approaches* (6th edn) (pp 513–31). New York: Oxford University Press.

Lee, M.Y., Ng, S.-M., Leung, P.P.Y. & Chan, C.L.W. (2009). *Integrative body-mind-spirit social work: An empirically based approach to assessment and treatment*. New York: Columbia University Press.

Legault, G. (1996). Social work practice in situations of intercultural misunderstandings. *Journal of Multicultural Social Work. 4*, 49–66.

Levinson, H.L. (1977). Termination of psychotherapy: Some salient issues. *Social Casework. 58*(8), 480–9.

Lindon, J. & Webb, J. (2016). *Safeguarding and child protection* (5th edn). London: Hodder.

Lindsay, T. & Orton, S. (2014). *Groupwork practice in social work* (3rd edn). London: Sage.

Livingstone, A. (2018). Privilege, oppression, and the intersections: The many faces of gender and identity. In S. Butler-Mokoro & L. Grant (eds) *Feminist perspectives on social work practice: The intersecting lives of women in the 21st century* (pp 59–83). New York: Oxford University Press.

Lloyd Davies, A.B. (1956). Psychotherapy and social casework II. In E.M. Goldberg, E.E. Irvine, A.B. Lloyd Davies & K.F. McDougall (eds) *The boundaries of casework* (pp 36–43). London: Association of Psychiatric Social Workers.

Local Government Association (2013). *Making safeguarding personal*. London: Local Government Association.

Loughran, H. (2011). *Understanding crisis therapies: An integrative approach to crisis intervention and post traumatic stress*. London: Jessica Kingsley.

Lovelock, R. & Powell, J. (2004). Habermas/Foucault for social work practices of critical reflection. In R. Lovelock, K. Lyons, & J. Powell (eds) *Reflecting on social work – Discipline and profession* (pp 181–223). Farnham: Ashgate.

Lyons, K. & Taylor, I. (2004). Gender and knowledge in social work. In R. Lovelock, K. Lyons & J. Powell (eds) *Reflecting on social work: Discipline and profession* (pp 72–94). Farnham: Ashgate.

Lysack, M. (2013). Emotion, ethics and fostering committed environmental citizenship. In M. Gray, J. Coates & T. Hetherington (eds) *Environmental social work* (pp 231–45). London: Routledge.

Macdonald, A. (2007). *Solution-focused therapy: Theory, research and practice*. London: Sage.

Macdonald, G. (2015). Cognitive behavioural social work. In J. Lishman (ed) *Handbook for practice learning in social work and social care: Knowledge and theory* (pp 190–210). London: Jessica Kingsley.

Macdonald, S.J. (2017a). Humanistic psychology: A stairway to Athena. In L. Deacon & S.J. Macdonald (eds) *Social work theory and practice* (pp 48–57). London: Sage.

Macdonald, S.J. (2017b). Psychoanalysis, psychodynamics and social work practice: The conflicted 'self'. In L. Deacon & S.J. Macdonald (eds) *Social work theory and practice* (pp 13–24). London: Sage.

MacIntyre, G., Stewart, A. & McCusker, P. (2018). *Safeguarding adults: Key themes and issues*. London: Palgrave.

Mackay, R. (2015). Empowerment and advocacy. In J. Lishman (ed) *Handbook for practice learning in social work and social care: Knowledge and theory* (pp 338–54). London: Jessica Kingsley.

Maclean, S. & Harrison, R. (2015). *Theory and practice: A straightforward guide for social work students* (3rd edn). Lichfield: Kirwin Maclean (103–8, Chapter 12; 167–8, Chapter 7; 187–90, Chapter 19).

Mainstone, F. (2014). *Mastering whole family assessment in social work*. London: Jessica Kingsley.

Marsh, P. (2015). Task-centred practice. In J. Lishman (ed) *Handbook for practice learning in social work and social care: Knowledge and theory* (pp 211–24). London: Jessica Kingsley.

Marsh, P. & Doel, M. (2005). *The task-centred book*. Abingdon: Routledge.

Marsiglia, F.F. & Kulis, S. (2009). *Diversity, oppression and change: Culturally grounded social work*. Chicago, IL: Lyceum.

Martin, R.R. (1995). *Oral history in social work: Research, assessment, and intervention*. Thousand Oaks, CA: Sage.

Mary, N.L. (2008). *Social work in a sustainable world*. Chicago, IL: Lyceum.

Maslow, A.H. (1971). *The farther reaches of human nature*. New York: Viking.

Maslow, A.H. (1999). *Toward a psychology of being* (3rd edn). New York: Wiley.

Matties, A.-L. & Närhi, K. (2018). Ecological theories. In N. Thompson & P. Stepney (eds) *Social work theory and methods: The essentials* (pp 202–14). New York: Routledge.

Mattinson, J. (1975). *The reflection process in casework supervision*. London: Tavistock Institute of Human Relations.

Mayo, M. (2009). Community work. In R. Adams, L. Dominelli & M. Payne (eds) *Critical practice in social work* (2nd edn) (pp 125–36). Basingstoke: Palgrave Macmillan.

McBroom, E. (1970). Socialization and social casework. In R.W. Roberts & R.H. Nee (eds) *Theories of social casework*. Chicago, IL: University of Chicago Press (327, Chapter 2).

McColgan, M. & McMullin, C. (eds) (2017). *Doing relationship-based social work: A practical guide to building relationships and enabling change*. London: Jessica Kingsley.

McDonald, C. (2006). *Challenging social work: The context of practice.* Basingstoke: Palgrave Macmillan.

McGaughan, N. (1978). Introduction: A framework for thinking about group work. In N. McGaughan (ed) *Group work: Learning and practice* (pp 13–21). London: Allen & Unwin.

McGlynn, P. (ed) (2006). *Crisis resolution and home treatment: A practical guide.* London: Sainsbury Centre for Mental Health.

McKinnon, J. & Alston, M. (eds) (2016). *Ecological social work: Towards sustainability.* London: Palgrave.

McLeod, E. (1994). *Women's experiences of feminist therapy and counselling.* Buckingham: Open University Press.

McLeod, J. (2013). *An introduction to counselling* (5th edn). Maidenhead: Open University Press (165–201, Chapter 7).

Mearns, D., Thorne, B. & McLeod, J. (2013). *Person-centred counselling in action* (4th edn). London: Sage.

Megele, C. (2015). *Psychosocial and relationship-based practice.* Northwich: Critical Publishing (162, Chapter 2).

Mendes, P. (2009). Tracing the origins of critical social work practice. In J. Allan, L. Briskman & B. Pease (eds) *Critical social work: Theories and practices for a socially just world* (2nd edn) (pp 17–29). Crows Nest: Allen & Unwin.

Meyer, C.H. (1993). *Assessment in social work practice.* New York: Columbia University Press.

Middleman, R. & Goldberg Wood, G. (1989). *The structural approach to direct practice in social work.* New York: Columbia University Press (47, Chapter 5).

Middleman, R. & Goldberg Wood, G. (1990). *Skills for direct practice in social work.* New York: Columbia University Press (49–53, Chapter 2; 73–88, Chapter 3).

Midgley, G. (2000). *Systemic intervention: Philosophy, methodology, and practice.* New York: Kluwer.

Miehls, D. (2011). Relational theory and social work treatment. In F.J. Turner (ed) *Social work treatment: Interlocking theoretical approaches* (6th edn) (pp 428–40). New York: Oxford University Press.

Millar, J. (2018). Working in the life space. In J. Lishman, C. Yuill, J. Brannen & A. Gibson (eds) *Social work: An introduction* (2nd edn) (pp 325–38). London: Sage.

Miller, L. (2012). *Counselling skills for social work* (2nd edn). London: Sage.

Miller, W.R. & Rollnick, S. (2013). *Motivational interviewing: Helping people change* (3rd edn). New York: Guilford (62–73, Chapter 4; 286–7, Chapter 16).

Milliken, E. (2018). Feminist theory and social work practice. In F.J. Turner (ed) *Social work treatment: Interlocking theoretical approaches* (6th edn) (pp 191–208). New York: Oxford University Press.

Milner, J. & O'Byrne, P. (2002). *Brief counselling: Narratives and solutions.* Basingstoke: Palgrave.

Milner, J., Myers, S. & O'Byrne, P. (2015). *Assessment in social work* (4th edn). London: Palgrave.

Mirabito, D.M. (2018). Social work theory and practice for crisis, disaster, and trauma. In F.J. Turner (ed) *Social work treatment: Interlocking theoretical approaches* (6th edn) (pp 117–30). New York: Oxford University Press.

Mirick, R. (2018). Not so crazed and confused: Unraveling women's mental health challenges. In S. Butler-Mokoro & L. Grant (eds) *Feminist perspectives on social work practice: The intersecting lives of women in the 21st century* (pp 153–76). New York: Oxford University Press.

Monroe, B. & Oliviere, D. (eds) (2007). *Resilience in palliative care: Achievement in adversity.* Oxford: Oxford University Press.

Moreau, M.J. (1979). A structural approach to social work practice. *Canadian Journal of Social Work Education. 5*(1), 78–94.

Moreau, M.J. (1990). Empowerment through advocacy and consciousness-raising: Implications of a structural approach to social work. *Journal of Sociology and Social Welfare. 17*(2), 53–68.

Morgan, E.D. (1962). Intake, a function of clinical social work. *Journal of the National Medical Association. 54*(2): 222–4.

Mullaly, B. (R.P.) (2010). *Challenging oppression and confronting privilege* (2nd edn). Ontario: Oxford University Press.

Mullaly, B. (R.P.) & West, J. (2017). *Challenging oppression and confronting privilege: A critical approach to anti-oppressive and anti-privilege theory and practice* (3rd edn). Don Mills: Oxford University Press.

Mullaly, B. (R.P.) & Dupré, M. (2019). *The new structural social work: Ideology, theory, and practice* (4th edn). Ontario: Oxford University Press.

Mullender, A., Ward, D. & Fleming, J. (2013). *Empowerment in action: Self-directed groupwork.* Basingstoke: Palgrave.

Munro, E. (1998). *Understanding social work: An empirical approach.* London: Athlone (72–87, Chapters 5 and 7).

Munro, E. (2008). *Effective child protection* (2nd edn). London: Sage.

Munro, E. (2011). *The Munro review of child protection: Final report: A child-centred system.* (Cm 8062). London: TSO.

Musson, P. (2017). *Making sense of theory: And its application to social work practice.* St Albans: Critical (31–6, Chapter 11; 37–54, Chapter 15; 55–69, Chapter 21; 84–93, Chapter 9).

Myer, R.A. (2001). *Assessment for crisis intervention: A triage assessment model.* Belmont, CA: Wadsworth.

Myers, S. (2008). *Solution-focused approaches.* Lyme Regis: Russell House.

Northcut, T.B. (ed) (2017). *Cultivating mindfulness in clinical social work: Narratives from practice.* Cham: Springer.

Norton, C.L. Holguin, B. & Manos, J. (2013). Restoration not incarceration: An environmentally based pilot initiative for working with young offenders. In M. Gray, J. Coates & T. Hetherington (eds) *Environmental social work* (pp 172–92). London: Routledge.

O'Donoghue, K. & Maidment, J. (2005). The ecological systems metaphor in Australasia. In M. Nash, R. Munford & K. O'Donoghue (eds) *Social work theories in action* (pp 32–49). London: Jessica Kingsley.

Okitikpi, T. & Aymer, C. (2010). *Key concepts in anti-discriminatory social work.* London: Sage.

Orme, J. (2009). Feminist social work. In R. Adams, L. Dominelli & M. Payne (eds) *Critical practice in social work* (2nd edn) (pp 199–208). Basingstoke: Palgrave Macmillan.

Page, T. (2018). Attachment theory and social work treatment. In F.J. Turner (ed) *Social work treatment: Interlocking theoretical approaches* (6th edn) (pp 1–22). New York: Oxford University Press.

Papell, C.P. & Rothman, B. (1966). Social group work models: Possession and heritage. *Journal of Education for Social Work. 2*(2), 42–55.

Parad, H.J. (ed) (1965). *Crisis intervention: Selected readings.* New York: Family Service Association of America.

Paré, D.A., Richardson, B. & Tarrgona, M. (2009). Watching the train: Mindfulness and inner dialogue in therapist skills training. In S.F. Hick (ed) *Mindfulness and social work* (pp 76–91). Chicago, IL: Lyceum.

Parker, J. (2007). The process of social work: Assessment, planning, intervention and review. In M. Lymbery & K. Postle (eds) *Social work: A companion to learning* (pp 111–22). London: Sage.

Parker, R.A. (1966). *Decision in child care: A study of prediction in fostering.* London: Allen & Unwin.

Parton, N. & O'Byrne, P. (2000). *Constructive social work: Towards a new practice.* Basingstoke: Macmillan (46–62, Chapter 10; 134–51, 140, Chapter 3).

Payne, M. (1995). *Social work and community care.* Basingstoke: Macmillan.

Payne, M. (2002). The politics of systems theory within social work. *Journal of Social Work. 2*(3), 269–92.

Payne, M. (2011). *Humanistic social work: Core principles in practice.* Basingstoke: Palgrave Macmillan (187–99, Chapter 6).

Payne, M. (2014). *Modern social work theory* (4th edn). Basingstoke: Palgrave Macmillan (127–42, Chapter 14; 150–83, Chapter 15; 243–70, Chapter 9; 373–401, Chapter 18).

Payne, M. (2017). *Older citizens and end-of-life care: Social work practice strategies for adults in later life.* Abingdon: Routledge.

Payne, M. & Oliviere, D. (2008). The interdisciplinary team. In D. Walsh (ed) *Palliative medicine* (pp 253–9). New York: Saunders Elsevier.

Payne, M. & Reith-Hall, E. (eds) (2019). *Routledge handbook of social work theory.* London: Routledge.

Payne, S. (2007). Resilient carers and caregivers. In B. Monroe & D. Oliviere (eds) *Resilience in palliative care: Achievement in adversity* (pp 83–97). Oxford: Oxford University Press.

Penhale, B. & Parker, J. (2008). *Working with vulnerable adults.* Abingdon: Routledge.

Perlman, F.T. & Brandell, J.R. (2011). Psychoanalytic theory. In J.R. Brandell (ed) *Theory and practice in clinical social work* (2nd edn) (pp 41–80). Thousand Oaks, CA: Sage.

Perlman, H.H. (1957). *Social casework: A problem-solving process.* Chicago, IL: University of Chicago Press.

Perlman, H.H. (1970). The problem-solving model in social casework. In R.W. Roberts & R.H. Nee (eds) *Theories of social casework* (pp 129–79). Chicago, IL: University of Chicago Press.

Petrie, P. (2011). *Communication skills for working with children and young people: Introducing social pedagogy.* London: Jessica Kingsley.

Phung, T.-C. (2018). Relationship-based social work. In J. Lishman, C. Yuill, J. Brannen & A. Gibson (eds) *Social work: An introduction* (2nd edn) (pp 267–79). London: Sage.

Pincus, A. & Minahan, A. (1973). *Social work practice: Model and method.* Itasca, IL: Peacock (272–85, Chapter 25).

Prochaska, J.O., Norcross, J.C. & DiClemente, C.C. (1994). *Changing for good: A revolutionary six-stage program for changing bad habits and moving your life positively forward.* New York: HarperCollins.

Prochaska, J.O., Redding, C.A. & Evers, K.E. (2008). The transtheoretical model and stages of change. In K. Glanz, B.K. Rimer & K. Viswanath (eds) *Health behavior and health education: Theory, research and practice* (4th edn) (pp 97–122). San Francisco, CA: Jossey-Bass.

Quinney, A. (2006). *Collaborative social work practice.* Exeter: Learning Matters.

Rapoport, L. (1970). Crisis intervention as a mode of brief treatment. In R.W. Roberts & R.H. Nee (eds) *Theories of social casework* (pp 265–311). Chicago, IL: University of Chicago Press.

Rapp, C.A. & Goscha, R.J. (2012). *The strengths model: A recovery-oriented approach to mental health services* (3rd edn). New York: Oxford University Press.

Ravey, M. (2013). Reflection. In A. Worsley, T. Mann, A. Olsen and E. Mason-Whitehead (eds) *Key concepts in social work practice* (pp 199–203). London: Sage.

Raymaekers, P. (2016). Social impact assessment for social workers. In J. McKinnon & M. Alston (eds) *Ecological social work: Towards sustainability* (pp 112–24). London: Palgrave.

Redmond, B. (2006). *Reflection in action: Developing reflective practice in health and social services*. Farnham: Ashgate.

Rees, S. (1975). How misunderstanding occurs. In R. Bailey & M. Brake (eds) *Radical social work* (pp 62–75). London: Edward Arnold.

Rees, S. (1991). *Achieving power: Practice and policy in social welfare*. North Sydney: Allen & Unwin.

Reid, K.E. (1981). *From character-building to social treatment: The history of the use of groups in social work*. Westport, CT: Greenwood.

Reid, W.J. (1975). A test of a task-centered approach. *Social Work, 20*, 3–9.

Reid, W.J. (2000). *The task planner: An intervention resource for human service professionals*. New York: Columbia University Press.

Reid, W.J. & Epstein, L. (1972). *Task-centered casework*. New York: Columbia University Press (192–9, Chapters 13 and 25).

Reid, W.J. & Shyne, A.W. (1969). *Brief and extended casework*. New York: Columbia University Press.

Reisch, M. & Andrews, J. (2002). *The road not taken: A history of radical social work in the United States*. New York: Brunner-Routledge.

Reith, M. & Payne, M. (2009). *Social work in end-of-life and palliative care*. Bristol: Policy Press.

Reynolds, J. (1970). Learning to work with anger. In Family Welfare Association London (ed) *The voice of the social worker* (pp 27–37). London: Bookstall Services.

Riggall, S. (2012). *Using counselling skills in social work*. London: Sage.

Roberts, R. (1990). *Lessons from the past: Issues for social work theory*. London: Tavistock.

Robinson, H. & Kaplan, C. (2011). Psychosocial theory and social work treatment. In F.J. Turner (ed) *Social work treatment: Interlocking theoretical approaches* (5th edn) (pp 387–400). New York: Oxford University Press.

Robson, T. (2000). *The state and community action.* London: Pluto.

Rogan, M. (2017). Beginning with the training: Training clinicians in essential methods for integrating mindfulness into clinical practice. In T.B. Northcut (ed) *Cultivating mindfulness in clinical social work: Narratives from practice* (pp 81–102). Cham: Springer.

Rogers, C.R. (1951). *Client-centered therapy: Its current practice, implications and theory.* London: Constable (85–8, Chapter 25).

Rogowski, S. (2013). *Critical social work with children and families: Theory, context and practice.* Bristol: Policy Press.

Ronen, T. & Freeman, A. (eds) (2007). *Cognitive behaviour therapy in clinical social work.* New York: Springer.

Rooney, R. (2018). Task-centered practice. In N. Thompson & P. Stepney (eds) *Social work theory and methods: The essentials* (pp 94–104). New York: Routledge.

Roscoe, K.D., Carson, A.M. & Madoc-Jones, I. (2011). Narrative social work: Conversations between theory and practice. *Journal of Social Work Practice. 25*(1), 47–61.

Rose, S.M. & Black, B.L. (1985). *Advocacy and empowerment: Mental health care in the community.* Boston, MA: Routledge and Kegan Paul.

Rosengren, D.B. (2018). *Building motivational interviewing skills: A practitioner workbook.* (2nd edn). New York: Guilford (51–163, Chapter 2).

Rothman, J. & Tropman, J.E. (1987). Models of community organization and macro practice: Their mixing and phasing. In F.M. Cox, J.L. Ehrlich, J. Rothman & J.E. Tropman (eds) *Strategies of community intervention: Macro practice* (4th edn) (pp 3–25). Itasca, IL: Peacock.

Rowe, W. (2011). Client-centered theory: The enduring principles of a person-centered approach. In F.J. Turner (ed) *Social work treatment: Interlocking theoretical approaches* (5th edn) (pp 58–76), New York: Oxford University Press.

Ruch, G. (2004). From triangle to spiral: Reflective practice in social work education, practice and research. *Social Work Education. 21*, 199–216.

Ruch, G. (2013). Understanding contemporary social work; we need to talk about relationships. In J. Parker & M. Doel (eds) *Professional social work* (pp 54–67). London: Sage.

Ruch, G., Turney, D. & Ward, A. (eds) (2018). *Relationship-based social work: Getting to the heart of practice* (2nd edn). London: Jessica Kingsley.

Ryan, T. (2013). Social work, animals, and the natural world. In M. Gray, J. Coates & T. Hetherington (eds) *Environmental social work* (pp 156–71). London: Routledge.

Rzepnicki, T.L., McCracken, S.G. & Briggs, H.E. (eds) (2012). *From task-centered social work to evidence-based and integrative practice: Reflections on history and implementation*. Chicago, IL: Lyceum.

Safeguarding Board for Northern Ireland (2018). *Safeguarding Board for Northern Ireland (SBNI) procedures manual*. Belfast: Safeguarding Board for Northern Ireland.

Saleebey, D. (2009a). *The strengths perspective in social work practice* (5th edn). Boston, MA: Pearson (93–107, Chapter 3).

Saleebey, D. (2009b). Introduction: Power in the people. In D. Saleebey (ed) *The strengths perspective in social work practice* (5th edn) (pp 1–23). Boston, MA: Allyn & Bacon (10, Chapter 9).

Saleebey, D. (2013). *The strengths perspective in social work practice* (6th edn). Upper Saddle River, NJ: Pearson.

Schmitz, C.L., Matyók, T., James, C.D. & Sloan, L.M. (2013). Environmental sustainability: Educating social workers for interdisciplinary practice. In M. Gray, J. Coates & T. Hetherington (eds) *Environmental social work* (pp 260–79). London: Routledge.

Schön, D.A. (1983). *The reflective practitioner: How professionals think in action*. New York: Basic Books.

Schwartz, W. (1971). On the use of groups in social work practice. In W. Schwartz & S.R. Zalba (eds) *The practice of groupwork* (pp 3–24). New York: Columbia University Press.

Scottish Government (2014). *The national guidance for child protection in Scotland*. Edinburgh: Scottish Government.

Scragg, T. & Mantell, A. (eds) (2011). *Safeguarding adults in social work* (2nd edn). Exeter: Learning Matters.

Seden, J. (2005). *Counselling skills in social work* (2nd edn). Maidenhead: Open University Press.

Seed, P. (1990). *Introducing network analysis in social work*. London: Jessica Kingsley.

Seligman, M.E.P. (2018). *Authentic happiness: Using the new positive psychology to realise your potential for lasting fulfilment*. New York: Atria.

Sharry, J. (2007). *Solution-focused groupwork* (2nd edn). London: Sage.

Sheedy, M. (2013). *Core themes in social work: Power, poverty, politics and values*. Maidenhead: Open University Press (92–3, Chapter 21; 101–2, Chapter 23).

Sheldon, B. & Macdonald, G. (2009). *A textbook of social work*. London: Routledge (95–111, Chapter 3; 99, Chapter 2).

Shemmings, D. & Shemmings, Y. (2011). *Understanding disorganized attachment: Theory and practice for working with children and adults*. London: Jessica Kingsley.

Shemmings, D. & Shemmings, Y. (eds) (2014). *Assessing disorganized attachment behaviour in children: An evidence-based model for understanding and supporting families.* London: Jessica Kingsley.

Shennan, G. (2014). *Solution-focused practice: Effective communication to facilitate change.* Basingstoke: Palgrave Macmillan.

Shepard, B. (2013). Community gardens, creative community organizing, and environmental activism. In M. Gray, J. Coates & T. Hetherington (eds) *Environmental social work* (pp 121–34). London: Routledge.

Sheppard, M. (2015). Assessment: From reflexivity to process knowledge. In J. Lishman (ed) *Handbook for practice learning in social work and social care: Knowledge and theory* (pp 163–73). London: Jessica Kingsley.

Sheppard, M. & Ryan, K. (2003). Practitioners as rule using analysts: A further development of process knowledge in social work. *British Journal of Social Work. 33*(2), 157–76.

Sheppard, M., Newstead, S., di Caccavo, A. & Ryan, K. (2000). Reflexivity and the development of process knowledge in social work: A classification and empirical study. *British Journal of Social Work. 30*(4), 465–88.

Shier, M.L. (2011). Problem solving and social work. In F.J. Turner (ed) *Social work treatment: Interlocking theoretical approaches* (5th edn) (pp 364–73). New York: Oxford University Press.

Shirran, A. (2018). Motivational interviewing. In J. Lishman, C. Yuill, J. Brannen & A. Gibson (eds) *Social work: An introduction* (2nd edn) (pp 365–79). London: Sage.

Shulman, L. (1971). 'Program' in group work: Another look. In W. Schwartz & S.R. Zalba (eds) *The practice of groupwork* (pp 221–40). New York: Columbia University Press.

Slesser, S. & Blair, J. (2018). Communication and ICT. In J. Lishman, C. Yuill, J. Brannen & A. Gibson (eds) *Social work: An introduction* (2nd edn) (pp 124–40). London: Sage.

Smale, G., Tuson, G., Biehal, N. & Marsh, P. (1993). *Empowerment, assessment, care management and the skilled worker.* London: HMSO.

Smalley, R.E. (1970). The functional approach to casework practice. In R.W. Roberts & R.H. Nee (eds) *Theories of social casework* (pp 77–128). Chicago, IL: University of Chicago Press.

Smethurst, C. (2011). Working with risk. In T. Scragg & A. Mantell (eds) *Safeguarding adults in social work* (2nd edn) (pp 168–79). Exeter: Learning Matters.

Smith, A. (1991). Feminist practice with teenage parents. In M. Bricker-Jenkins, N.R. Hooyman & N. Gottlieb (eds) *Feminist social work practice in clinical settings* (pp 91–104). Newbury Park, CA: Sage.

Smith P.B. (1978). Group work as a process of social influence. In N. McGaughan (ed) *Group work: Learning and practice* (pp 46–57). London: Allen & Unwin.

Smithson, R. & Gibson, M. (2017). Less than human: A qualitative study into the experience of parents involved in the child protection system. *Child and Family Social Work. 22*(2), 565–74.

Solomon, B.B. (1976). *Black empowerment: Social work in oppressed communities.* New York: Columbia University Press.

Statham, D. & Kearney, P. (2015). Models of assessment. In J. Lishman (ed) *Handbook for practice learning in social work and social care: Knowledge and theory* (pp 126–39). London: Jessica Kingsley.

Stepney, P. (2018). Community social work. In N. Thompson & P. Stepney (eds) *Social work theory and methods: The essentials* (pp 227–39). New York: Routledge.

Stepney, P. & Popple, K. (2009). *Social work and the community: A critical framework for practice.* Basingstoke: Palgrave Macmillan.

Stepney, P. & Popple, K. (2012). Community social work. In P. Stepney & D. Ford (eds) *Social work models, methods and theory: A framework for practice* (pp 181–200). Lyme Regis: Russell House

Strauss, R. (2017). Beginning with the modality: Learned helpfulness in mindful group work with individuals with serious mental illness. In T.B. Northcut (ed) *Cultivating mindfulness in clinical social work: Narratives from practice* (pp 173–90). Cham: Springer.

Sutherland, J.D. (1956). Psychotherapy and social casework I. In E.M. Goldberg, E.E. Irvine, A.B. Lloyd Davies & K.F. McDougall (eds) *The boundaries of casework* (pp 22–35). London: Association of Psychiatric Social Workers.

Taylor, B.J. (2017). *Decision making, assessment and risk in social work* (3rd edn). London: Sage.

Taylor, C. & White, S. (2000). *Practising reflexivity in health and welfare: Making knowledge.* Maidenhead: Open University Press.

Taylor, S.A. (2013). Social science research in ocean environments: A social worker's experience. In M. Gray, J. Coates & T. Hetherington (eds) *Environmental social work* (pp 88–101). London: Routledge.

Taylor, S.H. & Roberts, R.W. (eds) (1985). *Theory and practice of community social work.* New York: Columbia University Press.

Teater, B. (2014). *An introduction to applying social work theories and methods.* Maidenhead: Open University Press (56–73, Chapter 18; 204–20, Chapter 14).

Thomas, E.J. (1970). Behavioral modification and casework. In R.W. Roberts & R.H. Nee (eds) *Theories of social casework* (pp 181–218). Chicago, IL: University of Chicago Press.

Thomas, P. (1970). About experiencing the present. In Family Welfare Association London (ed) *The voice of the social worker* (pp 21–6). London: Bookstall Services.

Thomas, R. (2016). Boy trouble? Motivational interviewing and communication with black boys and their families. In C. Williams & M.J. Graham (eds) *Social work in a diverse society: Transformative practice with black and minority ethnic individuals and communities* (pp 199–215). Bristol: Policy Press.

Thomlison, R.J. & Thomlison, B. (2018). Cognitive behaviour theory and social work treatment. In F.J. Turner (ed) *Social work treatment: Interlocking theoretical approaches* (6th edn) (pp 54–79). New York: Oxford University Press.

Thompson, N. (2011). *Crisis intervention.* Lyme Regis: Russell House.

Thompson, N. (2016). *Anti-discriminatory practice: Equality, diversity and social justice.* London: Palgrave.

Thompson, N. (2018a) Crisis intervention. In N. Thompson & P. Stepney (eds) *Social work theory and methods: The essentials* (pp 105–16). New York: Routledge.

Thompson, N. (2018b). Theory and methods in a practice context: Theorizing practice. In N. Thompson & P. Stepney (eds) *Social work theory and methods: The essentials* (pp 9–25). New York: Routledge.

Thompson, N. & Stepney, P. (eds) (2018). *Social work theory and methods: The essentials.* New York: Routledge.

Thompson, S. & Thompson, N. (2018). *The critically reflective practitioner* (2nd edn). London: Palgrave.

Thorne, B. (2000). *Person-centred counselling: Therapeutic and spiritual dimensions.* London: Whurr (130–1, Chapter 5).

Thorpe, C. (2018). *Social theory for social work: Ideas and applications.* Abingdon: Routledge (124–42, Chapter 23).

Titterton, M. (2005). *Risk and risk taking in health and social welfare.* London: Jessica Kingsley.

Todd, S. (2009). Mobilizing communities for social change: Integrating mindfulness and passionate politics. In S.F. Hick (ed) *Mindfulness and social work* (pp 171–87). Chicago, IL: Lyceum.

Tolson, E.R., Reid, W.J. & Garvin, C.D. (2003). *Generalist practice: A task-centered approach.* New York: Columbia University Press.

Tosone, C. & Gelman, C.R. (2018). Relational social work: A contemporary perspective on practice. In F.J. Turner (ed) *Social work treatment: Interlocking theoretical approaches* (6th edn) (pp 420–7). New York: Oxford University Press.

Tracy, E.M. & Brown, S. (2018). Social networks and social work practice. In F.J. Turner (ed) *Social work treatment: Interlocking theoretical approaches* (6th edn) (pp 481–96). New York: Oxford University Press.

Trevithick, P. (2012a). Groupwork theory and practice. In P. Stepney and D. Ford (eds) *Social work models, methods and theories* (pp 236–54). Lyme Regis: Russell House.

Trevithick, P. (2012b). *Social work skills and knowledge: A practice handbook* (3rd edn). Maidenhead: Open University Press (229–32, Chapter 23; 253–74, Chapter 18).

Trotter, C. (2006). *Working with involuntary clients* (2nd edn). Crows Nest: Allen & Unwin.

Tunmore, J. (2017). General systems and ecological theory. In L. Deacon & S.J. Macdonald (eds) *Social work theory and practice* (pp 81–92). London: Sage.

Turnell, A. & Edwards, S. (1999). *Signs of safety: A solution and safety oriented approach to child protection*. New York: Norton.

Turner, F.J. (1995). *Differential diagnosis and treatment in social work* (4th edn). New York: Free Press.

Turner, F.J. (ed) (2018). *Social work treatment: Interlocking theoretical approaches* (6th edn). New York: Oxford University Press.

Valentich, M. (2011). Feminist theory and social work practice. In F.J. Turner (ed) *Social work treatment: Interlocking theoretical approaches* (5th edn) (pp 205–24). New York: Oxford University Press.

van Berkel, R. (2009). The provision of income protection and activation services for the unemployed in 'active' welfare states: An international comparison. *Journal of Social Policy*. *39*(1), 17–34.

Walker, S. & Beckett, C. (2011). *Social work assessment and intervention* (2nd edn). Lyme Regis: Russell House.

Walsh, F. (2011). Family therapy: Systemic approaches to practice. In J.R. Brandell (ed) *Theory and practice in clinical social work* (2nd edn) (pp 153–78). Thousand Oaks, CA: Sage.

Walsh, F. (2016). *Strengthening family resilience* (3rd edn). New York: Guilford.

Walsh, J. (2010). *Theories for direct social work practice* (2nd edn). Belmont, CA: Wadsworth.

Walsh, J. (2014). *Theories for direct social work practice* (3rd edn). Belmont, CA: Wadsworth (146–201, Chapter 15; 233–54, Chapter 9; 278–305, Chapter 10).

Ward, A. (2006). *Working in group care: Social work and social care in residential and day care settings* (2nd edn). Bristol: Policy Press.

Ward, A. (2018). The use of self in relationship-based practice. In G. Ruch, D. Turney & A. Ward (eds) *Relationship-based social work: Getting to the heart of practice* (2nd edn) (pp 55–74). London: Jessica Kingsley.

Ward, D. (2009). Groupwork. In R. Adams, L. Dominelli & M. Payne (eds) *Critical practice in social work* (2nd edn) (pp 115–24). Basingstoke: Palgrave Macmillan.

Watson, D. & West, J. (2006). *Social work process and practice: Approaches, knowledge and skills*. Basingstoke: Palgrave Macmillan (127–64, Chapter 25).

Webb, S. (2006). *Social work in a risk society: Social and political perspectives*. Basingstoke: Palgrave.

Webb, S. (ed) (2019). *The Routledge handbook of critical social work*. London: Routledge.

White, M. & Epston, D. (1990). *Narrative means to therapeutic ends*. New York: Norton.

White, S. (2013). Practising reflexively: Nurturing humane practice. In J. Parker & M. Doel (eds) *Professional social work* (pp 39–53). London: Sage.

White, S., Fook, J. & Gardner, F. (2006). *Critical reflection in health and social care*. Maidenhead: Open University Press.

White, V. (2006). *The state of feminist social work*. Abingdon: Routledge.

Wilks, T. (2012). *Advocacy and social work practice*. Maidenhead: Open University Press (24, 137, Chapter 17).

Williams, C. & Graham, M.J. (eds) (2016a). *Social work in a diverse society: Transformative practice with black and minority ethnic individuals and communities*. Bristol: Policy Press.

Williams, C. & Graham, M.J. (2016b). Building transformative practice. In C. Williams & M.J. Graham (eds) *Social work in a diverse society: Transformative practice with black and minority ethnic individuals and communities* (pp 3–19). Bristol: Policy Press.

Williams, F. (1996). Postmodernism, feminism and the question of difference. In N. Parton (ed) *Social theory, social change and social work* (pp 61–76). London: Routledge.

Woodcock Ross, J. (2016). *Specialist communication skills for social workers: Developing professional capability* (2nd edn). London: Palgrave.

Yeager, K.R. & Roberts, A.R. (eds) (2015a). *Crisis intervention handbook: Assessment, treatment, and research* (4th edn). New York: Oxford University Press.

Yeager, K.R. & Roberts, A.R. (2015b). Bridging the past and present to the future of crisis intervention and crisis management. In K.R. Yeager & A.R. Roberts (eds) *Crisis intervention handbook: Assessment, treatment, and research* (4th edn) (pp 3–35). New York: Oxford University Press.

Yeager, K.R. & Roberts, A.R. (2015c). Lethality assessment and crisis intervention with persons presenting with suicidal ideation. In K.R. Yeager & A.R. Roberts (eds) *Crisis intervention handbook: Assessment, treatment, and research* (4th edn) (pp 36–68). New York: Oxford University Press.

Youell, B. (2005). Observation in social work practice. In M. Bower (ed) *Psychoanalytic theory of social work practice: Thinking under fire* (pp 47–58). London: Routledge.

Zukin, E. (1991). *Landscapes of power: From Detroit to Disneyland.* Berkeley, CA: University of California Press.

Index

Note: Entries for authors in this index refer to mentions in the main body of the text

5WH mnemonic 54, 131

A

ABC analysis (CBT) 131
ABC analysis (cognitive restructuring) 134
ABC mnemonic (crisis practice) 124, 125
accessibility of agency 14
accurate empathy 66, 145
activation policies 111, 113
active listening 23, 33
activism 149, 154–5
Adult Attachment Interview 105, 109
adventure pedagogy 108, 217
advocacy, human and welfare rights 35–6, 147–56
 action sequence 151–5
 aims of 147, 149
 definitions 147
 dimensions of 152–3
 introducing to client 150
 level of advocacy 151–2
 policy advocacy 154–5
 representing people 153
 rights work 153–4
 things to think about 155–6
 types of 149, 152
 uses of 149
affective reactions to crises 124, 125
agency frame 32
agenda mapping 140
Alston, M. 213
amplified reflections 141
Andrews, J. 168, 196
applications process 13, 15
assessment 19–28
 action sequence 22–6
 aims of 19, 21
 analysis of information 23–4
 data collection 22–3
 definition 19
 introducing to client 21–2
 looking at issues or problems 24–5
 things to think about 26–7
 tools for 24
 towards planning 25–6
 uses of 21
attachment practice 103–10
 action sequence 106–10
 aims of 103
 attachment styles 106–7, 109
 contribution to social work practice 103
 interventions for adults 109–10
 interventions for carers 108–9
 interventions for young people 107–8
 introducing to client 105–6
 things to think about 110
 uses of 105
attribution errors 55–6

B

BASIC mnemonic 22–3
Bateman, N. 147
Beck, A. 128
Beck Depression Inventory 132
Beckett, C. 2
behavioural reactions to crises 124, 125
bereavement 109
best interest decisions 56–7
Biehal, N. 23
Bion, W. 168
biopsychosocial issues 188
Borden, W. 95
Bourn, D. 128
Bower, M. 98
Bowlby, J. 103
breathing techniques 71, 72
Brundtland Commission (1987) 220
Buckles, D.J. 178
Burford, G. 22

Burke, B. 157
Butler, G. 230
Butler-Mokoro, S. 205

C

Caplan, G. 120
caring role in families 208–9
case advocacy 147, 151–2
case files 17
Cassidy, J. 103
Castellanos, J. 208
cause advocacy 149, 154–5
chaining positive reinforcement 133
Chambon, A.S. 73
chaos and complexity theory 185, 187
Chevalier, J. 178
Cigno, K. 128
citizen advocacy 149
citizenship 77, 217
climate change *see* ecological and green practice
Coates, J. 213
cognitive behavioural therapy (CBT) 128–36
- action sequence 131–5
- aims of 128
- assessment 131–2
- definition 128
- interventions 132–5
- introducing to client 130
- things to think about 135–6
- uses of 128, 130

cognitive reactions to crises 120, 124, 125
cognitive restructuring 134–5
communication, advice, information 29–37
- action sequence 32–6
- aims of 29
- basics of 33–4
- definition 29
- introducing to client 31
- issues of 35
- participative decision making 35–6
- patterns of 34
- things to think about 36–7
- uses of 29, 31

community social work 181
community work and macro practice 176–84
- action sequence 179–83
- aims of 176
- definitions 176
- interventions 180–3
- introducing to client 179
- issues based 181
- network based 180–1
- participation based 181
- preparation 179–80
- strategic focuses 182–3
- things to think about 183–4
- uses of 178

compassion 66, 145
complex adaptive systems 185
complex reflections 141
complex systems 194
complexity theory 185, 187
Compton, B.R. 22
congruent 64, 66
consciousness raising 200
constructive practice 84
coping 80, 98, 120, 124, 125, 126
counselling 38–47
- action sequence 41–6
- aims of 38
- boundaries 46
- client-focused 41–2
- counselling skills 42–4
- definition 38
- interventions 44–6
- introducing to client 40–1
- things to think about 46–7
- uses of 40

counter-conditioning technique 133
Cournoyer, B.R. 22
creativity 64–5
crisis practice 120–7
- action sequence 123–6
- aims of 120
- assessment 123–4
- definition 120
- interventions 124–6
- introducing to client 122–3
- reintegration 126

things to think about 126–7
uses of 122
critical and structural practice 196–204
action sequence 199–203
aims of 196
definitions 196
interventions 200–2
introducing to client 198–9
and social identities 201–2
and social work responsibilities 202–3
things to think about 203–4
uses of 196, 198
see also feminist practice
critical reflection *see* ending and critical reflection
critical thinking 224
cultural competence 161–2

D

Dalrymple, J. 157
Dalzell, R. 26
DARN mnemonic 140
data collection 22–3
Davies, H. 228
decision making 26, 35–6, 56–7
decision trees 26
deep listening 86–7, 90
depth of understanding 67
Derezotes, D.S. 44
Dewey, J. 224
DiClemente, C.C. 137
disabilities, people with 36, 203
discrepancy 140
discrimination *see* empowerment, anti-oppressive practice and power
dismissing adults 109
disorganized attachment styles 106, 107
diversity 159, 161, 162
Doel, M. 111
Dominelli, L. 164, 205, 213, 217
Doran, G.T. 116
double-sided reflections 66, 141

E

ecocritical/ecocentric theory 213, 215
ecological and green practice 213–21
action sequence 216–20
aims of 213, 215
assessment 216
definition 213
focuses for intervention 217–19
interventions 219–20
introducing to client 215–16
and sustainability 220
things to think about 220
uses of 215
ecological systems theory 185, 194, 213
see also ecological and green practice; systems practice
Edwards, S. 55
Egan, G. 41, 42–3
ELLA mnemonic 208
empathy 35, 43, 66, 145, 209
empowerment, anti-oppressive practice and power 157–67
action sequence 160–6
aims of 157, 159
anti-discrimination and anti-oppression practices 162–3
approaches to 160
cultural competence and ethnic sensitivity 161–2
definitions 157
empowerment strategies 164–6
introducing to client 159
preventive approaches 165
and systems practice 187
things to think about 166–7
uses of 159
see also critical and structural practice; ethnic-sensitive practice; feminist practice
ending and critical reflection 222–34
action sequence 225–32
aims of 224
concept of 222, 224
and critical practice 203
critical reflection process 227–32
ending process 225–6
introducing to client 225
looking at ideas critically 230–1
and person-centred practice 65–6

ending and critical reflection (CONTD.)
- and social change 201
- things to think about 232–3
- uses of 225
- *see also* critical and structural practice; ethical reflection

entangled adults 109
Epstein, L. 111, 113
Epston, D. 84
equilibrium model (crisis practice) 120
ethical reflection 58–9
ethics of care 209
ethnic-sensitive practice 161–2
etiology 97
evaluation process 222, 224, 227, 228
Evers, K.E. 144
everyday teamwork 53
evoking 140, 142, 145
exchange approaches (assessment) 23
expectations, managing 64

F

family group conferences 22, 53, 193
family therapy 192
feedback, communication skills 36–7
Feldman, F.L. 156
feminist practice 205–12
- action sequence 207–11
- aims of 205
- and caring 208–9
- definition 205
- and identity 209
- and intimate and family relationships 209–11
- introducing to client 207
- and men 211
- strengths-based approach 207–8
- things to think about 211–12
- uses of 205, 207
- *see also* critical and structural practice; empowerment, anti-oppressive practice and power

first contact and engagement 11–18
- accessibility 14
- action sequence 13–16
- aims of 11
- areas of focus 15–16
- referrals and applications 13–15
- things to think about 16–17
- uses of 13

Fleming, J. 168
Fook, J. 196, 222, 224
Freeman, A. 128
Freud, S. 93

G

Galaway, B. 22
Gardner, F. 224, 227
Garvin, C.D. 111
gender *see* feminist practice
Germain, C.B. 213
Gibson, M. 35
Gilchrist, A. 176
Gilliland, B.E. 120
Gitterman, A. 213
Gloria, A.M. 208
goals, identifying 115–16
Goldberg Wood, G. 15
Goldstein, E. 93
Goscha, R.J. 75, 78
Grant, L. 205
Gray, M. 213
green practice *see* ecological and green practice
Greene, R.R. 48
group advocacy 149
group process 173, 174–5
groupthink 56
groupwork 168–75
- action sequence 171–3
- aims of 168, 170
- community work 178
- definition 168
- group process 173, 174–5
- interventions 172–3
- introducing to client 170–1
- solution-focused 81–2
- things to think about 174–5
- uses of 170

H

Hadley, R. 181
Halmos, P. 38

Hargie, O. 31
Hetherington, T. 213
Hick, S.F. 68
hindering growth 64
Hodgson, D. 2, 230–1
holding environment 97, 98, 101
Hollis, F. 97
Hood, R. 185
Horner, N. 2
Howe, D. 64
Hudson, C.G. 185
Hudson, R. 165
human rights *see* advocacy, human and welfare rights
humanistic person-centred practice 60–7
  action sequence 62–5
  aims of 60
  core conditions of relationship with clients 66
  definition 60
  focuses 63–4
  humanistic practice ideals 65
  things to think about 65–7
  uses of 60, 62

I

Ife, J. 147
implementation intention 142–3
inquiry and research 227
insecure-ambivalent attachment styles 107
insecure-avoidant attachment styles 107
instructed advocacy 147, 150, 152
  see also uninstructed advocacy
intake process 11, 14
intuitive thinking 58

J

James, C.D. 217
James, R.K. 120
Jeffs, T. 176
Jordan, B. 43

K

Kemp, S.P. 218
Kinloch, H. 228
Kirkman, E. 11
Koprowska, J. 34
Kroll, B. 16
Kulis, S. 161

L

Lavalette, M. 196
Lawson, J. 58
Lee, J.A.B. 15, 165
lethality 123
listening skills 23, 33, 50, 86–7, 90

M

MacLeod, S. 22
Marsh, P. 23, 111
Marsiglia, F.F. 161
masculinity 211
Maslow, A.H. 60
Matyók, T. 217
McGrath, M. 181
McKinnon, J. 213
McLeod, E. 205
McLeod, J. 38
Melrose, K. 11
mental capacity, and decision making 56–7
mentalization 106
Meyer, C.H. 27
Middleman, R. 15
Miehls, D. 93
Miller, W.R. 137, 142
Milner, J. 19
mindfulness 68–74
  action sequence 71–3
  aims of 68
  and awareness 72–3
  definition 68
  introducing to client 70–1
  techniques 71–3
  things to think about 74
  uses of 68
mindfulness-based cognitive therapy (MBCT) 68, 71
mindfulness-based stress-reduction (MBSR) 68
minority ethnic groups 161–2, 202, 218

mirroring 45
modelling 63, 98–99, 134, 173
motivational interviewing 36, 137–46
- action sequence 139–44
- aims of 137, 139
- definition 137
- evoking 140
- guiding 141–2
- introducing to client 139
- key communication skills 141
- moving to change 142–3
- pre-contemplation phase 139–40
- and resistance 143–4
- stage model 144–5
- things to think about 144–6
- uses of 139

Mullaly, B (R.P.) 157, 196
Mullender, A. 168
multiculturalism 162
multisystemic practice 194
multisystemic therapy 185
Munro, E. 48, 66, 185
Myers, S. 19

N

narrative practice 84–92
- action sequence 86–90
- aims of 84
- concept of 84
- deconstruction and externalization 87–8
- introducing to client 86
- reconstruction and re-storying 88–90
- things to think about 90–1
- uses of 84, 86

narrative truth 24
non-instructed advocacy 149, 152
non-spoken communication 33–4
Norcross, J.C. 137

O

OARS mnemonic 141
object relations 99
O'Byrne, P. 19, 24, 84
open listening 50, 199
operant extinction 133
oppression *see* empowerment, anti-oppressive practice and power

P

PACE mnemonic 145
Papell, C.P. 168
Parad, H.J. 120
paraphrasing 33, 35, 45
Paré, D.A. 72–3
participative decision making 35–6
participatory action research 178
Parton, N. 24, 84
Pennell, J. 22
person-centred practice *see* humanistic person-centred practice
person-in-environment 101, 188
person-situation reflection 98
policy advocacy 149, 154–5
positive psychologies 75, 84, 137, 145
positive reinforcement 132–3
poverty 156, 211–12
power
- balance of 101
- forms of 166–7
- power relations 25
- *see also* empowerment, anti-oppressive practice and power; feminist practice

practice concepts and theory 2–4
preventive approaches, and empowerment 165
privacy, and communication 32
procedural approaches (assessment) 23
Prochaska, J.O. 137, 144
psychodynamic relationship-based practice 93–102
- action sequence 96–100
- aims of 93
- assessing the problems 96–7
- definition 93
- interventions 97–100
- introducing to client 95
- things to think about 100–1
- uses of 93, 95

Q

questioning approaches/styles 23, 79–81
  Socratic questioning 135

R

radical social work 196, 205
Rapp, C.A. 75, 78
rational thinking 58
Redding, C.A. 144
referrals 13, 14
reflecting (motivational interviewing) 141 *see also* mirroring
reflection *see* ending and critical reflection
reflection-*for*-action 227
reflection-*in*-action 227, 228
reflection-*on*-action 227
reflexivity 224, 227, 228
Reid, K.E. 168
Reid, W.J. 111, 113, 116–17
Reisch, M. 196
relationship-based practice *see* psychodynamic relationship-based practice
representation work *see* advocacy, human and welfare rights
resilience, risk, safeguarding 48–59
  action sequence 51–8
  aims of 48
  areas of resilience 51
  decision making 55–7
  definitions 48
  ethical reflection 58–9
  intervention 57–8
  introducing to client 50
  risk assessment and management 53–4
  safeguarding process 52–3
  taking risks 54–5
  things to think about 58–9
  uses of 50
rewarding behaviour 132–3
Richardson, B. 72–3
Ringel, S. 93
risk *see* resilience, risk, safeguarding
Roberts, A.R. 123
Rogers, C.R, 60
Rollnick, S. 137, 142
Ronen, T. 128
Rothman, B. 168
Ruch, G. 93

S

SAD mnemonic 141
safeguarding *see* resilience, risk, safeguarding
Saleebey, D. 75, 82
Sawyer, E. 26
SCARED mnemonic 143–4
Schmitz, C.L. 217
Schön, D.A. 224
secure attachment styles 107
secure autonomous adults 109
self-actualization 60, 64, 65, 226
self-advocacy 149
self-efficacy 143, 149, 157
self-review 134–5
self-work 46–7
Seligman, M.E.P. 75, 84
shaping (CBT) 133
Shaver, J.R. 103
Shemmings, D. 103
Shemmings, Y. 103
Shennan, G. 75
signs of safety 55, 77
simple reflections 141
skilled helper model 41
skills training and modelling 134
Sloan, L.M. 217
Smale, G. 23
Smalley, R.E. 16
SMART mnemonic 116
Smithson, R. 35
social capital 164, 180–1, 219
social construction theories 75, 84
social control 26, 200–1
social impact assessment 216
social learning theory 130
social model of disability 203
social skills training 134
social work practice, concepts and theory 2
Socratic questioning 135
SOLER mnemonic 42–3

Solomon, B.B. 157
solution-focused practice *see* strengths and solution-focused practice
spiritual issues 188
state of active crisis 122, 123
steady state 120, 123, 124
Stepney, P. 3
strengths and solution-focused practice 75–83
 action sequence 78–82
 aims of 75, 77
 co-construction 78–9
 definitions 75
 groupwork 81–2
 introducing to client 77–8
 questioning techniques 79–81
 things to think about 82
 uses of 77
structural practice *see* critical and structural practice
sustainability 220
sustainment 97
systematic desensitization 133–4
systems practice 185–95
 action sequence 188–94
 aims of 185
 definition 185
 and environment 192–3
 interactional quality of 188–9
 interventions 190–4
 introducing to client 187–8
 and networks 193
 problems 194
 strategic approaches 192
 things to think about 194–5
 types of systems 190
 uses of 185, 187

T

Tarrgona, M. 72–3
task-centred practice 111–19
 action sequence 114–18
 aims of 111, 113
 and crisis practice 126
 definition 111
 and goals 115–16
 introducing to client 113–14
 task implementation sequence 116–18
 things to think about 118–19
 uses of 113
termination *see* ending and critical reflection
terminology ix–x
Thomas, R. 211
Thompson, N. 3, 157, 224
Thompson, S. 224
Tolson, E.R. 111
transference 99
transition model (crisis practice) 120
transtheoretical model of behaviour change 137, 144
traumatic events *see* crisis practice
Trotter, C. 25
tuning in 108
Turnell, A. 55
Turney, D. 93
Tuson, G. 23

U

uninstructed advocacy 149, 152 *see also* instructed advocacy
unresolved adults 109

W

Walsh, F. 48, 50
Ward, A. 93
Ward, D. 168
WASP mnemonic 135
Watts, L. 2, 230–1
Webb, S. 48
welfare rights *see* advocacy, human and welfare rights
West, J. 157
White, M. 84
White, S. 222, 224
Wilks, T. 147, 152–3
women *see* feminist practice
working through experiences 99

Y

Yeager, K.R. 123

Z

Zukin, E. 218

Printed and bound by CPI Group (UK) Ltd, Croydon, CR0 4YY

09/06/2025

14685899-0004